Roughton '95

D0954419

Spirit Poles
and
Flying Pigs

Spirit
Poles and

Flying Pigs

PUBLIC ART AND CULTURAL DEMOCRACY IN AMERICAN COMMUNITIES

Erika Doss

SMITHSONIAN INSTITUTION PRESS

WASHINGTON
AND LONDON

© 1995 by the Smithsonian Institution
All rights reserved

Copy Editor: Susan M. S. Brown
Supervisory Editor: Duke Johns
Designer: Kathleen Sims

Library of Congress Cataloging-in-Publication Data
Doss, Erika Lee.
    Spirit poles and flying pigs : public art and cultural democracy in American
communities / Erika Doss.
        p.   cm.
    Includes bibliographical references and index.
    ISBN 1-56098-464-3 (alk. paper).—ISBN 1-56098-534-8 (pbk. : alk. paper)
    1. Public art—United States—Public opinion. 2. Public opinion—United States.
I. Title.
N8835.D67   1995
701'03—dc20   94-26010

British Library Cataloguing-in-Publication Data is available

Manufactured in the United States of America
02 01 00 99 98 97 96 95   5 4 3 2 1

⊗ The paper used in this publication meets the minimum requirements of the American
National Standard for Permanence of Paper for Printed Library Materials Z39.48-1984.

For permission to reproduce illustrations appearing in this book, please correspond directly with the owners of the works, as listed in the individual captions. The Smithsonian
Institution Press does not retain reproduction rights for these illustrations individually, or
maintain a file of addresses for photo sources.

■■■

Contents

■■■

Preface and Acknowledgments

This is a book about public art, and why it is the source of so much controversy in contemporary America. And public art is controversial—scarcely a sculpture or a mural or any other work of art lately unveiled in the public sphere has not incurred some degree of friction and, in some cases, real rancor. This book attempts to explain why, to contextualize conflicted reactions to contemporary public art, and to show that fierce debate about public art is a sign that Americans still hold out for the possibilities of cultural democracy.

This is not a general survey of public art. Rather *Spirit Poles and Flying Pigs: Public Art and Cultural Democracy in American Communities* focuses on six public art episodes in scattered parts of the country. If many recent accounts of public art have tended to center on art in New York City (cf. the vast amount of attention given Richard Serra's *Tilted Arc*), this book offers a somewhat broader picture of contemporary cultural controversy by specifically analyzing public art projects in the Midwest and California and referring to many more in practically every region of the United States. From the *Spirit Poles* of Concord, California, to the *Flying Pigs* of Cincinnati, Ohio, each artwork considered in this book was chosen because it illuminates what I consider some essential aspect of the public art process. All together they show that today's wide-ranging public art battles are consistent with the abiding struggles

Americans continue to have over the meaning of democratic expression—and democracy in general.

The book opens with the story of a 1989 mural Barbara Kruger was commissioned to paint by the Museum of Contemporary Art in Los Angeles. The mural's location on the fringe of Little Tokyo, the cultural and economic hub of Los Angeles's Japanese American community, and the fact that it contained subject matter that that community found offensive and insulting were the primary factors in the controversy that Kruger's proposal aroused. After introducing many of the ideas and concerns that shape such public art controversies, each subsequent chapter of this book concentrates on what I find a particularly provocative and compelling public art story: the political consequences of angry public reaction to Gary Rieveschl's abstract sculpture called *Spirit Poles* in Concord, California (the *National Enquirer* called it the "ugliest tax-funded sculpture in America"); the significance of corporate and civic disdain for Claes Oldenburg's *Free Stamp* sculpture in Cleveland, Ohio; the issues of public access and eco-aesthetics as unfolded in the tale of Michael Heizer's *Effigy Tumuli* sculpture park in Ottawa, Illinois; the public engagement instrumental to the civic success story of Judy Baca's mural in Guadalupe, California; and the manner in which public art controversy was transformed into a meaningful episode in participatory democracy with Andrew Leicester's *Cincinnati Gateway* (aka *Flying Pigs*) sculpture. The book closes with a follow-up to Kruger's Little Tokyo mural, which, after a lengthy process of civic debate and negotiation, eventually emerged as an engaging and critically attuned (and temporary) public art project.

Taken as a whole this book considers why public art has become the focus of heated debate and how the public sphere has become the contested site of cultural authority as artists, arts agencies, politicians, corporations, and the public all vie for power in contemporary America. Yet at the same time this book aims to tell the story of cultural democracy. While the flood of recent public art controversy might be frightening to those who find conflict and debate irritating and unbearably complex, I think it is actually healthy and hopeful. The dynamics of public art controversy demonstrate just how important issues of culture and power are to Americans, often cynically miscast in the past decade as apathetic and uninformed. The public art stories related here show an ongoing American commitment to those meaningful and critical conversations that are the cornerstones of sustenance for an active democratic culture. The intent of this book, then, is to consider the value of public art controversy as the setting for democratic debate.

Since 1992 I have been a member of the Boulder Arts Commission, a city council–appointed body of volunteers mandated to oversee cultural directions (and the distribution of arts dollars) for the city. For the past several years, the commission has been trying to implement a public art process in Boulder and struggling to live down the specter of a failed public sculpture project from a decade ago (see Chapter 2). As a result of my involvement in this endeavor, I have developed a good deal of empathy for artists and arts agencies who aim to pursue more democratic forms of public culture and who often encounter adverse opinions about the public and their participation in the public sphere. Recently, for instance, during a talk that I gave to the Boulder City Council describing the large crowds that turned out to discuss the *Flying Pigs* in Cincinnati, the mayor of Boulder said, "The last thing I want to see is hundreds of people talking about public art in these chambers." In a lot of ways this book is for her and for others who fear (for whatever reasons) the dynamics of public debate. Perhaps the public art stories told here will help to convince us all of the cultural possibilities that remain to be realized in the public sphere.

Writing this book has been not unlike the process of public art itself. It is truly the result of several years of collaboration and cooperation, and I am indebted to the many who have shared information and helped shape the ideas expressed here. Likewise, I thank the University of Colorado for the financial assistance provided by the Graduate School and the IMPART Program that enabled me to conduct the research and travel necessary to this project.

I am particularly grateful to my students at the University of Colorado, where, in the several courses and seminars I taught on public art, I benefited from their astute critical responses to early versions of these chapters and from their own fascinating accounts of contemporary public art controversies. In this regard I want to thank especially Bill Anthes, Maggie Beyeler, Kathryn Charles, Carie Ferdani, Carl Gronquist, Karen Hoff, Bonnie Lawson, Rebecca McGrew-Yule, Rita Raley, Rayne Roper, Linda Slobodin, and Tim Weaver. Thanks also to Brendan Chuapoco, Heather Henck, Scott Lawson, Tom Rice, and Shane Stout, and the invaluable material they dug up in Linny Frickman's class.

Stimulating conversations with my colleagues, including Claire

Farago, Jerry Kunkel, Lucy Lippard, Mark Pittenger, Barbara Jo Revelle, Garrison Roots, and Antonette Rosato, have also been enormously influential in shaping the critical discourse that I hope this book provides. Similarly, I want to acknowledge the constructive feedback I've received from friends and scholars here in Boulder and across the country, including Karal Ann Marling, Elaine Tyler May, Lary May, Frances Pohl, Rickie Solinger, Shirley Wajda, and Jay Willis. For their insightful responses to versions of this material that I have presented at academic conferences, I'd especially like to thank Jonathan Katz, Richard Martin, John Peters-Campbell, Jules Prown, and George Sanchez.

For her generous help with this project, I am grateful to Sherry Wallace, and for their willingness to share information I'd like to thank a long list of people: Judy Baca, Dennis Barrie, Nancy Bless, John Blosser, Kathy Coakley, Kelly Dempsey, Jim Farrell, Julie Fehrenbach, Victor Garcia, Ann Goldstein, Lane Hirabayashi, Hawley Holmes, JoAnn Hustis, Ken Indermark, Bert Johns, Ariston Julian, Carol Kliger, Barbara Kruger, Norm Krumholz, Kats Kunitsugu, Walter Leedy, Andrew Leicester, Manuel Magana, Yvette Martinez, Ruth Meyer, Daphne Mitchell, Evelyn Muffler, Nick Natanson, Bill Patmon, John Perry, Rennie Pili, Mike Polensek, Jinnie Ponce, Rod Rolle, Ken Rosene, Jim Sanborn, Judy Schoenenberger, Mike Several, Wes Smith, Jane Tesso, Edmund Thornton, Sally Webster, and Derek Woodham. For sustenance and good humor on the road and in their homes I especially thank Beth Benezra and Rob Cordo, Kathy Culley and Dave Schwier, Lynne and Clay Cummins, Liz and Bernie Dominguez, Alice and Seale Doss, Donna Gartenmann, Evelyn Kane, Mary Ohlinger-Pray, and Sarah Rosner.

Finally, for their willingness to chauffeur and accompany me to the wilds of America in search of public art, I want to thank my very good friends Vanessa Jones and Lesley Sharp. I owe them each much more than a new pair of shoes.

Public Art in Little Tokyo
Part One

I n 1989 Barbara Kruger was invited by the Los Angeles Museum of Contemporary Art (MOCA) to paint an outdoor mural. Specifically, the New York artist was commissioned to make a gigantic billboard for MOCA's Temporary Contemporary (TC) building, an unmarked white elephant of a warehouse where the museum stores and displays much of its extensive collection of contemporary art. Located in central Los Angeles, about a block from the intersection of First Street and Alameda Avenue, the TC looms large on the northern fringe of Little Tokyo, the cultural and economic heart of Los Angeles's Japanese American community. Despite its enormous size (some 5,115 square meters [55,000 square feet]), the former paint factory is fairly anonymous. Planted at the edge of several parking lots, it doesn't look like a museum; art lovers trying to find it frequently get lost, often giving up their search and settling for lunch in Little Tokyo instead. Asked to remedy this situation, Kruger proposed an 8.8-meter (29-foot) by 66.5-meter (218-foot) mural for the TC's south wall, the wall facing and most clearly seen by those heading toward the museum—and by those who work in and frequent Little Tokyo (Fig. 1).

Kruger's plans were to monumentalize a bumper sticker, called *Untitled (Pledge)*, that she had made for MOCA's summer 1989 exhibition "A Forest of Signs: Art in the Crisis of Representation" (Fig. 2). As had

■ I. **Barbara Kruger,** *Untitled (Questions),* Version I, May 1989; proposed 8.8 meters (29 feet) by 66.4 meters (218 feet) mural design for south wall of the Temporary Contemporary, Los Angeles. Photo courtesy The Museum of Contemporary Art, Los Angeles.

the other artists in this critically celebrated show (including Jenny Holzer, Mike Kelley, and Sherrie Levine), Kruger tackled what MOCA director Richard Koshalek called "the central artistic issue" of our time: "the meaning of art in a media- and consumer-influenced era, and the meaning of representation within this art." Museum goers confronting Kruger's bumper stickers, which were plastered all over the museum, were encouraged to question the difference—if any—between her art and all the other examples of visual information glutting the world: "the 'forest' of signs and symbols that define contemporary culture: the flow of images from films, billboards, bus benches, magazines, television, and art that are with us daily."[1]

Since the early 1980s Kruger's take on visual glut has consisted primarily of photographic collages of words and pictures lifted from popu-

Who is bought and sold? Who is beyond the law? Who is free to choose? Who follows orders? Who salutes longest?

COMING SOON I PLEDGE ALLEGIANCE TO THE FLAG OF THE UNITED STATES OF AMERICA AND TO THE REPUBLIC FOR WHICH IT STANDS, ONE NATION UNDER GOD, INDIVISIBLE, WITH LIBERTY AND JUSTICE FOR ALL.

Who prays loudest? Who dies first? Who laughs last? Who does time? Who is beyond the law? Who is bought and sold?

■ 2. **Barbara Kruger,** *Untitled (Pledge),* May 1989; bumper sticker. Photo courtesy The Museum of Contemporary Art, Los Angeles.

lar media sources—such as print and television advertising. Mixing up those mass media texts and images, Kruger creates artwork aimed at leading audiences to a different and perhaps more critical understanding of their conventional sociopolitical significance: "I work with pictures and words and what they mean," she remarks. "Pictures and words have the power to determine who we are, what we want to be, and what we become. I'm interested in power—in how pictures and words relate to power."[2] In the red, white, and blue bumper sticker she designed for the 1989 MOCA show, Kruger played the Pledge of Allegiance against the shape and color of the U.S. flag, writing the pledge in white letters and placing it against a red background surrounded by a blue border. Within the border the following questions are written: "Who is bought and sold? Who is beyond the law? Who is free to choose? Who follows orders? Who salutes longest? Who prays loudest? Who dies first? Who laughs last? Who does time?" At the far left of the bumper sticker, large white letters announce: "Coming Soon."

In the context of the exhibition, Kruger's juxtaposition of patriotic symbols and insinuating questions was fairly clear. On one level it was the art world's countercultural sequel to those flag-waving spectacles of the 1988 presidential campaign—when George Bush arranged innumerable photo ops in front of oversize Star-Spangled Banners and decreed that the Pledge of Allegiance was the penultimate symbol of American loyalty. On another it embodied Kruger's angry denunciation of Bush's actual views of the rule of law, shown by his contemptuous response to the 21 June 1989 Supreme Court decision upholding flag burning as symbolic speech protected by the First Amendment. Posed against the king-size flag and the gargantuan figures of the Iwo Jima Memorial at an Arlington National Cemetery press conference held shortly after the decision was handed down, Bush proclaimed that "the flag represents and reflects the fabric of our nation—our dreams, our destiny, our very fiber as a people." Then he called for a constitutional amendment to make flag desecration illegal.[3]

Kruger's bumper sticker pierced these supercilious assumptions of American nationalism and identity, of Republican political hubris regarding the real meaning of the U.S. Constitution. Framing the Pledge of Allegiance—whose words "under God" were appended at the height of the Cold War, on Flag Day 1954—with questions such as "Who salutes longest?" and "Who is beyond the law?" Kruger queried the authority of America's neoconservative guardians of patriotism, and their astounding abuse of the country's slogans and symbols. "We were already nine years into incredibly oppressive stuff—the era of Reagan and Bush," Kruger comments. "The bumper sticker, and the mural design, were about power—about questions of power and authority." Other artists, equally angered by the patriotism-first hype of the 1980s, produced similar pieces: "Dread" Scott Tyler's *What Is the Proper Way to Display a U.S. Flag?* was exhibited at Chicago's Art Institute in February 1989 (Fig. 3). In order to answer that question, museum visitors were invited to step onto a U.S. flag—an act that infuriated members of the Veterans of Foreign Wars but more than met the artist's flag-desecrating and symbol-deflating agenda. Informed MOCA visitors, especially those familiar with the deconstructionist mind-set of artists such as Tyler, easily understood Kruger's bumper sticker critique of "the injustices of a nation parading a symbol of justice."[4]

But Kruger's plans to wrap the TC in this countercultural flag of resistance met with outright hostility—and not from flag-waving VFW xenophobes but from Little Tokyo residents. So that it would work effectively as a museum billboard, Kruger changed her bumper sticker by substituting the words "MOCA/AT THE TEMPORARY CONTEMPORARY" for "Coming Soon" in the upper-left corner, the star field of Old Glory. Other original design elements were retained—the Pledge of Allegiance laid out as the white stripes of the U.S. flag, the entire sign bordered by the provocative questions. It was Kruger's use of the pledge that especially outraged Los Angeles's Japanese American community.

The museum hoped to open its "Forest of Signs" exhibition in May

■ 3. **"Dread" Scott Tyler,**
What Is the Proper Way to Display a U.S. Flag? 1989; mixed-media installation in the student exhibition "A/Part of the Whole" at the School of the Art Institute of Chicago. Photo courtesy Michael Tropea, Chicago.

1989 with Kruger's mural in place at the TC. Following normal bureaucratic procedures, MOCA asked the city's Cultural Affairs Commission (CAC) to approve the outdoor mural. (Because it is owned by the City of Los Angeles, any design or addition to the TC is subject to the authority and final decision of this commission.) Approval was perfunctorily granted, and MOCA next presented Kruger's design to the Little Tokyo Community Development Advisory Committee (LTCDAC), a mayor-appointed citizen group (formed in 1969) whose mandate is to coordinate development and cultural resources in Los Angeles's Japanese American neighborhood. Much to MOCA's surprise, when Kruger's mural design was brought to a vote at the June 1989 meeting, it was resoundingly defeated.

Katsumi ("Kats") Kunitsugu, vice president of the LTCDAC and executive secretary of the Japanese American Cultural and Community

Center, introduced the motion rejecting Kruger's idea. Her distress about Kruger's proposal was shared by other longtime Little Tokyo residents who remembered what their community had been like before 1942. Up to then Little Tokyo—often called Japanese Town, J-Town, or Sho Tokyo (the term used by many Japanese today), and sometimes pejoratively called Jap Town—was the residential, economic, and cultural hub for Los Angeles's Japanese American citizens, the site of their houses and apartment buildings and businesses, the locus of the produce and flower markets, restaurants, banks, temples, newspapers, and schools central to the Japanese American community. It was home to more Japanese Americans than any other city on the U.S. mainland—about 37,000 Japanese Americans lived in Los Angeles County in 1940, many of them in or near the Little Tokyo neighborhood.[5]

But the racist hysteria that followed the bombing of Pearl Harbor turned Little Tokyo into a ghost town. Following Franklin D. Roosevelt's signing of Executive Order 9066 on 19 February 1942, some 110,000 Japanese Americans were forcibly removed from the West Coast and placed in "relocation centers" in remote, desert areas (many of them Native American Indian reservations) in California, Arizona, Utah, Idaho, Wyoming, and Colorado. During World War II Kats Kunitsugu spent three years of her childhood incarcerated in those "centers"—which Secretary of the Interior Harold L. Ickes recognized as American concentration camps:

> As a member of President Roosevelt's administration, I saw the United States Army give way to mass hysteria over the Japanese . . . it lost its self-control, and egged on by public clamor, some of it from greedy Americans who sought an opportunity to possess themselves of Japanese rights and property, it began to round up indiscriminately the Japanese. . . . Crowded into cars like cattle, these hapless people were hurried away. . . . We gave the fancy name of "relocation centers" to these dust bowls, but they were concentration camps nonetheless.[6]

Kunitsugu bitterly recalled the irony of the daily flag-raising ceremony in the camps and of Japanese American prisoners reciting the Pledge of Allegiance behind barbed-wire fences at Manzanar, Tule Lake, and Topaz (Figs. 4 and 5).

After the war Japanese Americans returning to the Los Angeles area settled in suburban residential communities such as Gardena rather than in Little Tokyo. Only in the last few decades has the downtown area

■ 4. **Dorothea Lange,** *Manzanar Relocation Center, 3 July 1942,* 1942; black and white photograph done for the War Relocation Authority. National Archives Still Pictures Branch, WRA 210-G-C-839.

seen an economic and cultural revival. Spurred by the Little Tokyo Redevelopment Association (formed in the early 1960s), numerous Japanese corporations have constructed office towers, hotels, and mixed-use commercial buildings in the area—and have hugely affected the visual look and overall economic picture of downtown Los Angeles. In 1988 L.A. took in $3.05 billion (over one-fifth) of Japan's North American real estate investment dollars. Local developers profited mightily from their involvement in various joint-venture projects—from Prudential's collaboration with Mitsubishi to build Citicorp Plaza to the multiple partnerships that generated the thirty-five stores, shops, and restaurants of Weller Court, Little Tokyo's chief retail and office complex. Some grumbled about the "Nipponization" of Southern California and of down-

■ 5. **Francis Stewart,** *Memorial Day Ceremonies with American Legion Members and Boy Scouts, 31 May 1942, Manzanar, 1942*; black and white photograph done for the War Relocation Authority. National Archives Still Pictures Branch, WRA 210-G-10D-538.

town L.A.'s seeming status as "second only to Tokyo as a financial pole of the Pacific Rim."[7] Such sentiments directly contributed to the controversy over Kruger's proposed mural.

If Little Tokyo's contemporary economic health was largely the result of an influx of Japanese yen, the LTCDAC (located on the third floor of Weller Court), was responsible for making sure that that surge of foreign development dollars did not totally destroy the area's few remaining older buildings and their physical contribution to Little Tokyo's Japanese American character. In 1986, after thirteen buildings in the Little Tokyo Historic District were placed on the National Register of Historic Places, these older brick storefronts began to be rehabilitated. Soon thereafter community and arts groups started to relocate to Little Tokyo and Japanese American suburbanites were drawn to the area.

Today, while Little Tokyo has almost no residential population, it has regained its reputation as the cultural core of Southern California's

Japanese American community (and is also a popular attraction for Japanese tourists). The Japanese American National Museum, in the former Nishi Hongwanji Buddhist Temple building, has frequent exhibitions, lectures, and festivals that aim to "make known the Japanese American experience as an integral part of our nation's heritage to improve understanding and appreciation for America's ethnic and cultural diversity."[8] For many in Los Angeles's Japanese American community, the mural that Barbara Kruger proposed for the south wall of the TC seemed to threaten this nascent renewal of Japanese American cultural— and perhaps economic—energies in Little Tokyo.

For others Kruger's mural design particularly stirred memories of forced evacuation and imprisonment. In 1989, when the mural was proposed, the site for the Japanese American National Museum (which opened in 1991) was remembered as the place where, in spring 1942, all persons of Japanese American ancestry in the Little Tokyo neighborhood were ordered to gather for internment. The future museum also housed many homeless (and penniless) Japanese American families after their release from the camps in 1945. Alan Furuta, chair of the Little Tokyo Community Development Advisory Committee, cautioned that the proposed TC mural—posed right across the street from this multivalent historic building—"would perhaps bring up old wounds and feelings." Furuta, whose parents and grandparents were imprisoned in the camps, added, "We gave up a lot of liberty and a lot of freedom. Do we have to be reminded of that lack of justice?"[9]

Highlighting the Pledge of Allegiance, Kruger's mural especially reminded older Little Tokyo residents of the disingenuous "loyalty tests" given in the internment camps. In 1943, anxious to make military use of the thousands of younger Japanese Americans in the camps, the U.S. War Department prepared a recruitment questionnaire directed toward male prisoners of military age. The War Relocation Authority (WRA), the official government agency that ran the camps, reshaped the questionnaire into a loyalty test for all Japanese Americans aged seventeen or older. Disguising it as an "Application to Leave Clearance," the WRA used the questionnaire to pose particular questions about patriotism and national allegiance. Question 27, for example, asked draft-age males if they would serve in the U.S. military, and Question 28 read: "Will you swear unqualified allegiance to the United States of America and faithfully defend the United States from any or all attack by foreign or domestic forces, and forswear any form of allegiance or obedience to the Japanese emperor, to any other foreign government, power or organization?" In other words, this oath basically asked Japanese nationals to forswear allegiance to Japan and was also tantamount to alien registration for Nisei (second-generation Japanese Americans). "Yes-yes" answers to questions 27 and 28 made male Nisei of draft age eligible for military service; "no-no" answers (or the more plausible response of "yes-if") led the WRA to segregate "loyal" Japanese Americans from "disloyal" prisoners, and many of the latter were transferred to high-security camps such as the FBI-run facility at Tule Lake. Asked essentially to defend the country that had violated their civil and human rights, some 65,000 of the 75,000 camp residents who filled out the questionnaires incredibly answered "yes" to these questions—and thereby affirmed their loyalty to the United States. A large number of men and women in the camps volunteered for military service, many men eventually serving in the 442nd Regimental Combat Team, the most highly decorated American fighting unit of World War II, and many women joining the Women's Auxiliary Army Corps (later the WAC).[10]

The thought of having to confront what they perceived as accusations of disloyalty again, on an everyday basis, in brightly painted letters five feet tall, was too much for Kats Kunitsugu and other members of Los Angeles's Japanese American community. "The pledge was such a slap in the face," Kunitsugu remarked. "The question of loyalty has always been a sensitive issue—people think we are not automatically loyal because we are not white." She also noted, "I thought that we had proved our loyalty. Friends of mine volunteered [for combat duty in the army] out of the camps and fought in Europe. I thought we paid our dues. The first impression that you get [of the mural] is this huge Pledge of Allegiance. Why facing Little Tokyo? Why now?"[11]

Indeed, the question Why now? is central to Little Tokyo's reaction to Kruger's proposed mural, especially since it came at a time when both Japan bashing and redress were making front-page news. Frustrated by a declining economy and seemingly insolvable domestic problems, recessionary America searched for a scapegoat and found it in the form of Japan and the Japanese. An outpouring of paranoid nonfiction treatises (*Yen! Japan's New Financial Empire and Its Threat to America* [1988] and *The Enigma of Japanese Power* [1989]) and novels (most notably Michael Crichton's 1992 thriller *Rising Sun*) conjured a new Fu Manchu to menace America. Yet, simultaneously, a long process of redress met with success in 1988, when Congress apologized to the 60,000 surviving Japanese Americans who had been imprisoned in U.S. concentration camps during World War II. Stating that their incarceration was "motivated largely by racial prejudice, wartime hysteria, and a failure of political leadership," the federal government set aside a $1.2 billion reparation fund and in 1990 began distributing a $20,000 check, and a signed letter of apology from President George Bush, to each of the former prisoners.[12]

Given the broader context of contemporary Japanese American relations, and the specific social and cultural dynamics of the Little Tokyo neighborhood, the reasons for the LTCDAC's unanimous rejection of Kruger's mural proposal become clear. While her aim was to stimulate awareness about the power and meaning of particular words and pictures—the Pledge of Allegiance, for example, and the U.S. flag—many members of Los Angeles's Japanese American community interpreted her proposal as a racial slur. Presumably democratic intentions in the public sphere were misread as evidence of artistic egocentrism and art museum arrogance.

Museum administrators and staff were clearly taken aback by the controversy that Kruger's mural design kindled in Little Tokyo. Director Koshalek remarked to one newspaper reporter, "Their reasons for being concerned came as a surprise to all of us. . . . I don't think any of us guessed that the situation in the 1940s could bring up this great sensitivity."[13] But, as this book demonstrates, this incident is by no means isolated: Public "sensitivity" to public art is widespread and vociferous. Nor did this particular tale of public art planners seemingly at odds with the public art audience end completely irreconciled—as the Epilogue to this book concludes. Public art happened in Little Tokyo, but not exactly the way it was first proposed.

Especially in the past decade, public art has become the site of conflict and the symbol of struggle over art style and authority in an increasingly complex and contested public sphere. *Spirit Poles and Flying Pigs: Public Art and Cultural Democracy in American Communities* tells the stories of this conflicted sphere, where artists, patrons, and audiences argue over opposing definitions of art and property, of public access and civic input. If today's public is "sensitive" about public art, it is because questions about public art—what is it? who is it for?—remain unanswered and open to interpretation. The ongoing debate over these questions is of fundamental importance, however, because the story of how public culture is created and contested—in Little Tokyo and across America—is the story of power and participation in the democratic sphere.

CHAPTER ONE

Contemporary Public Art Controversy
An Introduction

In 1983 artist Andrea Blum was hired by the Boulder Art Commission to create a public sculpture in a small park near downtown Boulder. But Blum's design for three concrete pavilions backfired, resulting in angry civic debate and a failed project.

In 1984 two abstract neon sculptures by Stephen Antonakos were installed in the Tacoma Dome in Tacoma, Washington. The art so infuriated citizens of this Puget Sound city that within months they voted to have the pieces removed, and by the end of 1985 they succeeded in repealing the municipal one-percent-for-art ordinance that had financed the public artwork.

In 1985 Sohio commissioned Pop artist Claes Oldenburg to make an outdoor sculpture for the company's new headquarters in downtown Cleveland. Oldenburg and partner Coosje van Bruggen designed *Free Stamp,* a gigantic metal replica of a rubber stamp with the word *FREE* embossed in capital letters 5.5 meters (18 feet) tall. But, after merging with British Petroleum in 1986, the company refused to install the sculpture and spent years trying to give it to the city, which viewed *Free Stamp* as an insulting corporate castoff.

In 1985 a 120.7-hectare (298-acre) sculpture park designed by Michael Heizer was dedicated on the site of an abandoned coal mine near Ottawa, Illinois. Within a few years the park was closed down, caught in the middle of a bitter dispute between local dirt bikers and the state Department of Conservation.

In 1988 citizens in Cincinnati protested the presence of bronze pigs in a scultural gateway created by Andrew Leicester. Local politicians went on record damning the "swine image" Leicester's flying pigs could create for Cincinnati.

In 1989 the town of Concord, California, unveiled an abstract outdoor sculpture designed by Gary Rieveschl. Shortly after its dedication hostile reaction to the sculpture, nicknamed *Spirit Poles,* swayed a general election: Candidates who promised to get rid of it were swept into office, and the lone incumbent—a city council member who had voted for the piece in 1988—was defeated. Topping off that political indignity, in March 1990 the *National Enquirer* called Concord's public art the "ugliest tax-funded sculpture in America."

These diverse episodes, all to be discussed in later chapters of this book, demonstrate how public art is the focus of heated civic debate in contemporary America. The 1980s opened and closed with two especially memorable public art quarrels—protests over the *Vietnam Veterans Memorial* and actions against *Tilted Arc,* an abstract sculpture removed from Manhattan's Federal Plaza in 1989—and such disputes continue. Public art controversy involves questions of art style and assumptions about audience, problems of placelessness, concerns about civic identity, and political posturing. Most of all, it centers on debates over the meaning of democracy, and especially how democratic expression is shaped in contemporary America.

Angered by perceptions of powerlessness and manipulation, growing numbers of Americans have targeted public art to question their role in the relevance and direction of civic life. Today's public sphere, that wide-ranging intersection of place, space, and human activity, has become a contested site of cultural authority as artists, arts agencies, politicians, and corporations vie for public favor and power. Public art discourse—debates, petitions, hearings, media accounts, artists' statements, political proceedings, and the art-making process itself—discloses widespread

American concern with this struggle for cultural, and social, control. Concentrating on a variety of recent public art controversies, this book explores the tense dynamics of today's public culture.

Public art controversy is, of course, nothing new. Early in the nineteenth century Davy Crockett criticized the first public art the U.S. government ever commissioned—Horatio Greenough's colossal marble sculpture called *George Washington* (1832–1841)—by proclaiming: "I do not like the statue of Washington in the State-House. . . . They have a Roman gown on him, and he was an American; this ain't right." Subsequently the sculpture was removed, from the rotunda of the U.S. Capitol to the Capitol's front lawn and, finally, to its current location by the escalator leading down to the cafeteria in the Smithsonian Institution's National Museum of American History. In 1855 rabid members of the Know-Nothings, a "semiclandestine political party that aimed to rid the country of Catholics and foreigners," sabotaged the construction of the Washington Monument by throwing blocks of the marble shaft into the Potomac River. They also interfered with funding for the 169.2-meter (555-foot) Doric obelisk and for "almost twenty-five years after this debacle, the monument stood as a pathetic stump in the very heart of the capital."[1]

In 1911 the *New York Times* denounced the *Maine Memorial,* a public sculpture commemorating the Spanish-American War, as a "cheap disfigurement" wrecking the views and landscape of Central Park. During the Great Depression of the 1930s, innumerable public murals came under siege—for being too modern, or not modern enough, or too much like propaganda. In 1933, before it was even finished, a mural by Diego Rivera in New York's Rockefeller Center, featuring a giant portrait of Lenin, was destroyed; in 1934 Victor Arnautoff's depiction of left-wing newspapers (and their readers) in a mural for San Francisco's Coit Tower became the focus of media sensationalism and political uproar. Egged on by anti–New Deal reactionaries, the entire process of public funding for the arts was subjected to violent congressional attack during the postwar era. Even the Iwo Jima Memorial became the target of intense scrutiny: Its 1954 unveiling in Arlington National Cemetery was met with media accusations of inauthenticity and outrage at its expense ($850,000).[2]

If even more complex, contemporary public art controversies are consistent with the long-standing struggle Americans have had over the meaning of democratic expression. Americans continue to respond angrily to public culture, so much so that it is rare today for any example of public art to be produced and then unveiled without heated argument and debate. The turbulent tones of these battles over public culture are certainly influenced by who the American public is and how that public is viewed by artists, arts agencies, politicians, and corporations. They are furthered by how the public—broadly and specifically—constructs itself in terms of race, sex, gender, and ethnic identity. And they are advanced by the disquieting sense that little of today's public culture is actually generated in behalf of "the people" and that notions of artistic autonomy, expert social vision, and political and corporate interest dominate the public sphere.

As posited by critic Jürgen Habermas in the early 1960s, the public sphere consists of a body of private people coming together to discuss common interests rationally. It is an ideal and detached realm distinct from the real-life tensions of politics, economics, and social difference—and so too is the public culture within that sphere. It is fictitious and utopian, and Habermas himself argued that this model is practically impossible under the tenets of late capitalism's pervasive corporate influence, mass media, and consumerism. Feminist philosopher Nancy Fraser argues that Habermas's concept of the liberal public sphere was not only an unrealized utopian ideal but "also a masculinist ideological notion that functioned to legitimate an emergent form of class rule." In deference to a model of a single, passive, and ideal public sphere, Habermas failed to recognize its inherent conflicts and the host of counterpublics—women, workers, racial groups, and so on—who were excluded from this ideal realm and who created their own public spheres and public cultures.[3]

Despite its failings this model of a limited and essentially problem-free public culture has been largely adopted by public arts agencies and public artists, as this book demonstrates. As a result it has dramatically informed the kind of art and the kind of audience response that shape contemporary debates about public art. Within the physical space of the supposedly passive public sphere, people have been encouraged to view objects—sometimes called monuments or memorials—uncritically, without discourse, and, quite literally, at face value. Public art objects are meant to exist in their "own dumb actuality"—silent, inert, and out of context, and public art audiences are expected to accept their mute but obvious presence.[4] Given this contemporary understanding, it is not surprising that Americans in Los Angeles, Boulder, Tacoma, Cleveland,

Ottawa, Cincinnati, Concord, and plenty of other places view public art as both irrelevant and a blatant symbol of their loss of autonomy in the public sphere.

Public anger about public art coincides with the recent development of the public art industry, a conglomerate of experts—artists, arts agencies, and consultants—charged with filling America's parks, airports, public buildings, and city streets with sculptures and murals. Today's public art industry is a flourishing enterprise: The expenditure on sculpture projects approved in 1991 alone topped $16 million.[5] Despite its nomenclature, however, it is an industry that often fails to engage citizens effectively in the development of civic culture. The National Endowment for the Arts (NEA), for example, which established its Art in Public Places program in 1966 and has since helped to commission and finance hundreds of public art projects across America, claims that the arts are to "be experienced and enjoyed by the widest possible audience."[6] The NEA's version of cultural democracy is predicated on the concept of consensus. Public arts agencies and public artists that follow this model seem to make little effort to assess the dramatic social and historical differences that exist in American communities, instead following the assumption that there is a generic American type and public art is for "him." Coupled with this denial of diversity is the presumption that culture is *for* the people, not *of* them. The public art industry rarely makes the effort to link public art with the cultural needs and direct participation of specific communities, and the result has been the widespread eruption of bitter controversy over what is perceived as elitist public culture.

Public art style plays a significant role in this controversy: Barbara Kruger's seemingly insensitive art world aesthetics clearly infuriated the citizens of Little Tokyo, and the abstract overtones of Gary Rieveschl's sculpture certainly heightened hostile civic reaction to public art in Concord. Further, it was *Tilted Arc*'s minimalist style that conditioned decisions leading to its removal in 1989. A decade earlier the U.S. General Services Administration (GSA) had commissioned Richard Serra to make a sculpture for Manhattan's Federal Plaza; *Tilted Arc,* an unadorned steel sculpture nearly the length of a city block (36.6 meters [120 feet] long and 3.7 meters [12 feet] tall), was placed in Foley Square, in front of the Jacob K. Javits Federal Building, in 1981. *Tilted Arc*'s unveiling met with considerable hostility: Nicknaming it "The Berlin Wall of Foley Square," some 1,300 employees of the Federal Complex signed petitions demanding the abstract sculpture's removal on the grounds that it "was ugly; that it spoiled the view; that it prevented the plaza from being used for concerts, performances, or social gatherings; that it attracted graffiti; that it made access to the building difficult."[7]

At first glance it would seem that the entire problem of public art controversy could be solved if artists abandoned modern art and catered to what appears to be public preference for sculpture along the lines of Mount Rushmore or the *Memorial to John Wayne* in the Orange County Airport. Indeed, representational bronzes à la Glenna Goodacre's *Pledge Allegiance* (Fig. 6) are popping up all over the country, ostensibly because audiences are drawn to their "realistic" sentimentalization of simpler times and "traditional" values. A closer examination, however, reveals that their public proliferation is largely the result of private marketing. The "public" art in Loveland, Colorado, for example, often cited as an outstanding civic venue for representational art, actually consists of private pieces donated or on loan from Loveland's High Plains Art Council, a private nonprofit group that often acts as a wholesaler for the city's famous bronze casting foundries. As a self-serving marketing ploy, malls and upscale suburban housing developments are also increasingly dotted with saccharine bronzes of frolicking kiddies and benign wildlife. One developer at Denver's Cherry Creek North Mall, where an outdoor plaza is filled with cloying bronzes of baseball players and dancing girls, remarks, "Our vision was to select friendly, more hands-on art. Art that you can walk up next to; art that is diverse, whimsical."[8]

And people often like this style of art—Goodacre, who was chosen to sculpt the *Vietnam Women's Memorial* unveiled in Washington, D.C., in November 1993, is probably the most successful sculptor in America. But representational art has also been the source of public art controversy, as Cleveland's enmity to *Free Stamp* and Cincinnati's affront to sculpted pigs both attest. Across the country numerous groups have indicted representational art for a variety of reasons: In San Jose, citizens objected to plans to erect a monumental bronze sculpture of a nineteenth-century U.S. Army captain, charging that it glorified militarism; in Denver the Commission on Cultural Affairs protested Barbara Jo Revelle's inclusion of portraits of Lauren Watson, founder of Denver's Black Panther Party, and Rodolfo "Corky" Gonzales, local Chicano activist, in a huge (182.9-meter, 600-foot) photomural at the city's Con-

■ 6. **Glenna Goodacre,**
Pledge Allegiance, 1992;
bronze, 4.6 meters (15 feet)
high, Loveland, Colo. Photo
by Fabrice, courtesy Glenna
Goodacre.

vention Center; in Pittsburgh, Luis Jimenez's 3.7-meter (12-foot) fiberglass sculpture *Hunky Steelworker* was attacked as a racial slur on Eastern European Americans.[9]

Not even Goodacre's art has been free from civic debate: At the height
of the Gulf War, *Pledge Allegiance* was criticized as an "alarming propa-
gandist depiction of social control." A year earlier, in 1990, some Albuquerque residents complained that her sculpture *Sidewalk Society,* a life-
size bronze tableau of six adults and three children, reinforced racial
stereotypes with its mustachioed, hard hat–holding depiction of a Hispanic male. Don Chavez, a member of Albuquerque's Hispanic Issues
Consortium, said Goodacre's sculpture insulted Mexican Americans:
"The statue portrays a very narrow, stereotypical image of a person who
is overweight and an underachiever committed to a career of toiling
labor for the rest of his life." Millie Santillanes, in contrast, president of
the city's Hispano Chamber of Commerce, called Chavez's comments
"arrogant" because of his insinuation that only Hispanic professionals

carrying briefcases had social status. A furious editorial writer in a local art magazine responded to the whole outcry with the following:

> In point of fact, the contested figure in *Sidewalk Society*, which symbol-izes Albuquerque's pride and confidence in its own future, is the highest possible compliment to Hispanics: for the building of the future of Albu-querque is being placed in that figure's hands—hands which, be it noted, are not holding a sombrero, nor is the man wearing a serape, nor is he at the back of the line of people dozing against an adobe wall.

Discounting local concerns about civic image and perceptions of racism that Goodacre's sculpture obviously stirred up, the writer concluded that the "moral" of this public art battle was that "fine art, which attempts to be timeless and universal, should be protected from political pressure groups, which are always wedded to a particular time and a particular selfish interest."[10]

Of course, public art debates over image and about the authority of special interest groups are hardly restricted to narrative and representa-tional forms of public art, as witnessed in the controversy surrounding Maya Lin's *Vietnam Veterans Memorial* in the early 1980s. Further-more, the depth of audience reaction to this work reveals the meaningful emotional response that abstract forms of public art can evoke: The monument is now the most visited public memorial in the nation's capi-tal. Any analysis of public art style, then, must realize the nuanced, com-plicated, and constantly shifting meanings that both styles and public spheres carry, especially as particular styles of public art carry different meanings in different contexts. It is doubtful that Orange County's *Memorial to John Wayne* would receive public accolade if placed on the Pine Ridge Reservation in South Dakota.

The problem of public art style is confounded by the quickening pace with which art styles are appropriated by various concerns fighting to control the public sphere. The styles of graffiti writing that inner-city teenagers tagged all over New York's subway trains, for example, were voraciously consumed in the early 1980s by the New York art world, and then by Madison Avenue. By the end of the decade, the dynamic, personalized rebelliousness of graffiti had become nothing more than a stylistic cliché, a backdrop for car advertisements, a design motif for T-shirts. Any style that lends cultural authority, even for a short period of time, is fair game in public culture. The overt manipulation of style, then, is central to contemporary public art controversy, especially when audiences sense the manner in which art styles are used to convey other, often hidden, agendas.

Indeed, controversies over public art style really unmask deeper concerns Americans have regarding their voice in the public sphere. Many feel marginalized by what they perceive as an unaccountable, self-referential group of experts: those in the public art industry but also city managers and politicians who claim to speak for "the people" yet seem willfully detached from real-life public concerns. Overwhelmed by social problems including homelessness, AIDS, and violent crime, Americans are frustrated by the failure of institutions, especially political parties but also state and local government, to solve those problems. Yet they also hold a certain degree of often healthy, often simply contrary, contempt for institutional authority (especially government), which blocks large-scale social problem solving. The number and nature of recent public art controversies suggest that many Americans have opted to vent their frustrations, and their inherent ambivalence about how to deal with so-cial problems, by assailing public culture. If the mercurial complexity of contemporary life seems unfathomable, if real-life problems seem in-surmountable and experts appear irresolutely unresponsive, the simple presence, the "thereness," of public art is a solid, knowable target. Of course, in the 1980s many neoconservative politicians and intellectuals attacked public culture on more disingenuous grounds, finding it both the cause and the cure for America's ills.

The readiness with which Americans assail public art is shaped by media accounts questioning how it is chosen and the high costs involved. A recent newspaper feature on public art at the Palm Beach International Airport, for example, criticized the "favoritism" of the "good old boy network" that selected art for the new airport and stressed that "one of the biggest problems [with public art] is that the public gets co-opted out of it."[11] Reader alienation about Palm Beach's public art was probably advanced by the color photographs supplementing the article, each cap-tioning the airport's art with its taxpayer-funded price tag in boldface type: *Untitled*, Ruth Duckworth, $30,000; *Zoetrope Ranch*, Ken Schnei-der, $7,500; *Passage*, Larry Kirkland, $50,000. Given the contemporary economic climate, it is not hard to imagine public reaction to the seem-ingly outrageous prices paid for public art—real or imaginary (Fig. 7). People see public art as a luxury and question its costs when other parts of contemporary society are so needy. American disgust with these costs is intensified by media focus on the fraudulent expenditure of public

Worst Case Scenario

MAKING ART PUBLIC

THE DENVER MAYOR'S OFFICE OF ART, CULTURE AND FILM HAS JUST ANNOUNCED THE PUBLIC COMPETITION FOR THE $448,700.00 COMMISSION OF ARTWORK FOR THE GREAT HALL IN THE NEW DENVER PUBLIC LIBRARY. IT'S THE LARGEST COMMISSION FOR AN ARTWORK THAT THE CITY HAS EVER OFFERED, AND ARTISTS ARE DIZZY WITH INSPIRATION. SO AM I. ALTHOUGH I'M JUST A CARTOONIST, I KNOW MY WAY AROUND A LIBRARY. I THINK ALL GREAT LIBRARIES SHOULD BE PROTECTED BY HUGE STONE LIONS. (IT'S A TRADITION!!) BUT SINCE THIS IS COLORADO, I PICTURE A HUGE STONE MOUNTAIN LION—WITH A BRIGHT SHINY FIBERGLASS ATHLETIC SHOE CLENCHED IN ITS JAW TO EMPHASIZE OUR OUTDOOR LIFESTYLE AND DRAMATIZE OUR INCREASINGLY TRAGIC CONFLICT WITH NATURE. WHILE $448,700 MAY SEEM EXORBITANT, NOTE ¼ OF EXPENSE IS TO BUY WORKERS COMP. INSURANCE, WHICH WINNING ARTIST MUST PROVIDE TO PROTECT THE CITY FROM A LAWSUIT IN THE EVENT OF AN ACCIDENT.

MOUNTAIN LION CHEWING ON A REEBOK

1992 Kenny Be

↑ **THE GREAT HALL.** WITH ART INSTALLATION AS SEEN FROM MAIN ENTRANCE.

Expenses

① 75-TON PINK GRANITE STONE FOR LION	$	500.00
② ITALIAN STONE SCULPTOR'S FEE	$	129,650.00
③ SHIPPING TO AND FROM ITALY	$	31,000.00
④ FIBERGLASS SHOE MATERIALS + INSTALL	$	29,000.00
⑤ BRASS PLAQUE	$	1,500.00
⑥ METAL PINES ON ZEPHYR BRACES 12 @ $4,000 ea.	$	48,000.00
⑦ INSTALLATION	$	6,000.00
⑧ SODIUM LIGHTNING RODS 12 @ $2,366 ea.	$	28,392.00
⑨ INSTALLATION BY MASTER ELECTRICIAN	$	32,000.00
⑩ VAULTED CEILING CLOUD MURAL	$	8,000.00
⑪ WORKERS COMP. INSURANCE	$	134,600.00
⑫ ARTIST DESIGN FEE	$	8.00
TOTAL	**$**	**448,700.00**

↑ LOOKING NORTH INTO THE GREAT HALL FROM 2ND FLOOR ADULT GENERAL COLLECTIONS.

■ 7. **Kenny Be,** *Worst Case Scenario: Making Art Public,* 1992; cartoon drawing. Courtesy Kenny Be.

■ 8. **Andrew Leicester,** *Paradise,* 1986; concrete, wood, water sculpture, 48.8 meters (160 feet) long by 18.3 meters (60 feet) wide by 4.6 meters (15 feet) high, "Old Max" Prison, Canon City, Colo. Photo: Andrew Leicester.

dollars and media reluctance to discuss the possible advantages of public art—beautification, artistic support, civic identity, and, most important, the role of public art in the manifestation of cultural democracy.

If Americans feel closed out by the public art selection process, they are incensed by examples of public art that literally exclude them. Public sculptures centerpiecing deserted urban plazas subtly substantiate this, but examples of completely unreachable publicly funded works of art also abound. A considerable body of public art, for instance, now exists in America's prisons—a concept that angers people even more by flying in the face of a widely held perception that prisons should be punitive. *Paradise,* a 1986 sculpture garden designed by Andrew Leicester for the maximum security prison in Canon City, Colorado, and financed through the State Arts Council's Percent for Art program, was not only inaccessible to the public but off-limits for prisoners (Fig. 8).[12] Accustomed to generating support for his public art projects by working closely with their intended audiences, Leicester was prohibited from contact with the prisoners while building this piece, a situation that dramatically affected its development and its reception. Although the prison warden was open to requests from visitors to view the sculpture, few were actually received—not surprisingly: Who wants to go to a maximum security pen to see public art? Deprived of either an in-house or an outside audience, *Paradise* was robbed of sustenance, and after a few years of neglect (despite contractual obligations to clean and repair the work), prison administrators decided to dismantle the sculpture. In 1992, unbeknownst to either the State Arts Council or the artist, *Paradise* was destroyed in Canon City—an event that raised no public ruckus whatsoever.

Kryptos (Greek for "hidden"), a 1991 granite and copper sculpture at the CIA's newly reconstructed headquarters in Langley, Virginia, was also funded with public monies (through the GSA). But located in the middle of The Company's off-limits grounds, it too is inaccessible to general visitors. ("The CIA does not conduct public tours," one agency spokesperson remarked.) The fact that it is inscribed in a mysterious code, which even experienced intelligence agents say they cannot decipher, makes it practically inaccessible to its CIA audience. The costs of these public projects infuriate Americans—some $79,500 for *Paradise*, and $250,000 for *Kryptos*—but the sense that they cannot possess what they've paid for (let alone ascertain why they paid for it) only heightens general outrage about public culture.[13]

Alienated by expert authority and aggrieved by perceptions of public culture as a costly and irrevelant social boondoggle, Americans center their discontent on public art. Ironically, their antipathy toward public culture has actually been fueled by a boom in public art. As critics and historians have recently noted, a "spectre of placelessness" characterizes much of today's built environment. Shopping malls, airports, office parks, and housing developments have such a "banal sameness" that it becomes difficult to distinguish one region or community from the next. The specificities of place, whether Boulder or Boston, are often reduced to a complete "lack of distinctive variation," a significant factor in the profound dislocation many feel from a sense of place, or community identity.[14] The difficulty with placelessness, of course, is the threat it poses to established social relations, the havoc that civic disaffection can play in terms of official authority, public passivity, and unanimity.

Throughout the 1980s one eagerly embraced solution to the problem of placelessness was public art—sculptures, murals, art parks, and landscape architecture. As social amenity, embellishment, and/or camouflage, public art was assigned the "mission," as critic Patricia Phillips cynically remarked, of "making people feel good—about themselves and where they live." Public art was thought to remedy social alienation and generate a sense of civic identity when treated as placemaking: the integration of site with aesthetics. A widespread interest in genius loci—spirit of place—emerged, with arts agencies especially attentive to "site-specific" works that helped turn places into "art."[15] Questions about whether a sense of place really does make people whole, or whose definition of place was being utilized in these public art projects, or of complicity between real estate developers and state and local government, largely went unexamined.

In any case, in the 1980s public art's appearance escalated. The American scene became dotted with abstract sculptures James Wines labeled "turds in the plaza" and with monuments and memorials that Karal Ann Marling called "the stuff of memory."[16] If an uncritical devotion to placemaking guided this public art boom, it really proliferated because of increased revenue generated through frenzied building and development schemes by both government agencies and private firms, and because of subsequent ordinances that mandated the allocation of a certain percentage of new construction costs for public art. But neither an interest in placemaking nor an ample money supply completely accounts for the growth of today's public art industry. Rather the public art movement has flourished because artists, arts agencies, corporations, and other interests have realized the cultural and political links between public art, public space, and public power.

Public space has always been an essential ingredient in the makeup of American culture, traditionally providing a dynamic locus for democratic engagement and debate by a richly diverse and perpetually shifting public. Despite the seemingly contradictory gesture of providing usually immutable visual and material models in such fluid spheres, public art has often played a role in that public debate. But prescriptive public spaces have changed dramatically in the past several decades, as has the potential for public invention and social examination. The public common and town hall have generally given way to private or commercial spaces that proclaim themselves as public spaces; the neighborhood tavern and barbershop and corner grocery have been replaced by national chains and relocated to suburban shopping centers. That is not to say that these new kinds of public space cannot provide an arena for democratic dialogue and debate—lots of civic groups meet for monthly breakfasts at McDonald's, for example—but it is to say that the central emphasis on consumption, on creating a dialogue between the individual consumer and the commodity, generally prohibits this.

It seems that today's public exists as a public only in malls, sports arenas, and concert halls, because consumerism is the primary factor in American social identity. Although civic events, such as parades and arts festivals, and spectacles sponsored by the private sector, such as the Olympics and Hands Across America, certainly provide opportunities for social interaction, they rarely provide forums for a critical analysis of that interaction. When public space is utilized for social practice, the emphasis is on unity and consensus, not on the fluctuating and eminently debatable dimensions of public culture. But contemporary public art controversy suggests a demand for the revitalization of that debate.

In the 1980s American debate over public culture was heightened by a considerably changed political atmosphere. The decade witnessed not only the final stages of a dramatic political shift, from a liberalism rooted in the New Deal to a postwar form of conservatism, but also the rise of a vocal political counterculture that challenged the dominance of neoconservatism. The agenda of both political groups was to influence and control public life, often without a genuine interest in or understanding of specific public needs and concerns.

Neoconservative intellectuals such as Daniel Bell, Hilton Kramer, Irving Kristol, Samuel Lipman, and Norman Podhoretz were obsessed with what they perceived as the crisis of authority in contemporary America, which they blamed on excessive liberalism and considered, Peter Steinfels explained, primarily in *cultural* terms, as "a matter of values, morals, and manners." Along with right-wing politicians and religious figures, they advocated the renewal of traditional, essentially patriarchal, values. As synthesized in the Republican presidencies of Ronald Reagan and George Bush, neoconservative ideology embodied supply-side economics and deregulation, anti–government intervention and state-oriented social policy, defense preparedness and geopolitical assertiveness, and an evangelical faith, as Reagan put it, in "an older American vision" of morality, religion, and family.[17]

Despite occasional paeans to a contemporary form of grassroots populism, neoconservative political culture showed itself to be, in fact, far more interested in elite leadership and social control. Determination to shape the public sphere was especially apparent in battles over arts fund-

■ 9. **Robert Mapplethorpe,** *Helmut, 1978,* 1978; black and white photograph. Copyright © 1978 The Estate of Robert Mapplethorpe.

ing: In the 1980s tax-funded culture became an easy neoconservative target. Attacks on publicly supported art exhibits that neoconservatives found incorrigible, such as Robert Mapplethorpe's photographs of gay men (Fig. 9) and naked children, are but one example.

Ironically, while many Americans protested the imposition of public art without democratic participation, pseudopopulist right-wingers such as Sen. Jesse Helms and Rev. Donald Wildmon attacked public culture on the ground that it needed to be even more tightly controlled, presumably by those aligned with them. Tapping into the popular theme of tax-dollar waste and exploiting sentiments of marginalization and voiceless-ness, these neoconservatives seized contemporary culture as a symbol of the "moral cancer in our society."[18] Suppressing First Amendment rights by criminally charging Cincinnati Contemporary Arts Center director Dennis Barrie with "pandering obscenity" for exhibiting Mapplethorpe's photographs, neoconservative moral crusaders imposed their authority in the cultural sphere.[19] Their cultural censorship had little to do with the art itself, as a comparison of Mapplethorpe's so-called obscene art and the socially/consumer-approved imagery of a 1990 Calvin Klein advertisement readily attests (Fig. 10). Nor was it motivated by genuine sympathy with the public interest. It was, rather, predicated on efforts to

■ 10. Calvin Klein
advertisement.

control public expression and direct it toward a neoconservative political and social agenda. Of course, if this agenda gained such acceptance in the 1980s it was largely because so many Americans seemed so disinterested in defending (let alone debating) the rights to free expression and democratic participation. Americans practically abandoned the public sphere, Laura Bergheim comments, when they "fled indoors under the blind, benevolent watch of the Reagan administration . . . reinstating the virtues of the tucked-away hearth and home as an excuse for shutting out the troubled world on the other side of the 'Welcome' mat."[20]

The neoconservative struggle for cultural dominance was no less evident in the arena of public art. Richard Serra, for instance, believes it was conservative political posturing that led to *Tilted Arc*'s dismantling, especially as the man most responsible for its removal, William Diamond, was a GSA regional administrator appointed by Reagan:

> My sculpture had been approved, commissioned and installed under a
> Democratic administration. A Republican administration decided that it

■ 11. **Frederick Hart,** *Three Fightingmen,* 1984; bronze, 2.4 meters (8 feet) high, Constitution Gardens, Washington, D.C.

should be destroyed. The governmental decree to destroy *Tilted Arc* is the direct outcome of a cynical Republican cultural policy that only supports art as a commodity. Relocation would, in fact, transform *Tilted Arc* into an exchange commodity in that it would annihilate the site-specific aspects of the work. *Tilted Arc* would become exactly what it was intended not to be: a mobile, marketable product.[21]

The story of *Three Fightingmen*—Frederick Hart's 1984 figural addition to the *Vietnam Veterans Memorial*—also seems to embody a neoconservative determination to influence the public sphere (Fig. 11). Angered by what they perceived as the funerary form and antiwar overtures of the memorial, a small group of veterans exerted pressure to have a flagpole and narrative sculpture erected on the grounds of Constitution Gardens 30.5 meters (100 feet) away. Their efforts were backed by James Watt, Reagan's first secretary of the interior, and Ross Perot, who had donated $170,000 to fund the original memorial competition but was upset that the winning design only commemorated the "guys that died." Two years after the *Vietnam Veterans Memorial* was completed, Hart's bronze sculpture was placed nearby. It was only then that President Reagan officially "accepted the completed memorial on behalf of the Nation," on Veterans Day, 13 November 1984.[22]

Although battle weary, Hart's larger-than-life-size figures (each about 2.3 meters [7.5 feet] tall) are idealized: They surmount their pedestal tough and erect, the bronze equivalents of Sly Stallone's *Übermensch* character in *First Blood* (1982) and *Rambo: First Blood Part II* (1985). Reflecting on Hart's sculpture in light of Reagan-era warmongering, writer Michael Clark remarked in 1986, "The hackneyed realism of these updated doughboys clashes aesthetically with the austere lines of the original monument, but the clichéd vision of dogged endurance and determined camaraderie behind Hart's statue is certainly more consistent with the history that was being written last spring than the silent mirror of the original memorial." Or as Jan Scruggs, the former army corporal who initiated the *Vietnam Veterans Memorial,* observed at The Wall's dedication in 1982: "Too bad it wasn't a simple war. Then we could put up a heroic statue of a couple of marines and leave it at that."[23] Unlike Maya Lin's memorial, Hart's superficial sculpture uncritically affirms the neoconservative position that the Vietnam War was an honorable episode in American history.

The Washington Mall's latest public art addition does much the same (Fig. 12). Glenna Goodacre's sculpture was instigated by the Vietnam Women's Memorial Project (VWMP), a group that formed in 1984 to erect a monument recognizing women's military service during the war. Featuring three army nurses grouped around a single wounded GI—one holding him à la the Pietà, one holding his helmet, one looking to the skies for a medevac chopper—the 2.1 meters (7 feet) tall bronze tableau (sited about 91.4 meters [300 feet] from The Wall) gives a warped glorification of war (and women's healing touch) typical of neoconservative revisionist accounts of America's Vietnam experience (and gender roles). Like Hart's sculpture, the *Vietnam Women's Memorial* makes heroes of all military veterans—not just those who died during the war (all of whom, male and female, are recorded on the walls of the *Vietnam War Memorial*). It not only elevates American guts-and-glory fantasies but turns wartime pain and sacrifice into nothing more than a bronze wet dream involving a GI and three nurses. It is interesting to note that Goodacre's original—and more acute—design included an army nurse holding a Vietnamese baby, but this was vetoed by VWMP board mem-

■ 12. **Glenna Goodacre,** *Vietnam Women's Memorial,* 1993; bronze, 2.1 meters (7 feet) high, Constitution Gardens, Washington, D.C. Photo: James Hart. Copyright © Vietnam Women's Memorial 1993, Glenna Goodacre, Sculptor.

bers. As one of their PR staff commented: "The baby represented an accurate portrayal of the war: many of the women who served over there took care of orphans. But given the proposed location of the memorial, I think the board members had to be careful not to make any political statements."[24] Of course, by avoiding allusions to the real context of American foreign policy, the *Vietnam Women's Memorial* shows itself as the perfect model of a thoroughly politicized right-wing recuperation of the war, sentimentalized as an altruistic, innocent, and unfinished American adventure.

Countercultural interests in the public sphere often demonstrate that they have their own political agenda, too. Barbara Kruger's MOCA mural, for instance, assailed neoconservative condemnation of contemporary art. Shaped like an American flag and posing questions such as "Who is free to choose?" and "Who is beyond the law?" it was clearly meant as a rejoinder to the culture wars of the past decade. But Kruger's (initial) insensitivity to Little Tokyo's dynamics suggests that many countercultural forms of public art are also predicated on moralistic assumptions about what audiences should believe in and care about. The ideological stance of such activist art often seems to take precedence over specific public interests, especially when it precludes civic participation.

Tilted Arc provides another compelling case illustrating how artistic presumptions made about and on behalf of "the people" can backfire. Even before *Tilted Arc* was unveiled, Serra made his aesthetic intentions clear: Utilizing an abstract sculpture to dissect Federal Plaza, he aimed to "dislocate or alter the decorative function of the plaza and actively bring people into the sculpture's context." As Michael Brenson notes, by reordering pedestrian traffic, Serra hoped to make people see their surroundings in a new way: "He wanted a sculpture that provoked relentless consciousness of the streets, office buildings and court around it. He wanted his steel gesture, with its sharp, sweeping movement, to be at the same time analytical and mythical, protective and subversive."[25] A "vocal leftist" who once worked in the steel industry ("quick money— the most you could get paid for slave labor," he once said), Serra anticipated that the "thereness" of *Tilted Arc* would lead Federal Plaza employees to rethink their physical space and their working conditions. The dire necessity for such a critique was substantiated in 1985, when disclosures of high lead levels in Federal Complex drinking water, which officials had known about for some time, were finally made public.[26] But Serra's countercultural aesthetics were not translated in ways that made sense to Federal Plaza employees, who saw his attempt at consciousness-raising only as another example of "ugly" public art.

Like those of many public artists, Serra's primary interests lie in the site-specific orientation of his sculpture. He spent months assessing Foley Square's physical character and determining an appropriate artwork for this space; one of his main arguments against *Tilted Arc*'s removal was that it was generated for Federal Plaza, and nowhere else. He is, as art historian Harriet Senie remarks, "scornful of the need to take the public's wishes into consideration." As Serra told her in 1984, "Trying to attract a bigger audience has nothing to do with the making of art. It has to do with making yourself into a product, only to be consumed by people. Working this way allows society to determine the terms and the concept of art; the artist must then fulfill those terms. I find the idea of populism art-defeating."[27] Thus insisting on *Tilted Arc*'s site-specific sanctity as an aesthetic object and ideological tool, Serra ignored the more complicated issue of discourse between public art and the public, and how that discourse shapes democratic expression in the public sphere.

His narrow frame of reference played right into the hands of GSA officials, who utilized public anger about *Tilted Arc* to substantiate their own authority. Public criticism of the sculpture died down after it was erected, and the GSA received few complaints for three years. Despite this, however, in 1985 the agency held a public hearing to determine if Serra's sculpture should be "relocated" to "increase public use of the plaza." Two-thirds of the speakers at the three-day hearing testified for the sculpture's continued presence (122 spoke in favor of retention, 58 in favor of relocation), but the hearing panel voted to have *Tilted Arc* removed anyway. Even as it skewed the democratic process, the GSA appropriated a populist tone: After the hearing GSA chief Diamond stated, "The people have spoken, and they have been listened to by their Government."[28] Serra pursued a series of legal actions based on breach of contract and *le droit moral* (the principle of the "moral right" of artists), but in 1989 the sculpture was removed. Cut up into several pieces, it was effectively destroyed.

Tilted Arc's removal would seem to suggest the victory of the public's voice in the public sphere: After it was dismantled Diamond told a newspaper reporter, "This is a day for the people to rejoice, because now the plaza returns rightfully to the people."[29] But *Tilted Arc*'s removal had less to do with public autonomy than with GSA sovereignty. Assuming that a majority of the 10,000 employees at the Federal Complex detested *Tilted Arc*'s abstract style—a claim that was never fully substantiated—the GSA further assumed *it* had the authority to determine the correct "public use" of the plaza.

If Serra reneged on populist discourse, the GSA seized on it by using the democratic procedures of petitions and hearings in a "textbook example of what Stuart Hall terms 'authoritarian populism': the mobilization of democratic discourses to sanction, indeed to pioneer, shifts toward authoritarianism."[30] Public anger about "ugly" abstract art was orchestrated to reinforce the GSA's claim on Foley Square; both the artist and the public were discounted in favor of state assumptions of a superior social vision. Federal Plaza is now "furnished with a few benches and planters ordered from a standard federal purchasing catalogue."[31] Although the mandate of the GSA's own percent-for-art legislation is to generate art for new federal buildings, the plaza currently stands empty of public art, and the GSA has not initiated any search for *Tilted Arc*'s replacement.

It is tempting to pinion contemporary public art controversy entirely on such politically motivated cabals, to blame "the state" or "the establishment" or "the cultural elite" or "the left." But this sort of polarization loses sight of the far more nuanced relationships involved: There is no "straight line linking intentions, actions, and effects," especially in the public sphere.[32] Even constructing the rigid categories of "neoconservative" and "countercultural" is strewn with difficulties: There is no neoconservative "look" in public art, nor is there a hegemonic cultural symbol of dissent. The physical presence of *Three Fightingmen,* for example, now conveys the neoconservative position on the Vietnam War, but it was instigated by a group of veterans who felt that The Wall's funerary focus on their fallen comrades failed to convey *their* role in the war, and their endurance afterward. Populist sentiments of voicelessness were thus manipulated to legitimate neoconservative insistence that Vietnam was a noble cause. This episode, like that of *Tilted Arc,* illustrates how the politics of the past decade have certainly helped shape the debate over public culture, but public art controversy involves much more than aesthetic accommodation or resistance to political culture.

In fact, the dynamics of public art controversy, the very process of dialogue that art making in the public sphere necessitates, suggest just how important contemporary debates about public culture are. While public art controversy abounds, it is genuinely healthy: It shows the continued vitality of civic engagement and reexamination in the United States. Debates about style and audience, about costs and censorship, about politics and participation are essential in the sustenance of an engaged, democratic culture. The various forms that public art controversy has taken in the civic sphere and in the corporate sphere, by politically engaged artists and those who consider themselves civic activists, provide the core of analysis in the following chapters. The intent here is to understand the meaning of public art controversy in its largest sense, as an arena for democratic debate.

CHAPTER TWO

Public Spirit and *Spirit Poles*
Public Art Controversy in the Civic Sphere

> In the arena of public art, everywhere across the country, people are saying, "Wait a minute. That's our money. You can have it in the museums, but we don't want it here, in our space."
>
> David Avalos, artist
> 11 June 1988[1]

In late 1989 the *National Enquirer* sponsored its "America's Ugliest Tax-Funded Sculpture" contest (Fig. 13). The winner was the *Concord Heritage Gateway,* a $500,000, five-block project along a downtown median strip in Concord, California (Fig. 14). Designed by Ohio artist Gary Rieveschl as a "unique city gateway," the sculpture was developed as a "living monument to Concord's past and a symbol for the City's present and future prosperity." The first three blocks, for instance, trace Concord's growth from Indian encampment to San Francisco suburb with trees, hedges, and ornamental flowers.[2] The last two blocks feature bricked walkways and ninety-one tapered aluminum poles ranging in height from 1.8 to 15.0 meters (6 to 50 feet). A Bay Area bedroom community, Concord had boomed in the 1980s, and Rieveschl's sculpture celebrated the town's dramatic expansion, as he explained: "The rhythmically varying heights and tilts of the poles represent cycles of growth—in a technological, political, and economic sense."

Governed by progressive Democrats, Concord had also pioneered some fairly liberal social programs in the 1980s, including an AIDS anti-discrimination ordinance, salary equity guarantees for city employees, and citywide child care. For Rieveschl, the *Concord Heritage Gateway* championed the city's contemporary reformist politics and linked them

35

Is America's Ugliest Tax-Funded Sculpture The Laughingstock of YOUR Hometown?

Does America's ugliest tax-funded sculpture sit right smack in your hometown?

If it does, we want to know about it — and if your nomination wins The ENQUIRER's latest fun contest, you will receive a $200 prize. Runners-up will collect $50 each.

There are lot of hideous examples around the country.

But to win, your entry will have to top "Dreams and Nightmares," which sits on the University of New Mexico campus in Albuquerque. It looks like a bunch of machine parts rusting in the sun — and it cost taxpayers $37,500.

If you think your town's tax-funded sculpture outuglies this one, send us a snapshot of it, along with

You Could Win $200 in Our New Contest

your name, address, daytime phone number and the sculpture's location.

Entries must reach our office by Dec. 19, 1989. Our editors will judge all submissions and their decision will be final.

Send your entry to: Sculpture, NATIONAL ENQUIRER, Lantana, Fla. 33464.

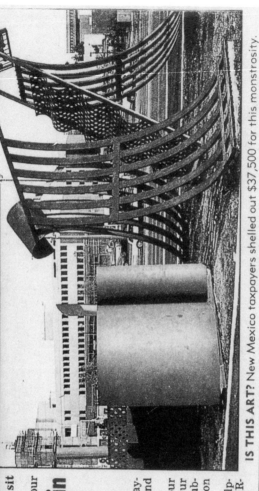

IS THIS ART? New Mexico taxpayers shelled out $37,500 for this monstrosity.

■ 13. *National Enquirer*, 5 December 1989. *Courtesy National Enquirer.*

■ 14. **Gary Rieveschl,** *Concord Heritage Gateway,* 1989; abstract outdoor aluminum sculpture and landscaping, five city blocks along Concord Avenue, Concord, Calif.

with its historical past: "Along the walkway you will find a 'Spirit Place' dedicated to everyone who has ever lived on this land. They have made Concord what it is today. Pausing in the Spirit Place to consider where we have come from, who we are, and where we are going, we have the opportunity to reaffirm our respectful responsibility to this land our children will inherit."

But Rieveschl's pseudo–New Age aspirations of creating a civic monument to spirituality and prosperity backfired. By the time the *Concord Heritage Gateway* was dedicated, in October 1989, it had been renamed *Spirit Poles* by the local press and "porcupine plaza" by an outraged citizenry. A Concord radio station "Save It or Trash It" poles poll revealed that 85 percent of callers wanted the sculpture "trashed," many volunteering to take chain saws and demolish it themselves. As *National Enquirer* contest winner Bobbie Oldenhoff, a forty-four-year-old Concord grocery clerk, said, "I have to drive past that thing all the time, and it just about makes me sick. What I can't understand is why they put the thing up in the first place, why they don't tear it down, and where they got the nerve to use taxpayer funds to pay for it."[3] Public hostility about the *Concord Heritage Gateway* was so pervasive it swayed the November 1989 city council election, and the entire tenor of Concord's political future.

Concord's public art controversy, like those in many other American cities, centered largely on the failure of public artists and arts agencies to engage citizens effectively in the development of public culture. The *National Enquirer*'s suggestion that Americans are mostly outraged by public art's "tax-funded" financing and its "ugly" looks is only partly right: Concerns about money and aesthetics mask deeper issues of authority and autonomy in the civic sphere. Pitting herself against the "they" who had engineered the *Concord Heritage Gateway* "in the first place," Oldenhoff summed up the frustration she felt about Concord's leadership—its city council and its arts agency experts. Angered by perceptions of powerlessness and manipulation, Oldenhoff and other Concord residents seized on the *Concord Heritage Gateway*'s abstract style and hefty price tag and targeted public art to question their role in the relevance and direction of civic life.

Concord's tangle with public art began in 1985, when the city council passed an Art in Public Places (AIPP) ordinance. Through this ordinance public art projects in central Concord were to be funded from two pots of money: a 0.5 percent tax on new downtown buildings and 1.0 percent of the annual tax revenue generated from business properties within the boundaries of the Central Concord Redevelopment Plan—several square kilometers of prime downtown real estate. The AIPP ordinance applied only to commercial properties, not to single-family homes, condominiums, or apartment complexes built downtown or anywhere else in Concord. Under its provisions, Concord's public art was to be paid for by new building or redevelopment funds—not by taxpayer dollars. And, because the art was to be financed with downtown development dollars, it could be located only downtown—not in the outlying suburban residential areas.

By 1986 some $700,000 had been collected in the two public art pots, the result of a building boom begun in 1976, when Bay Area Rapid Transit (BART) linked Concord to San Francisco, some 40 kilometers (25 miles) southwest. A Mexican land-grant community formerly called Todos Santos ("all saints"), Concord was renamed by a strong New

England constituency in 1869. Until the mid-twentieth century it was best known as a midsize market town for dairy and walnut farmers in the foothills of nearby Mount Diablo, its few downtown stores clustered around a public square called Todos Santos Plaza. California's explosive postwar growth completely transformed Concord, especially when its flat land was found perfectly suited for suburban tract housing. The town quickly developed as a bedroom community for blue-collar workers in the U.S. Steel and Shell Oil plants of nearby Pittsburg and Martinez, and the 1968 addition of the Sun Valley Mall on the city's outskirts enhanced Concord's mercantile reputation. The appearance of BART made Concord an easy San Francisco commute and increased the population to 112,000 by 1988.

The transit system also brought tens of thousands of new workers—many of them Hispanic, Asian, and Middle Eastern—to Concord, to new jobs in multistory office complexes built throughout the 1980s on readily available and affordable Concord land. A substantial gay and lesbian population was drawn to Concord as well, driven from San Francisco by high housing costs and decreased job opportunities. Concord had a cheaper housing stock and more jobs: The Bank of America Technology Center, for example, settled in Concord in 1985 and generated work for 5,000 employees. Long's Drugstore, Nationwide Insurance, and the Chevron Credit Card Company were other major corporations that chose to build national headquarters in downtown Concord in the 1980s, creating thousands of new jobs and hundreds of thousands of dollars for the city's public art fund. By the mid-1980s the former market town had become the capital city of Contra Costa County, second only to Orange County as California's fastest growing district. By the end of the decade Concord's transition from a predominantly white, suburban, middle-class community to a multiethnic and increasingly urban-affiliated middle-class population was obvious. A mix of languages—including Spanish, Tagalog, Korean, and Arabic—was heard on downtown streets; new businesses run by gays and lesbians changed the makeup of Concord's chamber of commerce. The sleepy suburb had become a multicultural city, and not everyone was happy about it.

Concord's speedy growth was encouraged, and carefully controlled, by a liberal city council, which dominated municipal politics through most of the 1980s. At the time of their ascent in the early 1980s, Concord was a typically sprawling and indistinct California suburb. It had neither the charming Victorian architecture of nearby Sonoma nor the outstanding physical presence of oceanfront towns such as Sausalito. Its four-block downtown was on the verge of financial collapse, eclipsed by the Sun Valley Mall and numerous minimalls; Todos Santos Plaza was decaying and disused. Aiming to revitalize Concord's failing city center to generate both a significant tax base and a flashy, upscale image, the new members of the city council urged developers to plant eleven-story glass office towers amid central Concord. At the same time the council taxed these buildings for community welfare. As John Gilkinson, a political consultant who worked with many of the council Democrats in the 1980s noted, "You get business to support you, and then you zonk them on the social programs."[4]

Led by councillor June Bulman, who had been the city's first female mayor, Concord developed a citywide child-care program in 1985 and paid for it with a 0.5 percent tax derived from the same source as the public art fund—new downtown development. In 1986 the five liberal Democrats on the city council created the Human Relations Commission after several episodes of racial violence, including the murder of a gay African American at the Concord BART station, were reported in the area press. "Concord is a growing urban community with many diverse ethnic, social, religious and cultural groups," the commission declared. "This diversity provides us with a wealth of human resources and presents us with a need for positive intergroup relations." In response, the Center for New Americans was established as an outreach service for arrivals to Concord. The city council also generated programs to feed the homeless in city parks, subsidized a rape crisis center, and instituted a comparable worth program for city employees whereby 2.0 percent of the annual budget went to boosting salaries in female-dominated jobs. In 1987 the council officially endorsed Gay Pride Week, and in April 1989 it adopted an AIDS antidiscrimination ordinance legally protecting those infected with HIV and those at risk of being HIV positive. As political analyst Alan Ehrenhalt remarks, in the 1980s Concord's city council was dominated by a "new breed" of baby boomer Democrats. With a political awareness grounded in 1960s idealism, these councillors saw municipal government as a primary means to a liberal social agenda.[5]

Ehrenhalt explains that Concord's city councillors were "political professionals," ambitious, full-time experts consumed by the desire to "make policy." They considered themselves civic problem solvers and trusted in institutional politics to help them out. Running for reelection in 1987, council member Ron Mullins said, "If I believed government wasn't an institution beneficial to society, I wouldn't give a tinker's damn about politics. I wouldn't waste my time on it."[6]

Such attitudes had been nurtured throughout the twentieth century, as widespread notions of technocratic efficiency and managerial expertise infiltrated society and citizens acquiesced to expert authority. Clear roles were established, whereby citizens were mostly marginalized by politicians who viewed themselves less as citizen representatives (much less advocates) than as political officeholders whose professional, institutional authority legitimated their expert decision making.[7] In the public sphere these roles made citizens spectators and politicians players, and isolated both. Even proponents of modern social liberalism, such as Concord's city council, were confined by the professional political power base they had constructed, which removed them from the real-life dynamics of their community—dynamics that in Concord were largely the result of a rapidly changing demographics. Concord's city councillors may have felt they were acting on behalf of their constituency, but the controversy that emerged over the *Concord Heritage Gateway* revealed otherwise.

The city council's expert-guided platform of civic reform was visually symbolized in Concord's public art program. In 1985 the councillors voted in a master plan for the city that included 1.5 million square meters (5 million square feet) of office space and 2,500 new apartments and condominiums. Urban planners had predicted a 75 percent increase in downtown vehicle traffic by the year 2000, and already Concord had grown so rapidly that its main arteries were desperately in need of redesign. Backed by the master plan, Concord Arts Committee (CAC) and AIPP staff advised the city council to couple utilitarian street widening with public art and landscaping.

As cultural managers, the arts experts of the CAC and AIPP understood civic aesthetics as "an area of investment and domestic public relations." Consuelo Underwood, visual arts coordinator for the AIPP program from 1985 to 1987, noted, "The city council wants the artwork to give a distinction to Concord so that it doesn't just keep blending into Pleasant Hill and Pacheco. Concord wants to be remembered for more than being an urban mass of Taco Bells and McDonald's."[8] Eventually, Concord's councillors approved nine sites for outdoor art in their city, including a five-block area encompassing the downtown traffic median of Concord Avenue from Market Street to Salvio Street (Fig. 15).

Concord's beautification program focused on entryways into the city

■ 15. Concord Avenue, Concord, Calif., before redevelopment in 1989. Photo from *City of Concord Newsette,* April 1986.

from surrounding freeways and on gateways into the central downtown. Everyone agreed that Concord needed some sort of dramatic visual hook—like St. Louis's *Arch*—to counter its strip-mall ambience. In 1986 a design competition for Concord Avenue's redevelopment as a downtown gateway off Highway 680 was underwritten with a $12,000 grant from the National Endowment for the Arts (NEA). Underwood selected a panel of arts experts—Bonnie Earl-Solari, director of the Bank of America's art collection; Jennifer Dowley, coordinator of Sacramento's Art in Public Places program; Mary Beebe, curator of the University of California, San Diego's art gallery; Leonard Hunter, a sculpture professor at San Francisco State University; and Minneapolis artist Andrew Leicester—to nominate artists for the site. Gary Rieveschl and New York artist Christopher Sproat were chosen. Their designs were displayed at a well-advertised (in the local press) but sparsely attended public forum held by the CAC in July 1986 (Fig. 16). Concord residents present at the forum voted 21 to 6 in favor of Rieveschl's design. A few weeks later the CAC chose Rieveschl and local landscape architect Michael Fotheringham to develop the *Concord Heritage Gateway* as a "unique city gateway" to central Concord.

The CAC's intention, following the lead of the city's 1985 master

■ 16. **Gary Rieveschl and Michael Fotheringham,** *Concord Heritage Gateway,* design for public sculpture, 1988.

plan, was civic improvement. The *Concord Heritage Gateway* was meant to revitalize "one of the city's busiest thoroughfares while inviting a sensory participation to all who drive or walk by." As a public art project, it was defined in terms of its place in a general program of urban redevelopment rather than its meaning within the specific context of Concord Avenue's site, history, and public audience. Such a definition meshed with federal arts agency ideas that public art exists to improve public, primarily urban, space. Consistent with the Great Society platform of the Johnson administration, the NEA was established in 1965 to foster American culture via federal funding. One year later the Endowment formed its Art in Public Places program, and in 1972 it helped revitalize the General Services Administration (GSA) Art-in-Architecture program. For the last three decades, the NEA has been directed by a well-educated, liberal cadre of arts professionals—the cultural equivalent of the expert managers dominating the political sphere. Their preference for particular art styles—mostly modern and mostly abstract— and their assumptions about American audiences and public space play a large role in today's public art controversies.

Jürgen Habermas's model of the public sphere—an all-inclusive space dominated by rational thinking, a realm where private individuals "freed from social compulsion and from political pressure" merge as like-thinking citizens, an essentially passive and problem-free space of consensus—has greatly informed the NEA.[9] That is, contemporary arts agencies seem to prefer a public culture in which audiences form a kind of democratic unity (or appear to do so) and in which the potential conflicts of political and social dissent are studiously avoided. They are partial to calm public spaces where "disinterested citizens may contemplate a transparent emblem of their own inclusiveness and solidarity, and deliberate on the general good, free of coercion, violence, or private interests."[10] Of course, as the sheer number of recent public art controversies reveals, the NEA preference for such an idealized public sphere is beset with problems, not the least of which is the viability of contemporary American consensus.

Elite preference for rational, problem-free public spaces developed especially after World War II, when changed perceptions of American audiences, and American art, emerged. If an earlier version of the American public (which was, of course, hardly inclusive) was characterized by its capable citizenship, autonomy, tolerance, and overall sense of commonwealth, postwar intellectuals and politicians tended to view "the people" as an irrational mass, easily swayed by dangerous political ideologies or consumerism, or both. Such fears were grounded in perceptions of the threat that uprooted mass movements, the social base for totalitarianism in China and the Soviet Union, might have in Cold War America; elite disdain for mass culture was based on perceptions of its inauthentic and conformist character. The response was a consideration of how best to contain, and thereby control, the public. It was predicated on two, often conflicted, liberal assumptions: that the public could be redeemed, or enlightened, yet pacified, or shaped into consensus, in a more rationally reconstructed modern society. In the art world no real theory of containment emerged, unlike that, for instance, which directed American foreign policy after World War II. What did evolve, however, was a liberal reverence for modern art and its vision of a rational, redemptive public culture.

If postwar elites feared the masses, they thoroughly distrusted mass culture. In 1939 critic Clement Greenberg published "Avant-Garde and Kitsch," an enormously influential essay that helped delineate the ideological framework for what would become postwar culture. Damning popular culture, which he called kitsch—a vast catalog of stuff ranging from Norman Rockwell's *Saturday Evening Post* covers to Civil War monuments—Greenberg championed, instead, modern, avant-garde art. Popular culture was dangerous, Greenberg said, because of its debased and vicarious character; put simply, it was escapist. And the danger of aesthetic escapism was that it could be utilized to reinforce equally dangerous political ideologies. Kitsch, explained Greenberg, was "the official tendency of culture in Germany, Italy, and Russia. . . . kitsch is the culture of the masses in these countries. . . . kitsch is merely another of the inexpensive ways in which totalitarian regimes seek to ingratiate themselves with their subjects."[11] Impugning the masses because of their easy and apparently willing manipulation at the hands of totalitarian politics, which, in the postwar era, he and other liberals viewed as America's greatest menace, Greenberg also impugned popular culture.

As did other postwar intellectuals, Greenberg found solace in modern art, especially that which held an agenda of shaping a rational, like-thinking society. On the one hand, Greenberg felt that one of modernism's essential features was its isolation and independence from mass culture—from, as he wrote in 1947, the "pedagogic vulgarization that infects everything." On the other hand, postwar society *needed* a culture based on "balance, largeness, precision, enlightenment." "Modern man," Greenberg wrote, "has *in theory* solved the great public and private questions." To put that theory into practice was the task of modern art:

> Only such an art, resting on rationality but without permitting itself to be rationalized, can adequately answer contemporary life, found our sensibilities, and, by containing and vicariously relieving them, remunerate us for those particular and necessary frustrations that ensue from living at the present moment in the history of western civilization.

Modern art had the capacity, then, to *contain* yet serve, or cultivate, postwar society. As Greenberg remarked, "Culture means *cultivation*. Only the enormous productivity of American industrialism could have led any society to think it possible to cultivate the *masses*."[12]

Of course, the idea that culture's task is to contain yet cultivate the public stemmed from the equally paradoxical concept of consensus—the postwar belief that the American majority shared the same assumptions, and if they didn't, they should. To resist communism—the most operative postwar motif—the decorum of public unity had to be maintained. The kind of cultural nationalism that emerged, while it hardly spoke literally to the politics of anticommunism, helped shape that unity. Modern art, and, specifically in the public sphere, modern abstract art, was seen as a great unifying force because it was seemingly apolitical and rational. Because it was nonfigurative, the postwar argument went, abstract art could not be used to prop up any deviant political ideology. Because it concentrated on itself—on the physical properties of paint, for instance, or steel—abstract art suppressed any romantic or subjective overtones and was thus inherently reasonable. The fact that such art had obvious links with consensus ideology was ignored, as were the passionate, often quite spiritualist intentions of many abstract painters and sculptors.[13]

Instead, because modern art meshed with the postwar elite's insistence that the public sphere *needed* to be ordered, and thus controlled, it was embraced by them as the most desirable aesthetic for the public sphere. Concomitant with postwar professionalism, elites saw themselves as the voices of cultural authority, the guides for what they hoped would be a radically transformed modern America. They rejected public distaste for and confusion about modern art, especially modern abstract art, as philistinism, the emotional response of the uneducated, the unenlightened. The kind of public advocacy characterized by federal support for the arts during the Great Depression—such as Works Progress Administration post office murals—declined in favor of support for individual artists whose work fit the modernist agenda, and for large-scale projects—such as urban renewal—that concentrated on trying to rationalize America's inner cities through slum clearance.

Indeed, beginning in the mid-1960s, these became the NEA's public art program mandates: urban renewal and individual artistic patronage. The GSA's mandate, originally conceived in 1962, has focused on incorporating fine art, especially that by living American artists, in the designs of new federal buildings; Richard Serra's *Tilted Arc* is a typical example. Federally funded, the NEA's public art program is based on municipal application and matching funds, whereas the GSA's Art-in-Architecture program (directed by the NEA) is based on architect interest and monies provided through 0.5 percent of the construction costs for new federal buildings. Both programs have tended to be staffed by arts professionals and consultants who view public art as a symbol of American unity and cultural largesse. As Arthur F. Sampson, acting GSA administrator under President Nixon, said in 1972, when the GSA was revitalized, "The President has said that 'only if the arts are alive and flourishing can we expe-

■ 17. **Alexander Calder,**
La Grande Vitesse, 1969; painted
steel stabile, 13.1 meters (43
feet) high by 16.5 meters (54
feet) long by 9.1 meters (30
feet) wide, Vandenberg Center,
Grand Rapids, Mich. Photo
courtesy City of Grand Rapids
Planning Department.

rience the true meaning of our freedom, and know the full glory of the
human spirit.' . . . The President's commitment is to forge a new partnership between Government and the arts 'to the benefit of the people of
America.'"[14]

The first town to request NEA funding for public art was Grand
Rapids, Michigan, where Alexander Calder's *La Grande Vitesse,* a gigantic red-painted steel stabile, was dedicated in 1969 (Fig. 17). Pursu-
ing a vigorous urban renewal program, the city wanted a large-scale
public sculpture to centerpiece a refurbished plaza, Vandenberg Center,
where free open-air arts festivals would be held. Civic boosters raised
some $85,000 in private funds, and the city received $45,000 from the
NEA to commission Calder. Today Calder's colossal sculpture is seen on
everything from city letterhead to the sides of garbage trucks—seeming
evidence of modern abstract art's success in the public sphere.

La Grande Vitesse was initially "greeted with a mixture of jubilation,
bemusement, and hostility," and heated debate about the work continued for a long time in the local press. The fact that the sculpture has
been embraced by local politicians and cultural cognoscenti—the two
groups responsible for its commission—does not substantiate its acceptance as a meaningful or vital symbol to Grand Rapids's citizens today.
Rather *La Grande Vitesse* may be an outstanding example of "official"
cultural authority, revealing elite concerns about the need for orderly,

unified public spaces. After all, it plops in an otherwise empty urban plaza whose open yet contained and secure and, above all, homogenous sensibility is the perfect postwar model of public space. Perhaps favorite son Gerald Ford told *La Grande Vitesse's* story best when he described his city's "Calder" to members of the House of Representatives:

> At the time I did not know what a Calder was. I doubt if many people here do today. It was somewhat shocking to a lot of our people out home. I must say that I did not really understand, and I do not today, what Mr. Calder was trying to tell us. But I can assure the Members that Calder in the center of the city, in an urban redevelopment area, has really helped to regenerate a city. . . . it was a good investment both locally and federally.[15]

In Concord elite concerns about slum clearance were less a driving force behind the interest in public art. Downtown Concord was not blight ridden or dangerous, it simply had no identity. Its anonymity stemmed from its postwar emergence as an "edge city," Joel Garreau's term for "high rised, semiautonomous, job laden, road clogged communities of enormous size, springing up on the edge of old urban fabrics where nothing existed ten years ago but residential suburbs or cow pastures."[16] As in the other East Bay Area communities of Pleasant Hill and Walnut Creek, the speedy, sprawling growth of Concord as a San Francisco outpost had generated a sense of placelessness for old and new residents alike. Its shopping malls, commercial strips, office parks, and housing developments were indistinguishable from those of the next community. The specificities of place, and the security and significance with which Concord's citizens may have related to those places, had remained undeveloped.

As had the political and cultural leaders in Grand Rapids, Concord's city council and arts agency experts opted for the remedy of public art. Hoping to generate a common civic identity, they searched for a physical image, a visual emblem, that might embody the dramatic economic and political changes they had put in place by the mid-1980s. The cultural model they selected was provided by the NEA. Hand in hand with its interest in urban renewal and artistic patronage, the NEA's perspective on public art has centered on its staunch allegiance to public unanimity and cultural largesse. The Endowment's first chairman, Roger Stevens, included the following among its objectives: "to provide the people with new opportunities in all aspects of the arts."[17] While notions of cultural democracy inform the NEA, Stevens's words are typical of Endowment assumptions that the American "people" are generally the same in their social, economic, and historical makeup.

Not surprisingly, art for "the people," or public art, has become directly attached to these notions of consensus. Mike Davis maintains that the "reformist vision of public space—as the emollient of class struggle, if not the bedrock of the American *polis*—is now as obsolete as Keynesian nostrums of full employment." Indeed, much of urban America is more like Victorian England, as Davis suggests, than any Middletown democracy; the "fortress" Los Angeles he describes is increasingly the locus of "spatial and social insulation."[18] Accordingly, while most of those involved in the public art industry, both liberal and neoconservative, insist that public culture's purpose is to shape civic and national unity, they base their belief on a contained vision of public space fronted by the elite. Pricking at that fictive balloon are the real-life tensions of late twentieth-century American life.

Prefacing a 1980 book on the GSA's Art-in-Architecture projects, art historian Sam Hunter wrote that public art

> serves an age-old need to rally the community around visible symbols and environmental amenities that soothe and heal social divisions even while affording aesthetic delight. A public context for art establishes a common ground of values and experience, liberating art from the cloistered museum and placing it in the public realm of shared purposes.

Writing for the neoconservative journal *The Public Interest* in 1982, Douglas Stalker and Clark Glymour asserted that public art should "realize and celebrate and exemplify a common tradition and shared political, cultural, and aesthetic heritage."[19] Based on the assumption that all Americans share "common ground," these sorts of remarks posit contemporary public art as a leveling device, a symbol—and, perhaps more important, a shaper—of consensus.

Coupled with these notions of American commonality were elite presumptions of cultural authority in the public sphere. Stevens's statement that the Endowment's aim is "to provide the people" with art conveys the postwar attitude that culture is properly the domain of a professional body of experts who apportion the arts; public art, then, has come to be something parceled out to "the people," not something created with their consultation or collaboration. Many are quick to declare that the NEA is no ministry of culture and that its complicated structure of panel and peer review keeps it from exerting too much pressure on artistic production. Indeed, during Livingston Biddle's chairmanship (1977–81), concerted efforts were made to create a more "populist" Endowment, with special emphasis on funding for community culture and public access.

Although Biddle's "Common Cause for the Arts" approach was assailed by those (especially in the 1980s) who insisted that Endowment dollars be returned to the elite realm of high art, the fact is that the congressional act which created the NEA inferred that a federal arts agency would take considerable responsibility for the patronage and direction of American culture. In the realm of public art, that government influence has been especially noticeable: According to one 1987 study, during the Endowment's first two decades, over 518 public art projects in forty-seven states and Washington, D.C., received NEA matching funds, and of 195 public art programs in the United States, 135 were supported with government funds, including NEA monies.[20]

Speaking to the Associated Council of the Arts in 1971, President Nixon upheld the NEA's public culture mandate:

> The important thing now is that government has accepted support of the arts as one of its responsibilities—not only on the federal level, but on the state and local levels as well. And increasingly, governments at all levels see this not only as a responsibility but an opportunity—for there is a growing recognition that few investments in the quality of life in America pay off so handsomely as the money spent to stimulate the arts.

The NEA's cultural responsibility was thus linked with opportunity, and influence. But, as NEA critic Edward Banfield remarks, "In the discussions leading to the passage of the law [creating the NEA], no one asked whether the anticipated benefits . . . were properly the concern of government. It was simply assumed that, if an end were worthy, the government ought to pursue it."[21]

In fact, public art's beneficence, its role in raising the "quality of life," has long been its resounding raison d'être among its elite advocates. The sentiment that culture is "good" for the public, that it brings "intellectual enlightenment and spiritual edification," is voiced again and again: "Public art is not a style or a movement, but a compound social service based on the premise that public well-being is enhanced by the presence of large scale art works in public spaces."[22] This may well be true, but the gift of public culture—and its anticipated role in shaping consensus—is often agreed upon apart from its recipients. To be sure, NEA support for public art stems first from local and state requests. But these mainly come from arts professionals and civic boosters—such as Concord's arts committee—who presume that public art will benefit the community and that the community will accept and appreciate this cultural gratuity. As critic Arthur Danto notes,

> One of the great failures in our public art programs . . . is that the public has been radically underinvolved and all the main decisions have been left to panels of "authorities." The assumption has been that art is good, so it must be good for people to have it, without anybody making much of an effort to translate the goodness of works that are not self-evidently good into terms people can grasp and respond to.[23]

In Concord the CAC did include the community in its public art process, but only after it and the city council had decided that Concord Avenue needed to be beautified with public art, and that Concord needed a certain physical symbol of unity, such as the *Concord Heritage Gateway*. When the public decides that the gift of public art is unacceptable—as it did in Concord—controversy erupts.

Some of the hostility surrounding the *Concord Heritage Gateway* stemmed from its modern art style—the style that postwar elites deemed most exemplary for the public sphere. Throughout the 1980s the NEA avoided funding public art projects that were specifically commemorative or representational. The archly conservative Heritage Foundation greatly overstates this in their frequent attacks on the NEA's "bias against traditional forms of art and traditional values in general." Still, a glance at the Art in Public Places grants awarded by the Endowment in 1980, for example, reveals a preference for modern abstract art in the funding of works by Athena Tacha, Richard Fleischner, Mary Miss, Stephen Antonakos, Robert Irwin, Tony Smith, Mark di Suvero, Siah Armajani, and Richard Serra. Only awards to Romare Bearden and Edgar Rodriguez, each to develop murals, can be construed as evidence of NEA support that year for narrative styles of public art. Summarizing the Endowment's 1980 awards, Visual Arts Director James Melchart noted, "It's a long way from the days when we thought of a public artwork as a statue of a prominent citizen on horseback." It seems that Greenberg's argument for an aesthetic of rational modernism that could enlighten the masses, and thereby contain them in consensus, remained accepted among many arts professionals in the 1980s. Of course, NEA trust in the "ideologic aegis of modernism" often led directly to the public art controversies detailed in this book.[24]

State arts agencies largely followed the model of their parent organization, some making their preference for nonrepresentational art very clear: The Philadelphia Redevelopment Authority's Percent for Art program mandated that it did "not approve of a Commemorative Work of Art when it is simply illustrative or is a literal portrait of a historical figure." But this "victory of abstraction," legal scholar Barbara Hoffman argues, has meant that the public art the NEA selects is "for the most part not public in the sense of shared aesthetic vocabulary, symbolism, or worldview between artists and their audiences."[25]

Public response to abstract art's supposed educative and unifying values ranges from apathy to outrage. Despite its long presence in the public sphere, abstract art is still viewed by much of the public as a hoax, an incomprehensible in-joke imposed on them by an art world elite. Abstract styles often generate outright public anger—as in Concord. On the other hand, abstract art often blends in so well with the banality of its equally modernist surroundings that people don't even see it. This does not mean that the public has finally come to *accept* abstract art—the claim of public arts administrators in places such as Grand Rapids, where initial "hostility" about *La Grande Vitesse* jelled into public silence. Rather it suggests that abstract forms of public art are often so irrelevant to social, economic, and political conditions that people don't respond to them. Whether they view it with anger or indifference, Americans often feel marginalized by modern art. Their ambivalence, however, actually fosters expert conclusions that abstract forms of art fit perfectly in the passive public sphere and its apparent affirmation of contemporary *communitas*.

The gap between public artists and their audiences also stems from the NEA's original mandate to support projects that aid artists and help them achieve standards of "professional excellence." This focus has led many arts agencies actually to start the public art process with the artist rather than with civic needs, community concerns, or even the site itself. Ignoring the dynamics of the public sphere and its audience, the trend in contemporary public art has been to honor the ideas of individual artists, often working in studios far removed from an intended site and audience. But by granting artists this kind of autonomy in the public sphere, the NEA risks alienating arts audiences. It is no wonder, then, that government-sponsored public art is frequently seen as "government-imposed" public art.[26]

Many government-sponsored public artworks can be described as localized extensions of the elite culture dominating modern museums, especially because the experts who initiate public art often look to museum collections for evidence of cultural authority. However, the contemporary art museum tends to focus on blue-chip artists of established "professional excellence" rather than local artists who might collaborate with their communities (or outsiders who might do the same). It has also tended toward modern styles rather than the diversity of cultures present in American communities. By appropriating these standards, contemporary public arts agencies further generate an elite model of public culture. There are occasional counterexamples, of course: In 1981 a community mural designed by Oakland artist Daniel Galvez was partially funded through the NEA's AIPP program; in the mid-1980s the small town of Villa Nueva, New Mexico, received a grant from the NEA's folk art program to create a tapestry about local history. Still, the NEA generally abides by a "continuing, restricted definition of the public arts in terms of elitist culture only." Endowment critic Edward Arian explains that the NEA rationalizes this by claiming that community-based arts programs "can only result in the dilution of standards and the triumph of mediocrity . . . elite consensus assigns little recognition to the concept of the average individual as an active participant in the 'doing' of art . . . [preferring] products of professional quality."[27]

Favoring the "professional" stuff of museum culture, arts agencies thus tend to commission the kind of public art most salient to an elite, art-smart, middle-class constituency. But at the same time they claim public art as a common social service. These conflicted notions also inform the contemporary museum, whose claims of a widely diverse audience are countered by recent studies. Writing in the early 1980s, Kevin Mulcahy noted that "there is no evidence, from studies conducted over the past fifteen years that cultural audiences are becoming more 'democratic,' that is, representative of the population-at-large in educational level and socioeconomic status."[28]

Contemporary America is increasingly complex; notions of consensus—which began thoroughly to unravel even as the NEA was created—are held together by only the flimsiest threads. It is ironic, then, that in the public sphere Americans are still surrounded by a kind of modern art born of elite authority and expectation and based on unanimity. As critic Michael Hall says,

Public in America is people—millions of them—brought up on the work ethic and Jeffersonian concepts of egalitarianism. Art in America is cult—arcane mysteries—practiced by misfits and understood only by aristocrats

53

and the power elite. Layered with the confusions generated by this contradiction, the picture of American public art in the eighties is more than a
little muddy.[29]

Muddy is an apt word to describe what happened when the *Concord
Heritage Gateway* was announced and then unveiled—it muddied the
formerly clear authority of the city's political, and cultural, liberal elite.
Confronted with a gift of abstract public art they found irrelevant and
alienating, and feeling neglected in the entire public art process, the citizens of Concord not surprisingly became incensed about the work. Clifford Geertz argues that incongruence between social and cultural structures provides the impetus for social change when cultural forms do not
satisfy social demands.[30] This is exactly what happened in Concord. Un-
sure about the dramatic socioeconomic changes they had witnessed in
their city and faced with a public art object that embodied the tenor of
those changes, a large body of Concord residents subjected the *Concord
Heritage Gateway* to intense scrutiny. Sensing that they were being manipulated by this form of public culture, they responded by evaluating,
questioning, and challenging that manipulation.

As mentioned previously, when designs for the *Concord Heritage
Gateway* were presented in 1986, few citizens responded—the Concord
Arts Committee forum drew only twenty-seven voting participants. For
whatever reasons, most of Concord reneged on the rights and responsi-
bilities of democratic participation in the public sphere. ("Too busy with
their crabgrass and their kids' braces to go to public hearings," one San
Francisco reporter gibed a few years later, after controversy over Concord's public art had erupted.)[31] Still, the CAC decided to go ahead with
Rieveschl and Fotheringham's design and asked the city council to approve their choice. The CAC had followed typical arts agency proce-
dure: writing a grant proposal and receiving an NEA grant, soliciting the
advice of arts professionals, and showing the selected designs at a public
forum. The council was reluctant to approve funding for the *Concord
Heritage Gateway,* however, until greater public interest was demonstrated—especially because the proposal carried a hefty $472,256 price
tag: $96,000 for the sculpture and $376,256 for the landscaping. From
1986 to 1988 CAC and AIPP staff developed public surveys, presented
the gateway design at local arts fairs, spoke with the media, and made
presentations about the project to the local Chamber of Commerce, Rotary Club, and Downtown Business Association. The committee's mar-

---

INTEREST SURVEY

YOUR COMMENTS ON THE PROPOSED GATEWAY DESIGN ARE NEEDED!

Please fill out this form and mail to:

City of Concord—CitiArts, 1950 Parkside Drive, Concord, CA 94519

☐ I like the proposed design! Here's why _____

_____

_____

_____

☐ *I cannot form an opinion based on what I see. Please invite me to a special viewing of models and illustrations so I can take a closer look.*

☐ I don't like the proposed design. Here's why: _____

_____

_____

_____

Optional:

Name _____

Address _____

Phone (Day) _____ (Eve) _____

■ 18. Interest Survey, used to gauge public reaction to Rieveschl and Fotheringham's proposed designs for Concord Avenue, Concord, Calif. From *City of Concord Newsette*, 1987.

keting scheme for the *Concord Heritage Gateway* was based on the premise that once Concord citizens saw the public art gift they were going to get, they would like it.

From the start, however, at least as indicated in survey results, public reaction to the design was less than enthusiastic. In February 1987 Concord citizens were invited to respond to a sketch of the project that appeared in the *City of Concord Newsette* (Fig. 18). Under the heading "I don't like the proposed design. Here's why" comments included

It looks like another abstract piece of junk that some doped up artist calls art.

I would like a sculpture along more traditional lines emphasizing Concord's Spanish past rather than a bunch of spikes.

It reminds me of a swamp full of dead trees or a barricade for tanks.

Ugly! Stark, cold, depressing! Not at all the spirit of Concord. Concord means harmony & agreement. To me, there is no harmony in this presentation. Please try again.

I don't care for the spending of money on a mess of jackstraws dumped in the middle of the road and called art. Better to spend our taxes on something useful.

It shows that the inmates have taken over the asylum!

Too stark, not esthetically pleasing. Can't see relationship to Concord history or spirit.

Aluminum poles! Downtown is not a high tech industrial park.

The long, jutting poles look foreign to the environment rather than harmonious with it. It didn't give me a welcome-gateway flavor.

It looks like it will give an overwhelming sense of agitation & disorientation—it seems to be seeking direction frantically.

A handful of the approximately 1,899 survey respondents wrote that they liked Rieveschl and Fotheringham's design, calling it an "exciting and interesting sculpture," a "design for tomorrow," and a "modern" work "in keeping with cultural events in Concord." But their support was outweighed by the opposition of hundreds of other Concord residents. Some of these revealed considerable misunderstanding about how the art was to be funded: Complaints that the proposal was a waste of taxpayer dollars showed that many Concord residents did not know that the *Concord Heritage Gateway* was to be paid for solely through downtown building and redevelopment monies.

Some of the hundreds of negative comments were misinformed and purely cantankerous, but many showed an astute aesthetic awareness that the design was too busy, too cold, too "overbearing." Some found it remote from the city's Hispanic heritage; others, apparently blind to Concord's obvious edge-city persona, wanted something more in keeping with what they believed to be their city's small-town image:

> The sculpture looks like sticks and is about as attractive as the palm trees that will be used in other roadways. Palm trees belong in So. Calif. Whatever happened to natural No. Calif. landscaping such as Redwood trees

and sophisticated country charm? Concord should not look like a city
metropolis. Most natives live here for the rural atmosphere and are disap-
pointed in the urban growth.

Rieveschl had recognized, of course, that Concord's "rural atmosphere"
had long since disappeared and had chosen to celebrate the city's contemporary high-tech look. But his image of Concord clashed with that
held by those who insisted on a public art project honoring their memories of an older, smaller, and more homogenous Concord.

To offset misperceptions about financing for the sculpture, CAC and
AIPP staff made numerous presentations to civic organizations emphasizing that the *Concord Heritage Gateway* would be paid for with funds
specifically earmarked for public art. A public relations outfit, the Heritage Gateway Committee, was formed to help sell the project. An "adopt
a pole" plan was proposed whereby individuals and organizations were
encouraged to pay $150 to sponsor one of the ninety-one poles; eventu-
ally, some $7,000 in private monies was raised, mostly from area busi-
nesses. And in September 1987 the gateway designs were displayed at
the city's annual Fall Fest. According to Hawley Holmes, who became
Concord's visual arts coordinator in mid-1987, "hundreds of people had
the opportunity to review and respond to the design" at the fest, and a
large majority "indicated their support for the installation of the project." Encouraged by this, and ignoring the survey responses, the CAC
once again proposed the project to the city council. In March 1988 the
council voted 3 to 2 in favor of the *Concord Heritage Gateway.*

The key design issue for Rieveschl and Fotheringham was accommo-
dating the project in the middle of a major urban street: It could not in-
terfere with traffic flow or visibility and had to be easily and inexpen-
sively maintained. Rieveschl wanted the art to reflect Concord's history:
"This is a 'site-specific' work about this place. The nature of the site and
how it would be viewed determined that the sculpture would have to include predominantly upright elements so that it could be seen by motorists traveling at 30 miles per hour. A sequence of vertical accents that
relate to each other rhythmically could also reflect the cyclical development growth of the City." Fotheringham agreed and treated the traffic
islands along the five-block site as a "sequence of landscape forms, reflecting the inherent subconscious pattern of development over time . . .
to remind the public of their historical roots."

Converting their Concord Avenue project into a "living monument to

Concord's past and a symbol for the City's present and future prosperity," Rieveschl and Fotheringham placed "The Tree in the Center of the World" in the first block, nearest Highway 680. This lone oak was meant as a monument to Concord's first inhabitants, the Ohlone and Miwok Indians. Writing that this tree symbolizes the "social unity achieved through individual integrity" among these Indian tribes, the artists hoped that it would remind Concord citizens "of the importance of nourishing a strong community feeling."

The next block of the gateway, called "The Orchards," features a grove of twenty-four flowering, nonfruit-bearing pear trees, referencing the agricultural development of Concord's first settlers, the Hispanic land grantees who called the town Todos Santos. The third block, "The Formal Gardens," continues the chronology with ornamental flowers and hedges representing the town's transformation into the City of Concord. These three blocks are fairly mundane examples of civic landscaping: There is no signage to inform drivers about the historical significance of the plantings, and there are no walkways for pedestrian accessibility. The first three blocks of the *Concord Heritage Gateway* go largely unnoticed.

But the next two blocks, the blocks holding Rieveschl's ninety-one poles, quickly demand public attention. The section titled "The Advent of Modern Technology" consists of a single line of conically tipped aluminum poles from 1.8 to 7.0 meters (6 to 24 feet) tall, set into modified flagpole foundations. Bricked walkways parallel the poles, allowing people to get close to them, and to the cars zooming past. Referencing how "mass-produced tools and consumer goods, along with modern building methods and materials, rapidly changed the face of Concord's landscape," the poles symbolize "the rise of technology in the lives of individual citizens." Installed in a serpentine pattern and varying in tilt from straight up to 15 degrees off-center, the poles are meant to suggest Concord's cycles of economic, political, and technological growth. The land between them was planted with an ivy ground cover that the artists hoped would climb up the poles and provide a contrast between natural and technological growth.

The last block of the *Concord Heritage Gateway,* called "The Age of Information," features a double line of poles ranging from 7 to 15 meters (24 to 50 feet) tall (Fig. 19). Their patterning "signifies our increasing interdependence in an electronic age on digitized information. The symmetrical lines of poles also represent our collective and synchronous

■ 19. **Gary Rieveschl and Michael Fotheringham,** *Concord Heritage Gateway,* 1989; detail of Block 5.

interconnection with the rest of the planet Earth." As in the previous block, the poles differ in height, angle of tilt, and linear placement, variations all based on sine curves. "In fitting the notion of cyclical growth to the linear character of the site," Rieveschl explained, sine wave curves "were designated as the backbone metaphor for our design solution—an image of cultural growth in linear terms."

The ninety-one poles on these last two traffic islands, according to a Heritage Gateway Committee press release, symbolize the Ohlone belief in a "spirit place": "During special festivals, each Ohlone hut was decorated with a ceremonial pole wrapped in fur and topped with a painted banner. In today's *Heritage Gateway,* we will replace the furs with vines, decoratively light the poles at night, and fly colorful banners when we celebrate our festive occasions." During the Gulf War the poles were hung with yellow ribbons; Memorial Day and Fourth of July celebrations find them strung with red, white, and blue banners. And one end of

■ 20. **Gary Rieveschl and Michael Fotheringham,** *Concord Heritage Gateway,* 1989; "Spirit Place."

this last block features an opening between the double line of poles, a "spirit place" where pedestrians can pause and contemplate Concord's and their own historical significance (Fig. 20). At the dedication ceremonies on 25 October 1989, Rieveschl encouraged Concord Avenue motorists to park their cars and "visit the project on foot and up close," to "walk inside it" and "give it a chance to speak to you about the spirit of our times."

It is doubtful that most drivers speeding down Concord Avenue equate the rhythm of the poles with sine wave curves, or spend much time contemplating the spiritual import of the *Concord Heritage Gateway.* The only text explaining the project is contained in a metal plaque mounted in the parking lot of TR's Restaurant, at the corner of Concord Avenue and Salvio Street. Still, unlike the bland blocks of landscaping, the kinetic, undulating poles are inescapably present to anyone driving past. Their pointed tips and seemingly haphazard tilts also render them unfriendly, unstable, and not a little oppressive. Many survey respondents commented on the "violent" nature of the poles, saying they looked like spikes or porcupine spines; others worried that they would crash during an earthquake and "impale" cars and drivers. Their fears have so far proved unfounded—the poles survived the late October 1989 earthquake unharmed and unharming—but this kind of reaction suggests that the art inspires feelings of insecurity rather than civic pride.

The congested, agitated placement of the poles especially seems to mimic the frenzied, anxious driving along Concord Avenue—where the 48 kilometers per hour (30 miles per hour) speed limit is rarely observed. Despite the inclusion of walkways near the poles, their threatening physical presence and their placement so near six lanes of loud, fast-moving traffic hardly encourage the casual Concord pedestrian to "visit the project on foot and up close" and interact with the art. Finally, California drought conditions all but destroyed Fotheringham's landscaping: The ground cover has never grown properly, the plantings are parched and dwarfed, and the lone oak seems forlorn and abandoned.

Rieveschl and Fotheringham's intentions were to generate a positive physical identity for Concord. But the image they created with the *Concord Heritage Gateway,* particularly in the blocks featuring the poles, conveyed the fast-growth, fast-lane pace of life in Concord in the 1980s—neither the ideal communitarian image they had originally proposed nor the folksy small-town image that many in Concord still subscribed to. Despite their aim of celebrating Concord's historical and spiritual past and linking it with what they saw as the city's promising and progressive future, the overwhelming sense that Rieveschl and Fotheringham's project generated was anxiety and disorientation. Perhaps one Concord citizen put it best when he wrote, "If this is someone's idea of the Concord family, no wonder the family is in trouble." With a completely different understanding of who the Concord "family" was (or thought they were), and with an aesthetic treatment of the Concord Avenue site that mostly generated public hostility, Rieveschl and Fotheringham's intention of fostering civic identity generated, instead, local uproar.

The controversy that ensued was heightened by one significant factor: Dedication of the *Concord Heritage Gateway* took place only two weeks before an important local election. Although it had been scheduled for completion in June 1989, technical difficulties and a strike by cement workers pushed the unveiling of the project forward by several months. During that time political tensions in Concord intensified over city council approval of an AIDS antidiscrimination ordinance and the proposed development of Crystyl Ranch, a planned subdivision of 725 half-million-dollar houses and a golf course at the foot of environmentally sensitive Mount Diablo. Pivotal to the November election were referendum petitions, signed by thousands of Concord voters, that placed both issues on the ballot. The race for three (out of five) city council seats was pursued by an unprecedented sixteen candidates, only one of whom (June Bulman) was an incumbent. Most of those competing for the three seats harped on their perception of an arrogant city council out of touch with the public. The clearest symbol of that arrogance was the *Concord Heritage Gateway.*

Even before the project was officially dedicated, it became the center of heated civic debate. Council candidates, some spending close to $50,000 to run for office, generated sophisticated campaign literature featuring pictures of Concord's public art and the cynical line "Your tax dollars at work. . . ." Disregarding the basic fact that the *Concord Heritage Gateway* was not funded by residential taxes, they fanned cultural alienation into a political bonfire. One candidate in particular, Rev. Lloyd Mashore, fundamentalist pastor of the Concord Christian Center and instigator of the referendum to repeal the AIDS antidiscrimination ordinance, shaped the election into a battle over "traditional" family values. Having led the fight against "special rights" for gays since 1987, when the city council had endorsed Gay Pride Week, Mashore conducted a particularly nasty campaign, which played as much to local homophobia as to citizen concerns about Concord's growth and environmental conditions. His flyers featured pictures of ACT-UP activists "in our Council chamber" and views of "the poles on Concord Avenue" accompanied by the bugle call "HAD ENOUGH YET?"

As the campaign progressed local newspapers printed letter after letter from people criticizing the art and the city council in the same breath: Thomas Sandow wrote that "the eyesore artwork . . . [is] ample evidence of a City Council that has lost touch with its constituency"; Chris H. Beyer called the art "a grotesque symbol of the council's foolishness"; and Geoffrey Hand, a council candidate himself, made his position clear by stating that "the City Council needs to learn that extremism in art or politics will not be acceptable in the City of Concord."[32] Incensed by what they perceived as the council's "special interest group" preference for gays and lesbians, angered by what they considered its unconditional support for growth and development, and simply overwhelmed by the actual physical and demographic changes that had occurred in Concord in the 1980s, a large group of citizens singled out the *Concord Heritage Gateway* as the primary object of their civic dissatisfaction.

Concord Arts Committee members tried to fight back: CAC Chair Phyllis Nishimori wrote a letter to the *Contra Costa Times* clarifying that funds for the project "did not come from city general funds [or] taxes levied against citizens" and noted that public forums had been held to choose the art—forums that few people attended. And Hawley Holmes, the public art coordinator responsible for the sculpture, called each person who had voiced opposition to the project in the local press and also tried to clear up public misperceptions about its funding.

But the political momentum of the city council election and the referendums, coupled with the art itself, led to predictable results. On 7 November 1989 a record 40 percent turnout of registered Concord voters repealed the AIDS antidiscrimination ordinance and defeated the Crystyl Ranch development. They also broke the liberal Democratic majority of the city council by electing three conservative Republicans: Mashore, Nancy Gore, and Byron Campbell—who was selected by the council as Concord's new mayor. Within days the new councillors made it clear that one of their top priorities would be dismantling the *Concord Heritage Gateway,* which at this point had been widely renamed *Spirit Poles.* Posing for pictures at the site, Campbell promised, "I'm the mayor now and we're going to get rid of this!"[33] A liberal city council and a group of arts professionals had anticipated that public art would generate community identity and consensus. The *Concord Heritage Gateway* did exactly this, but the conservative and intolerant civic image that emerged was hardly what they expected. Instead, milked by right-wingers and fundamentalists alike for all the political authority they could muster, *Spirit Poles* crystallized public cynicism about local politics and expert authority.

As a sort of public art version of NIMBY ("not in my backyard") neopopulism, Concord's civic debate over *Spirit Poles* is hardly unique. In 1984 two neon sculptures by Stephen Antonakos were installed in the Tacoma Dome, an amphitheater and arena (Fig. 21). The expenses related to this art so infuriated residents of the recession-blighted Puget Sound city that a citizen initiative group calling themselves the NO NEON committee spearheaded a recall move against the mayor and two city council members who had supported the $272,000 locally funded public artwork. The recall attempt failed, but in 1985 Tacoma voters repealed the municipal one-percent-for-art ordinance that had financed

■ 21. **Stephen Antonakos,** *Neons for the Tacoma Dome,* 1984; 2 neon tube panels, each 29.3 meters (96 feet) long by 3.7 meters (12 feet) high by 2.1 meters (7 feet) wide, Tacoma Dome, Tacoma, Wash.

Antonakos's art, thereby severing city funding for future public art projects.[34]

A year earlier, in Boulder, a similar situation erupted. After a former city dump was renovated, plans were made to turn it into a sculpture garden in honor of a local architect. The Boulder Arts Commission was asked by the Parks and Recreation Advisory Board to organize a public art competition for the site. Centrally located off a heavily used creek path and near a major highway leading into the Rocky Mountains, the site was well known to downtown residents, and any art located there had the potential of being broadly perceived as a civic metaphor. The commission secured a $30,000 grant from the NEA, and an expert panel of five was formed: two residents—a University of Colorado curator, and a local lawyer and art collector—and three nationally known art figures. Public meetings were held, although few attended, and, after considering more than 200 artists, the panel selected New York artist Andrea Blum.[35]

■ **22. Andrea Blum,** model for *Three Pavilions,* 1983; three 2.4 meters (8 feet) tall
white cast concrete structures within 0.6-hectare (1.5-acre) park site, Boulder, Colo.
Model on display in Boulder Public Library, April 1983. Photo: Jerry Cleveland,
courtesy [Boulder] *Daily Camera.*

Interviewed by phone in the Boulder *Daily Camera* shortly after she
received the commission, Blum said she was coming to Boulder "with
my own thoughts about things that have nothing to do with any place
specifically." She added, "What I like to do is to take a dull place and
turn it into a changed area." If Boulder residents didn't like her tone,
they detested her proposal, *Three Pavilions,* which consisted of three 2.4
meters (8 feet) tall concrete structures scattered throughout the 0.6-
hectare (1.5-acre) area (Fig. 22). Articles about the sculpture's incompat-
ibility with the site and about the "arrogant" stance of the arts commission and the expert panel appeared in the local press, followed by a
questionnaire inviting public comment (90 percent of 1,076 respondents
voted an emphatic "NO!" in terms of accepting the proposal). Blum
backers called Boulder residents "aesthetically immature," and Blum
critics piled broken skis, rusty car parts, and empty oil cans at the proposed sculpture site with a plaque saying, "Eat Your Heart Out Andrea

Blum." Blum revised her proposal, but the Parks and Recreation Advisory Board (which had final approval) voted 6 to 1 to reject her design. "We don't have the community behind us on this project in the fashion I'd like to see," said one board member.[36] A decade later the city remains wary about testing the public art waters. "How can we do it right this time?" one council member queried recently. "How can we make sure it's not another fiasco?"

Recognizing the antagonism with which Americans react to public art, the *National Enquirer* sponsored an "America's Ugliest Tax-Funded Sculpture" contest in December 1989. "Hideous examples" of public art are abundant in hometown America, the tabloid explained, but reader entries would "have to top *Dreams and Nightmares,* which sits on the University of New Mexico campus in Albuquerque. It looks like a bunch of machine parts rusting in the sun—and it cost taxpayers $35,000."[37] To win the $200 contest prize, readers were asked to send a snapshot of public art that "out-uglied" Albuquerque's and was clearly the "laughingstock" of their locale.

As had the city council election, the *National Enquirer*'s contest coincided with the unveiling of Concord's *Spirit Poles.* Thus, of the sixty-six contest entries, it is not surprising that twenty-eight came from Concord residents. In March 1990 the newspaper announced: "The ugliest tax-funded sculpture in America stands in Concord, Calif.—91 aluminum poles set in concrete! Taxpayers shelled out nearly $100,000 for the metal monstrosity, called 'Spirit Poles,' plus another $300,000 for the landscaping around it." Joint winners of the contest were Bobbie Oldenhoff and Eva Walthers, a seventy-seven-year-old longtime city resident. Driving past *Spirit Poles,* Oldenhoff wrote, "you start feeling like you're drunk. The darn things are traffic hazards. . . . They should take the guy who designed that mess and make him live in the middle of it. After the earthquake hit, we were hoping that they would all fall down, but when we drove by later, there they were—ugly as ever." Walthers added, "The city should tear those ugly things down. It looks like a big pile of aluminum knitting needles set in concrete. . . . This pile of junk is located on the road from the airport, so people visiting Concord for the first time have to drive past it. They must think this is a town full of crazy people when they see *Spirit Poles.*"[38]

Many disputes about public art in the past decade have been predicated on the question of cultural authority in the public sphere. While government funding for public culture has been assailed by neoconservative politicians and intellectuals, attempts to slash NEA budgets have been rebuffed and public art projects continue to be modestly funded. State and local arts agencies have assumed more cultural responsibility, but the authoritative model they have adopted has been based on the NEA. As a result, broad NEA notions of a passive public sphere have remained prevalent, and so have the physical emblems that arts professionals believe safely convey that ideal: modern, abstract works of art, which basically privilege an elite audience yet speak to visions of unanimity. In Concord, as in cities across the country, angry debate over this idealized and conflicted form of public art is clear evidence of the struggle for authority in the public sphere.

In this respect the neoconservative battle for America's cultural and moral future and the neopopulist revolt over public art in Concord were much the same: Both represented a larger struggle for control of democratic expression in contemporary America. Encouraged by conservatives determined to weaken the city's liberal political coalition, Concord residents made *Spirit Poles* the target of their challenges to elite cultural and political authority. *Spirit Poles* symbolized everything that this disgruntled group wanted to get rid of—homosexuals, growth, cosmopolitanism, diversity. Perhaps hoping to regain their suburban village, barbecue and bandstand, insulated and isolated, small-town image, these Concord residents voted out the city's liberal coalition and demanded that their political totem—*Spirit Poles*—be removed as well.

In 1990 Concord's new conservative city council voted to have the sculpture removed. *Spirit Poles* still stands, however, protected by state law—California is one of a handful of states with an artists' moral right, *le droit moral,* mandate—and by the artists' contracts, both of which prohibit moving or changing the piece without their consent. Both Rieveschl and Fotheringham have made it clear that they want the project to stay where it is, unchanged; Rieveschl has even intimated that he will sue the city if it doesn't stop "decorating" *Spirit Poles* with holiday banners—a design element that was strictly the idea of the Heritage Gateway Committee, not the artists. But even *le droit moral* may not protect *Spirit Poles* forever: A 1992 public sculpture built by Andrea Blum in Carlsbad, California, will be slowly dismantled and possibly completely razed over the next few years. Protesting that it blocked their ocean views, irate Carlsbad citizens demanded the removal of Blum's piece, called *Split Pavilion.* Local assemblymen introduced bills to overthrow the California law protecting the public sculpture, and the city of Carlsbad and Blum eventually reached a settlement regarding its removal.[39]

Rieveschl now sees Concord's reaction to *Spirit Poles* as a constructive civic exercise: In 1992 he was quoted as saying, "A proposal that fails to create any controversy has also failed to animate the healthy public debate that lies at the root of our democratic process."[40] His comments seem to echo those of the officials at the GSA, who appropriated the democratic procedures of petitions and hearings that emerged during the debate over *Tilted Arc* to substantiate their own authority in New York's Federal Plaza. In other words, democratic expression is a great and good thing—but subject to manipulation when it comes down to actually challenging the real authority that artists and arts agencies feel is theirs in the public sphere. Rieveschl, in fact, suggests that the blame for the controversy surrounding *Spirit Poles* actually lies with the public, not the art, Concord's arts committee, the city council, or himself.

To a degree, he's right. The fact that the initial CAC forum on proposed designs for the *Concord Heritage Gateway* drew only 27 participants—out of a population of 112,000—reveals that Concord citizens viewed cultural affairs, and democratic debate, with a collective yawn. Only after the poles started to go up and Mashore and Campbell seized them as political weapons, did that same constituency get its dander up. In June 1990, when the city council were still trying to get *Spirit Poles* removed, one local writer commented, "I say, let the poles stand as a monument to the complacency of a community which ignored the pleas of their public officials to participate in their own government. They are not soothing, but maybe that is what we need to be jarred out of our reverie and do some critical thinking about what we want Concord to be as we approach a new century."[41]

Public art should involve more than plopping a sculpture into public space; it should generate civic dialogue and centerpiece democratic debate. That dialogue and debate certainly took place with the *Concord Heritage Gateway,* but less as a conversation than as the one-sided voice of partisan politics—first as that of the city's liberal coalition, then as that of the right-wing Republicans who got elected in November 1989. Perhaps if Rieveschl and the CAC had more readily involved Concord citizens throughout the process of making the *Concord Heritage Gateway*—by listening to survey responses, for example, or earlier by considering what citizens wanted to see on Concord Avenue's median strip—a real conversation might have taken place.

Concord's city council and even some art critics continue to discount

Spirit Poles's controversial presence. Arguing that his constituency did not "like the work" but had "learned to ignore it," Mayor Campbell conveniently sidestepped the very symbol that got him his political authority. Insisting that outrage had "cooled" and people were beginning "to mellow" about the poles, one recent *ARTnews* writer quoted a Concord resident remarking, "We're all used to them now. . . . It would be a waste of time if you wanted to mess with them; they're there, so we might as well accept it."[42] Such resignation, however, is hardly testimony to public acceptance, nor does it discount *Spirit Poles*'s continued presence as a loathed reminder of expert political and cultural authority in the public sphere.

The cautionary tale of the *Concord Heritage Gateway,* aka *Spirit Poles,* suggests that Americans are less and less willing to tolerate cultural imposition without their representation. Public artists who assume that their autonomy is the basis for public culture should recognize the importance of engaging their audiences in a manner more truly indicative of cultural democracy. Arts professionals who have tended to treat public art as a tool of consensus should acknowledge the flaws inherent in that vision. City councils that have isolated themselves from community dynamics should seriously consider the ramifications that culture, specifically public art, has in terms of civic conflict and their own elite authority. Most important, the public should realize their potential for active participation in the public sphere—a topic to be discussed in future chapters. The fact that corporations, the entities to be examined in Chapter 3, increasingly look upon the public sphere as the site for their agendas makes the debate over contemporary public art even more multifaceted as private companies sponsor public culture.

CHAPTER THREE

Public Art in the Corporate Sphere
Public Relations/Public Seduction

I n 1985 Alton Whitehouse, chief executive officer of Sohio, commissioned Claes Oldenburg to create a large sculpture for his company's new corporate headquarters in downtown Cleveland. Oldenburg's plan was to produce a five-story desk stamp featuring the word "FREE" embossed in capital letters 5.5 meters (18 feet) tall (Fig. 23). Typical of his other magnified monuments to the mundane—such as Chicago's *Batcolumn* and Philadelphia's *Clothespin*—Sohio's *Free Stamp* was site-specific public art, expressly designed for the front of the new Sohio Building. It was inspired, Oldenburg said, by his impression of Cleveland as "an industrial city with strong, simple forms, such as chimneys and big factories." He added that *Free Stamp* further reflected "the ideals of freedom expressed in the neighboring Soldiers and Sailors Monument," a Civil War memorial across the street from Sohio's forty-five-story office tower. When asked if what was essentially an oversize rubber stamp was a "desirable image" for Sohio, Whitehouse replied, "It is a work of art, and it will stand by itself. . . . We have not bothered to think of a long-winded rationale that would relate to our company. We don't see that as a problem."[1]

Robert Horton, however, saw *Free Stamp* as a big problem. When Sohio was taken over by British Petroleum in 1986 and renamed BP America in deference to its new owners, "Horton the Hatchetman" be-

■ 23. **Claes Oldenburg and Coosje van Bruggen,** model for *Free Stamp,* 1985; proposed 14.6 meters (48 feet) tall painted steel and aluminum sculpture, Cleveland, Ohio. Oldenburg with model, August 1985, Cleveland, Ohio. Photo courtesy *The Plain Dealer,* Cleveland, Ohio.

came the company's new CEO and promptly axed *Free Stamp.* Declaring the sculpture an inappropriate corporate symbol for his multinational oil company, Horton broke Oldenburg's contract and initiated Cleveland to the lean, mean managerial style that had given him his reputation as "BP's number one troubleshooter" by age forty-six.[2] But getting rid of *Free Stamp* proved trickier than trimming capital spending and buying out shareholders. By the time Horton came onboard, *Free Stamp* had already been fabricated and was ready for assembly. More important, Oldenburg's contract specifically held that the sculpture would be placed in front of the corporation's new headquarters, on a special base designed by architect Gyo Obata.

Recognizing the nasty PR that might ensue if Oldenburg pursued a breach of contract action—particularly when fallout from their takeover (employee firings, salary reductions) was already making hysterical local headlines—BP America backed down on their rejection of *Free Stamp* by

■ 24. **Claes Oldenburg and Coosje van Bruggen,** *Free Stamp,* 1991; painted steel and aluminum sculpture, 8.5 meters (28 feet) high by 14.6 meters (48 feet) long by 7.3 meters (24 feet) wide, Willard Park, Cleveland, Ohio. Owner: City of Cleveland.

promising to place it somewhere in central Cleveland, a free gift to the city. Early in 1987 Oldenburg and art partner Coosje (pronounced "Cosha") van Bruggen informed city officials that they wanted to see the sculpture in Willard Park, a small common next to City Hall. For the next four years, however, the city council hemmed and hawed about accepting BP America's gift, some councillors echoing constituency complaints that *Free Stamp* was an insulting corporate castoff, others saying that a huge rubber stamp suggested collusion between city government and big business. At the height of the Gulf War, Councilman Mike Polensek told the press he would rather see an Iraqi tank next to City Hall than a monster stamp.[3] Finally, however, the city accepted *Free Stamp*—and BP America's promise to maintain the sculpture and the park in perpetuity—and in late 1991 it was dedicated at Willard Park (Fig. 24).

■ 25. **Michael Heizer,** *Levitated Mass,* 1982; Vermont granite, stainless steel, and water sculpture/fountain, 7.8 meters (25.5 feet) by 5.0 meters (16.5 feet) by 0.8 meters (2.5 feet), IBM Building, New York City.

Money and culture mixed it up in the 1980s like Brie and white wine. Corporate support for the arts skyrocketed: By the middle of the decade, companies were pumping close to $1 billion a year into the art market. Corporate art collections flourished: More than 60 percent of Fortune 500 companies (including BP America) held collections of mostly contemporary art. Artists responded to corporate America's new Medicean persona by acting more and more like businessmen—reading the *Wall Street Journal,* hiring agents and accountants, investing in tax shelters, becoming more and more astute about corporate yearnings for the patina of contemporary art.[4]

Nowhere was this power lunch of business and culture more obvious than in the public sphere. Hardly a single corporate headquarters was built without some sort of public art accompaniment: Michael Heizer's *Levitated Mass* at IBM's outdoor plaza in New York (Fig. 25), Terry Allen's *Corporate Head* in Citicorp Plaza in downtown Los Angeles, Anne and Patrick Poirier's *Promenade Classique* at the TransPotomac

Canal Center in Alexandria, Virginia (see Figs. 27 and 28), Oldenburg's *Free Stamp* in Cleveland.

Not only did the number of corporate commissions for public art proliferate but overall business interest in public life—and determination to influence that life—soared. Put simply, in the 1980s corporate America saw culture as a tool of public seduction. Less interested in improving the quality of life (ostensibly a motivation behind government arts funding), corporate cultural sponsorship centered on corporate benefit. A 1988 brochure published by the Business Committee for the Arts, Inc., an organization formed to encourage such support, explained: "Business is investing its resources in the arts because it increases sales, attracts employees, enhances relations with employees and customers, helps develop new markets, broadens public awareness of business, and in some instances, increases property values." Or, as a Mobil Oil spokesperson bluntly put it in 1987: "All of the projects we sponsor must meet a corporate objective or a direct business need. We don't sponsor events just because they're cultural."[5]

Profit ruled during the so-called greed decade, and the manner in which commerce and culture mixed it up had a profound impact on public life. The public realm, writes critic Richard Bolton, was increasingly "brought under corporate control," a move sanctioned politically and aided aesthetically:

> Conservatism has extensively restructured cultural production. The corporation that performs as a good citizen doesn't really donate its capital, it *invests* it, developing a corporate culture and extending business's reach into all walks of life. The role of the corporation as a shadowy government is strengthened. Citizens become accustomed to official art.[6]

Ranging in style from Heizer's abstract sculptures to Oldenburg's grossly cloned Pop icons, the public art sponsored by corporate America in the 1980s carried the baggage of private interest.

Rigid distinctions between "public" and "private" are tenuous—family life, for instance, obviously spans both realms. In the 1980s, however, encouraged by economic, legal, and political permissions (such as deregulation), corporate America sought to muddy those distinctions more thoroughly by manipulating the public sphere for private motives. Contemporary notions of public and private blurred as corporate dollars subsidized public development (for instance, in Cleveland's Willard Park) and public dollars financed private development (most notably at

New York's Battery Park City, but examples abound).[7] More important, as corporations sought more of a presence in the public sphere, they used culture to gain legitimacy. Public art was an obvious symbol of that quest, although, as the *Free Stamp* saga reveals, the route to such legitimacy was hardly direct.

The neoconservative politics of the 1980s helped pave the way for this. At his 1981 inaugural Ronald Reagan intoned, "In this present crisis, government is not the solution to our problem. Government is the problem." The crisis was economic ("We suffer from the longest and one of the worst sustained inflations in our national history"), and the cure was Reaganomics, a simplistic (and thus highly appealing) economic strategy that involved reducing taxes and government spending (except in defense) to encourage corporate America—flush with billions in a deregulated, free-market renaissance—to take on the responsibility of the nation's social and cultural services. Big government was Reaganomics's bugaboo, and big business was its savior. In his account of the 1980s, *Sleepwalking through History*, Haynes Johnson described Reagan's "basic contempt" for government:

> Reagan believed in dismantling government and advocated selling off major public assets, such as naval petroleum reserves and parkland, federal power marketing operations like the TVA, and the National Technical Information Service. His mission was to privatize government's functions and turn them over to market-oriented entrepreneurs who would operate them as private concerns.[8]

Such laissez-faire attitudes dominated the cultural realm as well.

Reagan's plans to privatize public culture were announced in his first State of the Union Address, delivered to Congress 18 February 1981:

> Historically, the American people have supported by voluntary contributions more artistic and cultural activities than all the other countries in the world put together. I wholeheartedly support this approach and believe Americans will continue their generosity. Therefore, I am proposing a savings of $85 million in the federal subsidies now going to the arts and humanities.

While greatly overstating American altruism, Reagan was right on one count: Historically, government funding for the arts in the United States has been very limited. But his administration's disdain for government funding hit the NEA (National Endowment for the Arts) and the NEH (National Endowment for the Humanities) disproportionally harder than any other groups—in 1981 it was these agencies that were "scheduled initially for the greatest percentage reductions in the budget." In an interview that year, Aram Bakshian, Reagan's special assistant for cultural matters, remarked that "the President and his wife are performing artists, and they feel very strongly about the arts." But, he added, presumably echoing Reagan, "It wouldn't be the end of the world for any art forms or institutions if arts funding were cut."[9]

Following this lead, Office of Management and Budget (OMB) hit man David Stockman proposed 50 percent budget cuts for both endowments, on the ground that their funding had "resulted in a reduction in the historic role of private individual and corporate philanthropic support" in the arts and humanities. National Endowment for the Arts Chair Livingston Biddle countered by explaining that corporate support for the arts had actually grown from $22 million in 1966 (the year after the NEA was founded) to $435 million in 1981—and it had grown *because* of the NEA's catalytic role. Congress eventually challenged the Reagan campaign to dismantle these agencies by approving endowment budgets significantly higher than those proposed by the OMB. Still, there were large-scale cuts—the NEA budget declined from $158.6 million in 1981 to $119.3 million in 1982. Public culture was not, one critic writes, "a popular idea in the Reagan administration."[10]

Fiscal conservatism accounts only partially for this attack on public culture—even combined, the 1981 NEA and NEH budgets totaled less than $310 million, a practically invisible fraction of federal spending. Nor can the Reagan administration alone be credited with engendering such opposition—many leading neoconservative intellectuals willfully argued against government arts subsidies in the 1980s. Their antipathy toward what they dubbed "The National Endowment for the Frills" was rooted in political disgust with the "populist excesses" of the Carter administration, particularly Biddle's attempts (from 1977 to 1981) "to democratize and regionalize the distribution of cultural subsidies" at the NEA. Biddle's "Common Cause for the Arts" approach tried to make the Endowment "more responsive to the constituency it serves—developing audiences for the arts and groups who have not been considered in the past such as minorities, Hispanics, women, labor, community groups, neighborhood arts organizations."[11]

Fearing that their own government funding might altogether dissipate in the face of the NEA's apparent interest in a more democratic culture, disgruntled supporters of elite arts organizations (such as the Metropolitan Opera) charged Biddle with "politicizing" the Endowment by pandering to Carter's kind of grassroots populism. Others equated NEA efforts to diversify federal arts funding with lower cultural standards. Public culture became negatively tied to political populism—still a big source of concern for many mob-fearing conservatives—and aesthetic mediocrity.

Whatever populism was present in public culture during the 1970s—particularly during Carter's term—was discounted in the 1980s by neoconservative politicians and critics alike in favor of a decidedly more elitist agenda. In a replay of the antipublic hysteria that had gripped postwar intellectuals such as Clement Greenberg in the 1950s, fears of American pluralism—now called multiculturalism—surfaced with renewed vigor. Journals such as *The New Criterion* (launched in 1982) bewailed American culture's "fateful collapse in critical standards" and pinned the blame on "the leftward turn in our political life," responsible, said its editor, Hilton Kramer, for "the introduction of kitsch into the museums" and "the decline of literacy in the schools." Toward the end of the 1980s, the target became multiculturalism, a "cultural revolution," said Kramer, "that has succeeded in making race, gender, and class the touchstones governing every question that concerns the life and thought of the nation, which means that it has succeeded in undermining the very principles upon which our nation was founded."[12]

From the onset *The New Criterion* was determined to turn the cultural life of the nation to its definition of those "very principles." As a sort of neoconservative house organ, *The New Criterion* held culture responsible for both the country's ills and its redemption. Generously subsidized by the right-wing Heritage, Olin, and Scaife foundations, *The New Criterion* declared its task to be "the defense of high art in a democratic society," a smoke screen for attempts to revalidate modernism at a time when feminism and multiculturalism were making important cultural inroads. In the journal's inaugural issue, Kramer aspersed postmodernists as "philistines" and proclaimed modernism "the only really vital tradition that the art of our time can claim as its own."[13] Threatened by how America had become more and more a multiculture over which they seemed to have little direct influence, neoconservatives struggled to keep culture static by sustaining the modernist agenda.

The New Criterion focused on revamping notions of culture broached in the 1950s, when the supposedly apolitical and rational culture of modernism was deemed best able to meet the demands of consensus. Neoconservative views of democracy were similar: While insisting they were the authentic voice of the American folk, their idea of a like-thinking, narrowly defined, and nonparticipatory electorate betrayed their real interest in social control, in containment. Much of their antagonism toward contemporary culture was based on the assumption that Americans shared a single standard of "public taste." Art that veered from that standard, such as Robert Mapplethorpe's photographs or Martin Scorsese's 1988 movie *The Last Temptation of Christ,* was, as columnist and presidential aspirant Pat Buchanan put it, "anti-American, anti-Christian, and nihilist."[14]

In the 1980s the neoconservative path to cultural—and moral—consensus was economic: the economics of free-market capitalism. Publisher Samuel Lipman declared that *The New Criterion* was "a marriage of an essentially modernist artistic outlook with an essentially pro-American democratic society outlook. That of course includes capitalism. We are, in fact, anti-Socialist; we are pro-capitalist; we are very much pro-America. And we're attempting to bring those two ideas together." Kramer, bristling at the Marxist underpinnings of revisionist criticism, demanded that its adherents recognize that "capitalism, for all its many flaws, has proved to be the greatest safeguard of democratic institutions and the best guarantee of intellectual and artistic freedom—including *their* freedom—that the modern world has given us."[15]

Kramer and Lipman made no bones about their disgust with federal funding for the arts: Not only did it threaten their free-market vision of culture but it dangerously encouraged a populist culture of lowbrow "entertainment" such as blockbuster museum exhibitions and *Masterpiece Theatre.* There was some difference, of course, between their critique of public culture and that based on right-wing political and religious posturing. Pat Buchanan, Jesse Helms, and Donald Wildmon attacked American culture on more obviously moralistic grounds, damning the "cultural elite" for infecting America with threats such as *Mighty Mouse*—Wildmon pressured CBS to remove a three-second scene from the Saturday morning cartoon, insisting the character was sniffing cocaine. Witless, unyielding, and unconscious (much less supportive) of the rational modernism held in such high esteem by the intellectual neoconservatives, these sanctimonious right-wingers aimed to purge America of all undesirable cultural—and hence political and moral—elements. Buchanan's rhetoric, Carol Vance notes, is "chillingly reminiscent" of Hitler's: "As with our rivers and lakes, we need to clean up our culture: for it is a well from which we must all drink. Just as a poisoned land will yield up poisonous fruits, so a polluted culture, left to fester and stink, can destroy a nation's soul."[16]

The staff at *The New Criterion* more subtly embraced the same agenda. Along with Allan Bloom and E. D. Hirsch, the journal assailed popular culture (Kramer demanded that courses in popular culture be removed from university curricula) and called for the revitalization of "traditional" cultures—classical and modern. A basic ideological suspicion of a diverse, active public culture informed their critique, as did their assumption that popular culture, or any culture rooted in public taste, was inauthentic and inferior. Neoconservative criticism was also shaped, George Lipsitz argues, by a certain refusal to admit the "complex realities of American history."[17] Constructing a past based on progress, expansion, and common ground, neoconservatives conveniently ignored the "other" side of American historic reality—ethnic diversity, class conflict, and gendered inequity.

Historical amnesia also informed *The New Criterion*'s assault on public culture and the NEA. "Few observers of art," Lipman wrote in 1983, "would credit the NEA with having had other than a marginal effect on the development of American culture during the nearly two decades of its existence." In the realm of public art alone, Lipman's claims can be challenged: The NEA is largely responsible for ensuring that works by modernists such as Sol LeWitt, Robert Morris, Isamu Noguchi, and Richard Serra bedeck and bear influence on the "development" of American culture. Despite their distaste for the NEA, both Lipman and Kramer were closely involved with the Endowment: From 1981 to 1987 Lipman served on the National Council for the Arts, the presidentially appointed advisory body to the NEA, and in 1983 Kramer participated in an Endowment Visual Arts Criticism Seminar, an event he wrote about with such bile that it hardly seemed a coincidence when, a few months later, then NEA Chair Frank Hodsoll decided to suspend all grants to art critics.[18]

While *The New Criterion* never advocated axing the NEA—which many other neoconservative voices did—it demanded that federal arts funding be reformed to promote high culture, not mass entertainment. The journal sided with the Heritage Foundation's *Mandate for Leader-*

ship, a 1981 report that greatly influenced the Reagan administration. The chapter on cultural policy (which Lipman helped write) said the NEA had unwisely overexpanded by trying to reach an "unsophisticated mass public." It advised the Endowment to retrench, to "finally acknowledge that the enduring audience for art is largely self-selecting, a relatively small public."[19] Likewise, in *The New Criterion,* Lipman insisted that culture and democracy be kept separate:

> Just because government in the United States is responsive to political constituencies, there will inevitably be increasing pressures to use public power to make culture serve the needs of what I have called an all-encompassing definition of democracy. To capitulate to these pressures would be to reduce culture to a mere expression of the democratic impulse. . . . Our need today is not for a forced unification of culture and democracy, but for their amicable separation.[20]

Likening the "impulse" of cultural democracy to mob tyranny, Lipman and other neoconservatives argued that government funding for the arts should reach the people—all of them. But their interest in public culture was motivated by the desire for consensus, for social order, and the control of democratic expression:

> The state should support art, construed not as amusement but as one of the chief carriers of civilization. Here in America this mission can be seen as having a particular relevance to our national mission of making one people out of many, of building social unity out of a pluralistic culture. Whatever the future of our society, we can hardly doubt that Western civilization can and must serve as a binding force.

It is not surprising that neoconservatives, remarkably conflicted about culture's role in the restoration of conservative ideology, with its challenge to government authority and its regulation of public expression, wavered on what role the NEA should actually play in orchestrating public taste. By and large, though, the Endowment's role was redefined as "cultural uplift for all": no more PBS populism, no more art for audiences' sake, no more (or at least no further) American multiculturalism. Failing this, and Lipman for one was not so convinced that the NEA—with its "interest group pressures" and "constituency demands"—was truly capable of "communicating our civilized heritage," neoconservatives appealed to the private sector, to corporations, to finance and foster the arts.[21]

Antistatists in the 1980s insisted that the "inflation of expectations" that came about through federal arts funding—as different groups competed for a piece of the NEA pie—overburdened the government agency and ultimately rendered it and the arts illegitimate. Pluralism, populism, multiculturalism—all were blamed for the crisis of authority looming in America. The neoconservative response was to see government's "burden" reduced and return culture to the marketplace, assuming, as Jürgen Habermas wrote, that "the more the state withdraws from the economic process, as by privatizing public services, the better it can escape the legitimation demands that arise from its general responsibility for the burdens resulting from a crisis-ridden capitalism."[22]

Neoconservatives trusted in the "magic of the marketplace" (a favorite Reagan adage) to sort out the mess multiculturalism had made of democracy. As Lipman explained,

> The chief justification for a private system of cultural patronage . . . is that our reliance on the private sector, with all its richness, its power, and even its arrogance, is a manifestation of liberty. Because of the *private* patrons' power, this liberty extends even to the rights of artists to resist, criticize, and even replace supporters as the artists themselves see fit.

Assigning capitalism the task of restoring *their* version of a culturally moralized democracy, neoconservatives assumed that private sector patronage would also ensure aesthetic quality. Lipman, at least, recognized that this would not be easy: Mobil and Philip Morris, after all, were the primary benefactors of the lowbrow PBS and museum culture he despised. The solution was to encourage corporate America to make "educated, sophisticated decisions about cultural matters, decisions which are based not upon the public relations imperative of advocacy or the mindless praise for all art, any art, and every art."[23]

Neoconservative naïveté—or disingenuousness—about the magical marketplace discounted, of course, the reality of contemporary capitalism. Ignoring its dependence on profit and hence on mass—not elite—taste, its mammoth complexity, and its sheer power, neoconservatives put their own agenda at risk. For corporate patrons, notions of aesthetic quality are based on art's blue-chip cachet not its value as a hallmark of modern civilization. The "liberty" of capitalism lies in its power to drive prices up and down—witness the incoherent financial brouhaha that surrounded Van Gogh's *Irises,* sold at $53.9 million in 1987 and then resold at an apparently lower price in 1990—not in disinterested cul-

tural appreciation.[24] Nor is the marketplace full of eager arts patrons—
the idea that contemporary artists, particularly those with critical social
or economic views, can pick and choose their sponsors is laughable. Unless it meets investment and/or public relations demands, art is ignored
by business. But, romanticizing the marketplace as the site of contemporary cultural Darwinism, where good (modern) art rises to the top and
the rest falls by the wayside, neoconservatives implored corporate America to take the lead in the cultural realm.

Which it readily did. In 1985 alone American business provided
$698.0 million to the arts (compared with NEA funding of $163.0 million). For a good deal of the 1980s, some $30.0 million was spent annu-
ally subsidizing the museum blockbusters *The New Criterion* hated so
much: Philip Morris paid more than $3.5 million sponsoring the Metro-
politan Museum's "Vatican Collections" show in 1983, and Ford put up
around $5.0 million for the "Treasure Houses of Britain" exhibition at
the National Gallery two years later. More insidious, perhaps, were the
numbers of corporate chairs who exerted their influence on the art museum boards they came to dominate in the 1980s: Paine Webber CEO
Donald Marron, for example, was the president of the board of the Museum of Modern Art. Several corporations actually served as museum
satellites: Equitable Life Assurance Society, Philip Morris, Champion International, and IBM and Park Tower Realty all operated annexes of the
Whitney Museum of American Art, underwriting the museum's installation and operating expenses in their own corporate facilities. Millions
more were expended purchasing art for corporate headquarters: By
1986 Equitable had spent more than $7.5 million on paintings and
sculpture for their new fifty-four-story midtown Manhattan building,
commissioning contemporary works by Sandro Chia, Sol LeWitt, and
Roy Lichtenstein and spending $3.4 million for Thomas Hart Benton's
1930 mural *America Today*.[25]

The most visible sign of corporate America's cultural investiture in the
1980s was public art—the sculptures, murals, and artparks that sprouted
in and around corporate venues. Cray commissioned a sculpture by Andrew Leicester for the front entrance to their Mendota Heights, Minnesota, facility in 1981. Wells Fargo commissioned a stainless steel sculpture by Michael Heizer for the outdoor lobby of their forty-eight-story
Los Angeles building in 1982; the same year IBM commissioned him to
make the sculpture-fountain *Levitated Mass* (Fig. 25) for the Madison
Avenue entrance to their forty-three-story headquarters. Kaempfer Co.

commissioned Miriam Schapiro's *Anna and David* sculpture for the plaza entrance to their Rosslyn, Virginia, building in 1987. Equitable put Roy Lichtenstein's 20.7 meters (68 feet) tall *Mural with Blue Brush-stroke* in the atrium of their midtown building; Creative Artists Agency put a Lichtenstein mural in the main hall of their Beverly Hills headquarters in 1989. The National Geographic Society hired Elyn Zimmerman to design an entry plaza for their Washington, D.C., building in 1984. Savage/Fogarty hired Anne and Patrick Poirier to design a 3.2-hectare (8-acre) sculpture park for an Alexandria, Virginia, office and retail complex in 1986 (see Figs. 27 and 28). The list was endless: A casual drive past the office towers and industrial parks of American business in the 1980s showed countless examples of public art—outdoor, indoor, large, small, abstract, figurative, steel, stone, autonomous, interactive.

Despite neoconservative suggestions otherwise, corporate America's astounding cultural patronage in the 1980s was hardly motivated by newfound feelings of responsibility for a realm government didn't want to nurture. Nor was it inspired by interest in a neoconservative version of cultural morality (although this may have been the end result). It wasn't especially the result of aesthetic altruism either—few justified raiding the company treasury on the ground that art is a nice thing to look at. In practical terms, it was motivated by tax benefits and Reagan-era business maneuvers; less prosaically, perhaps, it was stimulated by image-making incentives, by what artist Hans Haacke describes as the corporate goal of public seduction.[26]

From 1981 to 1986 IRS deductions for corporate giving to charity increased from 5 to 10 percent. During this five-year span corporate art collections, museum sponsorship, and public art commissions flourished. Chockful of cash from deregulation and merger mania, corporations came to depend on culture to launder their money—and improve their public image. When tax laws were changed in 1986 and write-offs for charity came to be worth less, corporate philanthropy slowed; when the stock market crashed in 1987, it fell off dramatically.[27]

Financial gain is a given, but Americans remain conflicted about big money. Perhaps because of our republicanist roots, we love seeing "bad" capitalists such as J. R. Ewing and Donald Trump take the fall. True, ostentation went unquestioned through most of the 1980s—few cried foul at the $209,508 price tag for Nancy Reagan's new Lenox china in 1981, and cheers, not cries of moral outrage, greeted Ivan Boesky in 1985 when he told a Berkeley crowd, "Greed is all right. . . . You shouldn't feel guilty."[28] But apprehension about how corporate America was acquiring its greed-decade billions and how that affected the country endured—particularly as leveraged buyouts and hostile takeovers took their toll on local economies and corporations seemed to thrive while U.S. family income and standards of living steadily declined.

Throughout the 1980s (or at least until the 1987 crash), corporations relied on art to make sure they were seen as "good" capitalists, such as Bobby Ewing and Malcolm Forbes. Corporate cultural citizenship was calculated as a form of public relations designed to appease misgivings about business practice and profit. In part this reflects the changed postwar nature of the business class. "While fewer than 50 percent of top executives had some college education in 1900," Paul Mattick writes, "76 percent did by 1950. The postwar rise of the professional manager helped break down the traditional barrier between the worlds of business and culture."[29] The educated CEO came to recognize the investment and PR potential of art. Eventually, too, he recognized how corporate philanthropy could be skewed to supplant an older (and more costly) business world notion of paternalism. As workers were laid off or fired, corporations dealt with the backlash by upping their support for orchestras and art museums—maybe on the assumption that culture could take care of the workers they had abandoned. Flint, Michigan's ridiculous Auto World, a $100 million amusement park, which opened just as GM finished closing its last factory in the city, was a perfect example of the cynical culture-circus mentality of the 1980s—as Michael Moore's 1989 movie *Roger and Me* aptly revealed.

By and large, corporations tended to advertise their pursuit of cultural patronage less flagrantly—although one Exxon executive's observation that his company's "support of the arts serves the arts as a social lubricant" inspired artist Hans Haacke's observation that corporate philanthropy really amounted to "social grease." For the most part, corporations marketed their cultural "lubrication" as a tremendous opportunity for the arts and for artists, a boon that enhanced the quality of life for all citizens. As one AT&T ad in *ARTnews* put it: "From the beginning, we've been committed to achieving excellence in communications. It's only natural for us to support excellence in the arts that communicate."[30]

Corporations gave other reasons for supporting the arts, too. First Bank System, a huge Minneapolis-based banking concern, claimed their support for the arts—which grew into a 3,000-piece contemporary art collection valued at over $10 million—benefited worker creativity. (Instead, it generated employee outrage and was dismantled in early 1990.) Equitable Life Assurance explained that their cultural patronage was undertaken "foremost for love of art." (It was more bluntly bait to draw high-paying tenants to their new building—to get Park Avenue rents in midtown Manhattan.) *Sports Illustrated* said *Monument to Joe Louis* (1986), a $350,000 public sculpture they commissioned from Robert Graham, was a gift to the people of Detroit, an altruistic memorial to the world heavyweight champion who made his home in the city. (It was more of a calculated PR move on the part of the Detroit Institute of the Arts, accused of financial mismanagement and community isolation in the mid-1980s.)[31]

Underlying their philanthropy, Tom Wolfe argues, is corporate America's quest for the "legitimation of wealth." Business patrons long to be seen as multinational Medicis with reputations for refinement, not just rapacious capitalism: "We are long past the age when autocrats made aesthetic decisions based on what *they* wanted to see in public. Today corporations . . . turn to the [art] clerisy, saying, in effect, 'Please give us whatever we should have to certify the devoutness of our dedication to art.'" But links between corporations and culture, from Mobil and *Mystery!* to Sohio and *Free Stamp*, do more than enhance corporate public image, they legitimate corporate public influence. Corporate financing turns culture into a lobbying tool, Haacke remarks, "with potentially far-reaching consequences for public policy."[32] Corporate pursuit of a Medicean persona is concomitant with the manipulation of public culture for private interest.

The entire issue of corporate control is admittedly slippery: Corporations usually hire art experts (Wolfe's "clerisy") to make cultural decisions for them. The diversity of interests at work in decentralized, bureaucratic, large-scale businesses makes any cause and effect relationship between corporations, their art collections and/or museum sponsorship, the art itself, and the public very tentative. Nevertheless, in the 1980s many multinational corporations translated neoconservative importunity to take responsibility for culture as an invitation to take over public culture. Corporate largesse was seen as a manifestation of corporate *rights*.

There is perhaps no better example of this than Philip Morris's blatant monopolization of the First Amendment. The corporation is best known as the world's largest consumer packaged goods company, manufacturer of products ranging from Cheez Whiz and Miller Lite to Marlboros. In the 1980s double-page ads (Fig. 26) for various exhibitions that Philip

Which is "primitive"? Which is "modern"?

Maybe you can tell at a glance, maybe you can't. But before you leap to the answers down below, put another question to yourself: How do they relate to each other, and we to them? It is a fascinating question which we can only now fully explore for the first time—in an exciting and enlightening new exhibition "'Primitivism' in 20th Century Art: Affinity of the Tribal and the Modern" at The Museum of Modern Art.

In over 350 works—150 modern and 200 tribal—we can now get a definitive view of the similarities and differences, the influences and affinities which have intrigued us for nearly a hundred years. It is a show which sheds new light on, and challenges much of our "received wisdom" about both "primitive" and modern art and their relation to each other. It may be the first art exhibition you've ever seen which asks and answers so many questions about art—and about ourselves.

That's one reason we sponsored this exhibition, and why we urge you to see it at the times and places listed below. In our business as in yours, we must constantly ask ourselves new questions, and be prepared for answers quite different from those we expect—from the endless resources of our individual imagination, individual creativity and individual innovativeness. Sponsorship of art that reminds us of these things is not patronage: it's a business and human necessity.

If your company would like to know more about corporate sponsorship of art, write Hamish Maxwell, Chairman of the Board, Philip Morris Incorporated, 120 Park Avenue, New York, N.Y. 10017.

Philip Morris Incorporated
It takes art to make a company great.

Makers of Marlboro, Benson & Hedges 100's, Merit, Parliament Lights, Virginia Slims and Players; Miller High Life Beer, Lite Beer, Lowenbrau Special and Dark Special Beers, Meister Brau and Milwaukee's Best; 7UP, Diet 7UP, LIKE Cola and Sugar Free LIKE Cola.

"'Primitivism' in 20th Century Art: Affinity of the Tribal and the Modern" appears at The Museum of Modern Art, New York, September 27, 1984—January 15, 1985; The Detroit Institute of Arts, Detroit, February 27—May 19, 1985; Dallas Museum of Art, Dallas, June 23—September 1, 1986.

■ 26. Philip Morris advertisement in *Art in America*, October 1984. Courtesy Philip Morris Companies, Inc.

Morris sponsored—such as "Primitivism in Twentieth Century Art" at the Museum of Modern Art—included the following text: "In our business as in yours, we must constantly ask ourselves new questions, and be prepared for answers quite different from those we expect—from the endless resources of *our individual imagination, individual creativity and individual innovativeness.* Sponsorship of art that reminds us of these things is not patronage: it's a business and human necessity."[33]

Then in 1989 the company started an extensive advertising campaign celebrating the two-hundredth anniversary of the U.S. Constitution. Free copies of the Bill of Rights were distributed through a 1-800 telephone number, and an original copy even went on tour to all fifty states in a glitzy exhibit designed by the company. Promoting themselves as the cultural sponsor of the Bill of Rights, Philip Morris implied that they—not the Founding Fathers—had actually engineered the U.S. Constitution. Public and congressional proposals to ban all cigarette advertising account for Philip Morris's real interest in America's Noble Experiment. Taking the Bill of Rights on tour and touting the oxymoron of corporate "individuality" in its art exhibition advertising, Philip Morris rather transparently utilized American history and culture to declare *their* First Amendment rights—and to intimate that any ban on cigarette advertising would violate their constitutional guarantee of freedom of speech. Ironically, while distributing copies of the Bill of Rights, Philip Morris was also heavily financing the 1990 reelection campaign of North Carolina senator Jesse Helms, a "great friend" of the tobacco industry whose political agenda at the time was to place legal constraints on the NEA. Hans Haacke's indictment of all this was a mixed-media work called *Helmsboro Country* (1990), an Oldenburg-esque sculpture of a huge pack of cigarettes with the "Marlboro" logo replaced by "Helmsboro" and the surgeon general's advisories replaced by quotations from Philip Morris and Helms.[34] Haacke understood that Philip Morris's take on free expression was motivated by private interest.

The idea that corporations, like American citizens, are entitled to the benefits of the First Amendment is ludicrous, as Herbert Schiller persuasively argues. In 1942, in *Valentine* v. *Chrestensen,* the U.S. Supreme Court unanimously ruled that commercial speech is *not* entitled to constitutional rights. During the postwar years, however, and especially in the 1980s, court rulings expanded the legal definition of corporations as "persons." This, along with deregulation and privatization, served increasingly to legitimize corporations as individuals entitled to citizen rights. As the corporate persona shifted, or widened, conventional dis-

tinctions between "public" and "private" blurred. Corporate appropriation of a public identity conformed to neoconservative efforts to "reduce, even eliminate, the public realm in favor of the corporate sector."[35]

The NEA, for instance, started an "Art in the Marketplace" program,
giving federal funds to the Rouse Company, the nation's leading real estate development firm and owner-operator of shopping malls and "festival marketplaces" across the country—such as Baltimore's Harborplace,
Seattle's Westlake Center, and Boston's Faneuil Hall. Rouse spent the
NEA money ($150,000, which the company matched) on arts events
(jazz festivals, senior art shows) in their own malls. Bob Johnson, a
Florida state senator, was the only member of the Endowment's advisory
body (the twenty-three-person National Council on the Arts) to object
to the NEA-Rouse merger, saying, "I don't think we should spend federal
money in privately owned, for-profit malls." Endowment Chair John
Frohnmayer (largely responsible for arranging the liaison) defended the
public-private partnership by stating that "the shopping center of today
reflects the fairs and marketplaces of Renaissance times." This may be
true, but the Supreme Court has yet to accord such sites "public forum
status for First Amendment access," and the Rouse Company's primary
intention as a business is to make a profit by renting mall space, not to
patronize the arts.[36] The fact that NEA dollars subsidized corporate interests suggests that in the neoconservative era of Reagan and Bush, public culture became pivotal to the development of private concerns.

Countless examples support this suggestion. Public art boomed in the
1980s because corporations recognized that it, like museum exhibitions
and art collections, is a highly visible form of public persuasion. Explaining why Rouse & Associates, for instance, commissioned seventeen
larger-than-life-size steel sculptures of Washington Redskins football
players and various other sports figures for their 60.8-hectare (150-acre)
Ammendale Technology Park in Prince George's County, Maryland, general partner Mark Dishaw said, "It's a way people can remember your
project. And sometimes that's half the battle in this area because it's so
competitive."[37]

A few miles away *Promenade Classique,* a 1986 plaza at the Trans-
Potomac Canal Center in Alexandria, Virginia, was likewise designed to
entice business clients (Fig. 27). Financed by Savage/Fogarty Real Estate,
Inc., a Dutch development firm, *Promenade Classique* was the public art
capstone to a $125 million, four-building, 152,400-square-meter
(500,000-square-foot) office and retail center built along the abandoned
docks of Alexandria's waterfront. Like the art at the Equitable, *Prome-*

■ 27. **Anne and Patrick Poirier,** *Promenade Classique,* 1986; Carrara marble, bronze, brick, and water sculpture/fountain, TransPotomac Canal Center, Alexandria, Va.

nade Classique was an amenity designed to sell space—which is exactly how it was advertised in a Canal Center prospectus:

- Spectacular views across the Potomac River to Downtown Washington, D.C.
- Award-winning Landscaping
- World Class Art Sculpture
- Cascading Water Fountain

As Savage/Fogarty Vice President Jeffrey Riddel remarked, "We wanted to capitalize on the location and provide a museum and waterfront park to maintain the city's heritage. They are amenities that are combining to promote the marketability of the project."[38]

French artists Anne and Patrick Poirier helped "market" the Canal Center with *Promenade Classique.* The $5 million plaza consists of huge fragments of pseudoclassical ruins—obelisks, columns, sculpted heads, torsos—casually strewn throughout a 3.2-hectare (8-acre) space. Fountains, reflecting pools, terraces, walkways, marble boulders, and a 9.1-

■ **28. Anne and Patrick Poirier,** *Promenade Classique,* 1986; detail of shallow rectangular pool with classically carved mouth spouting 3-meter (10-foot) water stream, TransPotomac Canal Center, Alexandria, Va. Photo courtesy Savage/Fogarty Real Estate, Inc.

meter (30-foot) bronze arrow transform the former docklands into a picturesque and entirely mythical space. Certain motifs—such as the 12.2-meter (40-foot) obelisk at the bank of the Potomac—reference the art and architecture of the capital city across the river, where classical styles have long served to legitimate American notions of democracy and government.

If *Promenade Classique*'s neoclassical appropriation legitimizes Savage/Fogarty's corporate interests, it also amounts to a perfect neoconservative view of history, in which the crisis of contemporary America is pinioned on cultural decline rather than on greed-decade economics and politics. The plaza's classical specimens, its broken fragments of pseudo-Greek and Roman sculpture, intimate longing for a past when culture was more durable, more entrenched; its contrived ruins imply the wane of that culture, the erosion of morality, the loss of empire (Fig. 28). Ig-

91

noring Alexandria's real past—its industrial workers, its massive shipping operations, and even its canal lock, after which, ironically, the TransPotomac Canal Center was named—the false history of *Promenade Classique* propped the private concerns of its corporate sponsor.

In addition to rewriting Alexandria's history, *Promenade Classique* legitimized Savage/Fogarty's incorporation of public space. The TransPotomac Canal Center, like several other office complexes developed along a twelve-block stretch of Alexandria's waterfront in the 1980s, was built on open space. Anxious to flee the high rents of downtown Washington, 9.7 kilometers (6 miles) away, firms looked to the Beltway suburbs—and Alexandria's city council and chamber of commerce eagerly accommodated them. Former public spaces, especially those along the waterfront, became corporate environments. Pedestrian walkways, landscaping, a maritime museum, and *Promenade Classique*— public amenities all sponsored by the waterfront's new private interests—helped render this transformation more palatable to Alexandria residents and potential corporate employees.

Some citizens' groups, challenging the loss of public space, fought the development in federal court. Former city council member Ellen Pickering angrily remarked, "That was public land given to private hands for private profit. I think it is a crime, a white-collar crime."[39] Most of Alexandria, however, acquiesced to the corporate takeover on the waterfront and abandoned claims on the space, literally and psychologically. Escalating housing prices forced many of them out of the gentrified areas that sprang up around the corporatized shoreline. And while the Canal Center is close to the city's well-trafficked Old Town district, *Promenade Classique* is usually deserted. Locals don't seem to know it exists, and those who do assume that, because it is on private property, it is off-limits. Although *Promenade Classique* has been praised as an outstanding example of public art, many in Alexandria see it as a private playground on corporate turf.

Similarly, fears that *Free Stamp* validated BP America's private interests are central to the heated debate that surrounded the Cleveland sculpture during the late 1980s and early 1990s. On the one hand, Robert Horton, for example, was obviously uneasy that Oldenburg's giant sculpture might make a laughingstock of the oil company he had just taken over. Some members of Cleveland's city council, on the other hand, worried that *Free Stamp* might intimate another kind of takeover—such as corporate America's appropriation of local government.

The story of *Free Stamp* is about the intersection of those fears, in a city where image and influence have always been touchy subjects.

John D. Rockefeller (1839–1937), who incorporated the Standard Oil Company in Cleveland in 1870 and maintained a residence in the city until 1917, spent a good deal of his life trying to counter his image as the most hated man in America. Standard was one of the first American corporations to hire a public relations outfit, a damage control necessity in light of Rockefeller's ruthless monopolization of the oil industry (Standard controlled 90 percent of the nation's oil refineries by 1882) and his son's implication in the Ludlow Massacre (John Rockefeller, Jr., controlled the Colorado properties where dozens of miners died in a 1914 labor war).[40] Fallout from Ida Tarbell's muckraking and federal antitrust action in 1911 forced Standard's dissolution and spawned many of today's oil companies, including Sohio, Mobil, and Exxon. Philanthropy became Rockefeller's (and eventually Mobil's and Exxon's) primary means of buying public goodwill—from doling out "Rockefeller dimes" to bequeathing millions to medical research. In Cleveland fears of "tainted money" prohibited much acceptance of Rockefeller beneficence, however. Offers to bankroll Cleveland's Western Reserve University or its Case Institute of Technology were apparently spurned. The University of Chicago received Rockefeller millions instead.

Suspicions about the sway of corporate influence resurfaced in Cleveland in the 1980s, when the city was wrestling with its own disastrous public image. The Cuyahoga River caught on fire in 1969, an event that was immediately lampooned in Randy Newman's hit song "Burn On" and that became fodder for comic jabs from *Laugh-In* to *Letterman* over the next two decades. In 1975 the Brookings Institution rated Cleveland the second worst city in America for social and economic problems (Newark, New Jersey, took top honors). The city defaulted in 1978, the first large American city to do so since the Great Depression. Deindustrialization (Cleveland lost 86,100 manufacturing jobs from 1970 to 1985) and depopulation (the city shrank from 914,000 people in 1950 to 573,000 in 1980) were the basic factors in Cleveland's fiscal catastrophe, and further eroded civic confidence.[41] Formerly the "Best Location in the Nation," Cleveland became the "mistake on the lake."

In the 1980s Cleveland challenged that image, so much that *Time* magazine called it the "comeback city." The comeback, however, focused almost completely on the city's corporate community. Like Pittsburgh, Cleveland dealt with rust belt decline by encouraging downtown and waterfront development and basically ignoring the neighborhood decay, factory closures, double-digit unemployment, drug wars, and disillusion that racked the city. Declaring major downtown areas blighted, the city won $132 million in Urban Development Action Grants from the U.S. Department of Housing and Urban Development.[42] With these public subsidies and offers of substantial property tax abatements, Cleveland lured corporations downtown.

In order to catch Sohio, the city added the bait of open space, made available by condemning two landmarks—the Cuyahoga Building, designed by Burnham & Root in 1892, and the Williamson Building, designed by George B. Post and Sons in 1900. Ironically, Sohio had put a lot of money into refurbishing the Cuyahoga Building in the late 1970s and maintained offices there with several hundred employees. But concomitant with corporate image making in the 1980s (and Sohio's own sheer wealth), the prestige—and visual power—of a new forty-five-story office tower won out over the charm of Burnham & Root's older eight-story building. The new building would consolidate Sohio operations from nine locations and house 3,000 employees. Breaking ground for their $250 million Public Square corporate headquarters in 1982, Sohio stood to monopolize downtown Cleveland as much as Standard had once controlled the entire oil industry.

"Cleveland," George Will wrote in 1979, "is the only major American city where the original city center is still the city's hub." Public Square, the center of the city, is thus an ideal location for a corporate headquarters. Across the street from the city's main transit base in Terminal Tower, in line with the celebrated Cleveland Mall Plan (Daniel Burnham's 1903 "city beautiful" design, only partially realized), and central to Cleveland's main arteries (Euclid, Superior, and Ontario avenues), a Public Square locale guaranteed Sohio a visible corporate presence and Cleveland the economic stimulus and architectural showcase it desired. But it also guaranteed civic controversy: Public Square has always been a conflicted public space. Originally conceived as a city common in 1796, the 4.1-hectare (10-acre) park was ringed with commercial blocks by 1870. It was seen as an obstacle to progress by Gilded Age merchants, who fought court battles to make sure commercial traffic could bisect the square. It was the site of civic riot in the 1890s, when plans to replace a statue of Admiral Oliver Perry, erected in 1860, with a Civil War memorial were announced. It took an Ohio Supreme Court decision to

■ 29. **Gyo Obata,** architect, *BP America Building,* 1985; Cleveland, Ohio. Dominating downtown Cleveland's Public Square, Obata's building faces the 1894 Soldiers and Sailors Monument in the center of the square. *Free Stamp* was originally planned for a pedestal placed in front of the building and across the street from the monument. Photo courtesy BP America.

allow the new memorial, dedicated as the Soldiers and Sailors Monument, on 4 July 1894.[43]

Whether or not Sohio knew Public Square's contentious history, they became embroiled in it themselves through *Free Stamp.* Actually, controversy had ensued earlier—many citizens were furious that landmarked properties were demolished to make way for Sohio's new office tower (Fig. 29). Others complained that architect Gyo Obata's postmodern building contrasted too much with Terminal Tower, Cleveland's most familiar landmark (completed in 1927), across the street. Obata responded by saying that he had actually been inspired by Burnham's original designs for downtown Cleveland and by the city's older architecture, explaining that the Sohio Building's eight-story atrium, a vast space of gardens, fountains, and restaurants, was rooted in the open space intentions of Burnham's Mall Plan and the Terminal Tower's gradated facade. Calling the atrium "a gift to the city of Cleveland," Obata remarked that as the Sohio Building unfolded it had become "an important public space more than just an attractive magnet for building investment." Indeed, the inviting glass-covered atrium was expressly designed as a public amenity on private property, as other principles explained: "It extends the pedestrian-scale environment of Public Square and Euclid Avenue into the corporate center."[44]

Just a few stories shorter and a good deal bulkier than the sleek and lacy Terminal Tower, Obata's building dominates Public Square. The recessed atrium entrance is a postmodern public fancy, backed by the requisite modern office tower, the "box" that has dominated the corporate zone since midcentury. Sohio wanted this image: They specifically asked Obata's firm to design an office building with a durable "look," one whose stone facade would convey the power and stability of their multinational oil operations.[45] At the same time, Sohio wanted a user-friendly image: Consumer relations, after all, are a primary corporate concern. The skylit atrium, with its botanical gardens, street-level shops, indoor art gallery, and large-scale lobby sculptures by George Rickey and Richard Lippold, helped Sohio's corporate persona seem less threatening and seductively positioned the company as the primary agent of Cleveland's public interest. Commissioning *Free Stamp*—instead of the huge clocks and thermometers that were pro forma additions to earlier twentieth-century office buildings—was Sohio's most blatant attempt at public amenity. Placed right outside the atrium's arched doorway, Oldenburg's sculpture would draw people to the Sohio Building's "public" space. *Free Stamp* might also add a little levity to Sohio's tower of power.

In the 1980s Sohio—like their Standard siblings Mobil and Exxon—needed as much levity and public approval as they could muster. Despised for their horrific environmental record (it was an *oil slick*, after all, that set the Cuyahoga River on fire), their gasoline price jockeying, and their "pornographic" profits (as one union spokesman called them), big oil courted culture in order to appease and distract the public. "The energy crisis," Tom Wolfe writes, "was the greatest bonanza in the Public Broadcasting Service's history. The more loudly they were assailed as exploiters and profiteers, the more earnestly the oil companies poured money into PBS's cultural programming."[46]

Of all the greed decade's corporate patrons, big oil were also the most blatant about their cultural intentions. Herbert Schmertz, Mobil's vice president for public affairs, matter-of-factly remarked, "We remove the arts and humanities from the category of things done because they're

■ 30. **Hans Haacke,** *MetroMobiltan,* 1985; fiberglass construction, three banners and photomural, 3.6 meters (11.7 feet) by 6.1 meters (20.0 feet) by 1.5 meters (5.0 feet). Photo: Fred Scruton. Courtesy John Weber Gallery, New York.

nice . . . and we demonstrate instead that patronage is just another aspect of the marketplace, another move you make there to sell your products and enlarge your share." Hans Haacke has had a field day with Mobil's cultural conceit, explicating their philanthropy in installations such as *MetroMobiltan* (1985, Fig. 30). Critiquing the real reasons behind corporate support of the arts, Haacke assailed Mobil's sponsorship of the Metropolitan Museum of Art's "Treasures of Ancient Nigeria" exhibition in 1980, mounted at a time when the company dismissed a shareholder resolution to ban sales to South Africa. Utilizing the PR slogan "Art, for the sake of business," Mobil made their cultural interests rather obvious.[47]

If Mobil had the Met and *Masterpiece Theatre,* Sohio had Obata's "public" building and Oldenburg's "public" sculpture, and used both to justify their substantial private interests. By the late 1970s Sohio was a leading producer of crude oil, the result of majority ownership in the Prudhoe Bay, Alaska, oil fields. In 1969 the company had merged with British Petroleum, which financed Sohio's Alaskan exploration by swapping their northern U.S. mineral rights for shares of Sohio stock. The merger made for *spectacular* profits: By 1980 Sohio held more than $4 billion in cash and liquid assets. Rather than retire their debts, pay off dividends, and buy back shares (BP had become a majority shareholder in 1978), Sohio chose to expand and diversify: spending $2.4 billion on oil and gas exploration during 1978–82; spending $1.8 billion to acquire the Kennecott Corporation (a huge mining concern) in 1981.[48] Certain that energy prices, and hence profits, would continue to rise in the 1980s (an error soon realized), Sohio marked their success in Cleveland's Public Square, laundering $250 million of their crude oil cash flow in the construction of a new office tower.

Such corporate fortune was met with public outrage, especially when big oil's profiteering (in 1979, Sohio's third-quarter earnings were up 191 percent over the previous year) followed long lines and high prices at the gas pumps. In rust-belted, job-hungry Cleveland, Sohio softened resentment by promising that their new building would employ thousands and contribute to downtown revitalization. Masking profits with philanthropy, the company announced in August 1985—just as the doors to the new headquarters opened—that Oldenburg's *Free Stamp* would grace the front of the Sohio Building. Chief Executive Officer Alton Whitehouse remarked, "Our goal in commissioning public sculpture is to create a stimulating and aesthetically pleasing environment for visitors to our building and downtown Cleveland."[49] The city's Fine Arts Advisory Commission and City Planning Commission concurred and unanimously approved Sohio's sculptural addition to Public Square, scheduled for dedication in spring 1986.

Despite what cynics said in the subsequent media fallout—the *Wall Street Journal* headlined one piece "If Cleveland Is Sick of Bad Jokes, Why Is It Making This So Easy?"—Oldenburg's decision to inflate a rubber stamp into a 14.6-meter (48-foot) sculpture was predicated less on big oil bashing than on his Pop art fascination with monumentalizing the mundane. Hans Haacke he's not—few Oldenburg sculptures (most notably a proposed El Salvador monument) can be construed as serious sociopolitical critiques. Oldenburg is far more concerned with scale, with how everyday objects—electrical plugs, toothbrushes, buttons, flashlights—take on different meaning when grossly enlarged. Discussing the Cleveland piece, he and van Bruggen noted,

> The Stamp subject was an immediate response to our first sight of the new Standard Oil Company building: the ponderous main structure with its foot-like extension into an atrium and the inclusion of a large pad-like pedestal in the design.
>
> Since the site was in front of the office building we felt the subject should be associated with the office. The stamp . . . is a form experienced by every office worker in a tactile way and lends itself to expansion in scale.

By making the ordinary enormous, van Bruggen explained, she and Oldenburg created a certain "tension between concreteness and abstraction." "We're trying to take something that people know . . . to something they don't know."[50]

While Pop art's droll cynicism is inescapable in *Free Stamp*'s huge scale, both artists also expressed an interest in the sculpture's social context—its physical setting and audience response: "Our preference in large-scale projects is for a public situation. We stressed in accepting the commission, that, from our point of view, the stamp would be a 'monument' for the city of Cleveland, not a company emblem, since it faced the Public Square, a focal point in Cleveland and a gathering place for shoppers, workers and commuters in the downtown area." Accordingly, Oldenburg and van Bruggen originally designed *Free Stamp* with a walk-in interior surrounded by sloping walks and stairs. Such interactive elements were identical in the other big Public Square sculpture, the Soldiers and Sailors Monument across the street. A "stupendous pile, a granite-and-bronze clutter of guns and fierce warriors," Cleveland's Civil War monument features an elevated base containing a tablet room listing Cuyahoga County residents who served in the Civil War.[51] Spatial considerations forced Oldenburg and van Bruggen eventually to abandon plans for a room inside their sculpture, but audience engagement remained crucial to them: Viewers could only "read" *Free Stamp* by walking around it and peeking under the pad at the edged outline of its raised letters.

A far cry from "turd in the plaza" public art—of which *Portal,* Isamu Noguchi's 1976 sculpture in front of Cleveland's Justice Center, is a prime example (Fig. 31)—*Free Stamp* integrated Pop humor with its Public Square site, with local history, and with the Sohio Building's an-

■ 31. **Isamu Noguchi,** *Portal,* 1974; steel sculpture, Justice Center, Cleveland, Ohio. Photo courtesy *The Plain Dealer,* Cleveland, Ohio.

ticipated audience. If the sculpture itself was actually rather simple—an upright maroon office stamp with a letter base pressed into a pink pad— the letters that Oldenburg and van Bruggen chose for it changed the entire nature of the project. As they explained,

> We saw our sculpture as mediating between the new Standard Oil Company building behind it and the well-established Memorial it faced, in the process becoming a kind of contemporary paraphrase of the latter.
> Critical to the concept was what word the stamp would be stamping. . . . We wanted a brief word with maximum possibilities. After considering many words, we selected FREE, which was also the most positive word we could think of. We linked its paradoxical relationship to the physical situation of being (op)pressed by the stamp. . . . FREE echoed the word LIBERTY inscribed on a shield at the top of the Civil War Memorial.

As a "contemporary paraphrase" of the 1894 Soldiers and Sailors Monument, their sculpture, Oldenburg and van Bruggen explained, celebrated the heroism of daily existence, not of wartime valor: "One is reminded that the *Free Stamp*, despite its 48 feet, is a hand-stamp, something used by an individual. Perhaps this suggests that, even within an office situation, sandwiched between power groups, the individual may make his/her mark through an independent act." Oldenburg further explained how, when he was a nine-year-old immigrant to the United States (his father was a Swedish diplomat), the individual action of a bureaucratic stamp holder could make all the difference in an application for U.S. citizenship: "'Free' is a word that works in many different ways. If you're an immigrant into the U.S., such as I am, you're always involved with a lot of stamps. The ultimate result of all the stamping is that you're free, if you come from a place that's not free."

By selecting a word for their stamp whose meaning, especially in 1980s America, was as hotly contested as Public Square itself—and public culture in general—Oldenburg and van Bruggen intentionally opened Sohio's corporate art commission to civic controversy. The absurd scale alone of their sculpture might imply that they—and their corporate sponsor—saw freedom as an absurdity; likewise, *Free Stamp*'s inert monumentality might imply that they considered freedom burdensome and inflexible. Still, the company certainly knew what they were in for: In newsletters and in-house magazines, Sohio writers discussed other "controversial" works the artists had made in Chicago and Philadelphia and explained how public antagonism often turned into appreciation. Anticipating the heated debate *Free Stamp* might produce, Oldenburg commented, "I think that it is good that people voice their feelings about art in public places. I will be interested in opinions and reactions."[52]

Within days he got what he wanted, as Cleveland became embroiled in a fury of newspaper cartoons, columns, editorials, and letters that the city hadn't seen since its last public art controversy—in 1976, when Noguchi's *Portal* was dedicated. At the *Plain Dealer* (Cleveland's sole daily), one cartoonist sketched the stamp with a huge garbage can next to it, perhaps predicting what would eventually happen to the corporate commission. Editorials more or less approved Sohio's sculpture choice—one predicted that *Free Stamp* would "add a measure of fun and whimsy to a slab of a building that expresses neither." Likewise, columnists praised the sculpture's "irony" and Sohio's bold "willingness to commission a work that is both elegant and critically evocative."[53]

Of the many letters that the *Plain Dealer* published, only a few shared this view. Douglas Seim of Shaker Heights, for instance, saw *Free Stamp* as an expression of American liberty:

> Most of us have difficulty understanding what a rubber stamp and freedom have in common. . . . Many of us Americans have ancestors who arrived on Ellis Island and endured an assembly line of filling out forms and seeking stamps of approval. . . . Sure, to those of us who are free, a rubber stamp symbolizes repetition, drudgery, bureaucracy. To many others, a bureaucracy holds the path to freedom; if they can only obtain the necessary stamp.[54]

Most of the *Plain Dealer*'s readership, however, saw the sculpture as yet another assault on Cleveland's fragile self-image. Taking Oldenburg to task for making Cleveland the butt of the ultimate Polish joke, Kenneth Harwood of Rocky River wrote, "I was looking forward to the opening of the Sohio Building in our struggling city, but now it is to be marred by this tacky object that must have strained Oldenburg's imaginative powers for all of five minutes. It seems to me that the joke is on Cleveland. Is Oldenburg trying to expand our 'white socks' image?" Helen Amato of Independence called *Free Stamp* "a ridiculous waste of money," and Jean Sokol of Cleveland called it "an ugly monstrosity." Ben Berkey of Cleveland Heights said Sohio would have been better off choosing a sculpture about "the discovery of oil," and Madeline Parvin of Cleveland said she "would have appreciated something more spiritual." Patricia Pierce of Shaker Heights summed up the opinion of many Clevelanders: "In 50 years, this Cleveland-chosen sculpture will be embarrassing, a real 'rubber-stamp,' a copy of every other idea in the field in the last thirty years. There must be something 'larger than life' in our society, other than plugs, clothespins, and rubber stamps—probably the check written to the artist!"[55]

Sohio chief Whitehouse defended the commission: "Many people love it. Others hate it. I think this is good—and exactly what you should expect from an Oldenburg. Controversy, argument, and smiles. . . . The fun of *Free Stamp* comes from deciding for *ourselves* what we want it to mean and say. We're free to think whatever we like." Interested in free and open democratic exchange—or at least saying he was to defend his commission of *Free Stamp*, Whitehouse responded positively to public outburst. Cleveland's arts community backed him, pleasantly shocked that stodgy Sohio had actually commissioned something by a well-known artist with a reputation for stirring up public controversy ("Everyone dropped their jaws," said a member of the Fine Arts Advisory Commission). By March 1986 *Free Stamp* had been entirely fabricated into "railroad-car-sized sub-units" at the Chicago Bridge and Iron steel plant in Kankakee, Illinois, where workers awaited the go-ahead to ship the pieces to Cleveland for on-site assembly.[56]

But then *Free Stamp* got stomped. The oil boom went bust, racked by overproduction and declining demand, and oil prices plummeted nearly 50 percent in the first three months of 1986. With the market glutted with Prudhoe Bay crude selling for less than twelve dollars a barrel but costing eighteen to twenty-five dollars a barrel to produce, Sohio shareholders saw their dividends shrink. Worse, the company's Kennecott acquisition proved a major disaster—the $1.8 billion investment had generated more than $700 million in operating losses by 1986. Although somewhat cushioned by their extraordinary prebust cash flow, Sohio retrenched—selling exploration leases and mineral properties, cutting operations, eliminating corporate offices. They even changed their name back to Standard Oil Company, trying to reclaim some of the power and prestige of Rockefeller's original outfit.[57]

All this wasn't enough, however, for their major shareholder. Just as Standard was set to report a 26 percent earnings drop for the first quarter of 1986, British Petroleum stepped in. Whitehouse was fired and replaced by BP Managing Director Robert Horton, dubbed "Horton the Hatchetman" for his ruthless corporate efficiency. His nickname, Horton complained, was "very unfair. It is just that I have been given a number of difficult things to do. I do not like cutting off heads or closing things down, but unfortunately survival is important." Apparently, *Free Stamp* threatened Standard's survival, because only a few weeks after he took over the company, Horton axed it. His only comment, made at the company's annual shareholder meeting on 24 April 1986, was "I don't want to destroy a work of art . . . but I don't think the symbolism is appropriate." One stockholder yelled out from the crowd: "Put it in the middle of Lake Erie!"[58]

Hired to rescue Standard from economic disaster, Horton went right to work, starting with changing the company name to BP America. Major cutbacks in capital spending and exploration were announced, Kennecott holdings were sold off (at substantial losses), staff were sacked. At the new Cleveland headquarters, the number of on-site staff went from 3,000 to 1,800 (by the end of 1990). And although *Free Stamp* had already been paid for (costs have never been disclosed), it too was cut—another chapter in Public Square's conflicted history. Maybe it reminded the new corporate regime of the excesses of the past. More likely, the idea of a huge rubber stamp fronting the oil empire he now commanded struck Horton as a not particularly funny joke at his expense.

Dependent on BP America for jobs, for their charitable giving (Standard had given some $17 million annually), and for their role in Public Square's renaissance, Cleveland viewed the shake-up with trepidation. Admittedly, some cheered Horton's decision to ax *Free Stamp*: "All praise to Robert B. Horton for stopping the erection of *Free Stamp* in front of the Standard Oil building," Donald Miller of Cleveland wrote to the *Plain Dealer,* adding, "We should try to get him to run for mayor. Maybe he could get the ugly 'sewer pipe' removed from the Justice Center." Arthur Tuscany of Brecksville attempted canonization: "Greater Cleveland should be thankful for two residents of exceptional perception—Art Modell of the Cleveland Browns and Robert Horton of Standard Oil."[59]

Most of Cleveland's arts community, of course, hardly saw Horton as a saint, perhaps fearing that his capricious cultural behavior presaged worse examples of corporate privilege. A week after he announced his intent to ax *Free Stamp,* about fifty people protested in front of BP America's new headquarters, wearing black armbands and holding signs of stamps with the words *free* and *cancelled* on them. The *Plain Dealer* gave front-page attention to the company's about-face; one story, headlined "STAMPED OUT! Oldenburg Hurt and Angry at Standard Rejection," clearly called Horton's action into question. The national press seized on the incident too: "In Defense of Stomped Stamp Art" fronted a *Chicago Tribune* story about the Kankakee steelworkers who made the sculpture; "The Wrong Impression?" headlined one *Industry Week* article. Bids to take *Free Stamp* off of Standard's hands came in from all over the country: Oberlin College President Frederick Starr telegrammed Horton offering "permanent asylum for Oldenburg's foundling" at his campus; Hirshhorn Museum director James Demetrion exclaimed, "We'll gladly take it! Wow! You mean they don't want it?"; Walker Art Center director Martin Friedman commented, "So, the fat is in the fire. Send it to me. Put it on a flat-bed truck. I'll take it at once."[60]

Oldenburg and van Bruggen were hardly so amused by Horton's cancellation of *Free Stamp* and told the *Plain Dealer* that they viewed it as a breach of contract, which "has to have consequences." Angered because Horton's decision threatened to destroy a sculpture designed for its Sohio Building site, and nowhere else, the artists were also annoyed by company refusal to discuss why the commission had been canceled. "We have been asking for reasons and they have not given any," Oldenburg said, adding, "They treat *Free Stamp* as a boxcar or an oil tank that can go anywhere as long as they pay for it. They miss the point of its being, which is the site as part of the work of art. That is something that we will have to approach from a legal aspect."[61]

Beset by protests at the new building, by taunting media innuendos, and by art world offers implying he was a twit for rejecting *Free Stamp*, Horton had to realize his corporate decision to can the sculpture had backfired. Whatever humiliation BP America might have suffered with a 14.6-meter (48-foot) stamp sculpture at their door was being surpassed by the sort of negative PR the company hardly needed in the wake of a corporate takeover. Although he had come close to canonization in the eyes of some Clevelanders for axing the sculpture from its intended Public Square site, Horton knew his company would have to act diplomatically or face the "consequences" of a potentially nasty court battle.

After about a year of legal wrestling, a compromise was reached: *Free Stamp* would stay in Cleveland, a free gift to the city. BP America would pay for its assembly and maintenance in perpetuity, in a spot the artists selected, and they would also pay to have that spot refurbished. Oldenburg and van Bruggen chose Willard Park, a small common named after Archibald Willard (1836–1918), Cleveland-born painter of *The Spirit of '76*. Located only a few blocks from BP America, the park already featured a fountain and a monument to Cleveland's firefighters. But Oldenburg, van Bruggen, and a number of city officials felt that the site, next to City Hall (where the original version of Willard's famous 1876 painting hangs in the rotunda) and across the street from the Celebrezze Federal Building (where immigration matters are handled), was perfect for *Free Stamp*. As the Cleveland City Council president put it, Willard Park was the most "appropriate site for a work which likewise celebrates freedom."[62] City Planning Director Hunter Morrison even envisioned turning the site into a mini–theme park with flags from different nations, the Firefighters Monument, and *Free Stamp* all symbolizing democratic government at work. Redesigned to fit its new site, the 34,050-kilogram (75,000-pound) maroon metal sculpture would no longer stand upright but would lie on its side, 14.6 meters (48 feet) long, 8.5 meters (28 feet) high, its stamp bottom with the 5.5 meters (18 feet) tall hot pink embossed letters FREE clearly visible.

If Horton thought his company now stood clear of the *Free Stamp* debacle, he was wrong. The corporation and the artists had reached an agreement, but the sculpture still needed the legislated approval of the Cleveland City Council to be officially accepted and erected. For the next four years the council made it clear they were not interested in routinely endorsing BP America's corporate largesse. Free gift that *Free Stamp* might be, council members asked why they should accept something the corporation had refused, argued about what the sculpture meant and who it benefited, and, most important, questioned BP America's assumptions about the city's public interest.

A lot of their opposition was purely political. City Council President George Forbes, "the undisputed ringmaster of Cleveland politics," completely roadblocked *Free Stamp* for two years because he feared the sculpture's presence next to City Hall might imply his own innumerable intrigues with Cleveland's business community throughout the 1970s and 1980s. (City developers and corporations strongly supported him during all his political campaigns and arranged for his defense when he was indicted on kickback charges in 1978.) Not until November 1989, when Forbes lost a mayoral bid and Jay Westbrook became council president, did Cleveland's twenty-one council members even begin to debate the *Free Stamp* issue.[63]

Convinced of the prestige *Free Stamp* could bring to Cleveland, Westbrook began campaigning to see it erected in Willard Park. He turned for help to the arts community, especially the Committee for Public Art and the Cleveland Museum of Art, where Director Evan Turner hosted a special dinner and slide-lecture for city council members, soliciting their votes of approval for *Free Stamp*. In a letter to Oldenburg and van Bruggen, Westbrook pledged the support of his council colleagues and declared, "It is fitting that in this unique time, when the winds of change are blowing over Eastern Europe and Southern Africa, Clevelanders should have the opportunity to celebrate their common heritage and deep love of freedom in this unique way."

The post of city council president is all-powerful in Cleveland, but Westbrook's championship of public art hardly met with blanket approval from his colleagues. Perhaps testing his first-term authority, and certainly feeling their oats after almost two decades under Forbes's thumb, council members delayed legislation on *Free Stamp* for months. Some raised serious public art issues: Many felt *Free Stamp* was simply too big for the relatively small space of Willard Park, and a few lamented that the Firefighters Monument, a sculpture consisting of two short granite slabs listing the names of the firemen, would be eclipsed by *Free Stamp*'s domineering size and neon colors. A few councillors were simply ornery: Ward 7 Councilwoman Fannie Lewis worried that the city might be "getting a cheap piece of junk"; Odelia Robinson of Ward 3 argued that the sculpture was more appropriate "outside a paper mill or an office equipment company."[64]

Other council members cited constituency complaints that the sculpture was an insulting corporate castoff. "BP got rid of the butt of jokes and dumped it on City Hall," Ward 11 Councilman Mike Polensek complained. "I don't think that's the way you treat a sculpture. I think you start with a location. But BP commissioned it and then they didn't want it, so it's stuck here." Oldenburg and van Bruggen more or less assisted this popularly held view when they changed the sculpture to lie on its side, looking, as they said, as if some corporate giant had thrown it "from the top of the BP building."[65]

Free Stamp's new look may have been Oldenburg and van Bruggen's sly comeback to corporate rejection, but accepting BP America's throwaway art, argued Ward 8 Councilman Bill Patmon, would intimate complicity between big business and local government. "I feel that the sculpture makes a mockery of what we stand for here at City Hall," stated Patmon, representing Cleveland's mostly African American neighborhood along Martin Luther King, Jr., Drive. "It says that government is considered a rubber stamp for private interests in this city." Other council members concurred, feeling *Free Stamp*'s approval "would suggest City Hall had become a rubber stamp for wealthy developers," several of whom had recently been granted tax abatements.[66]

Charges of collusion were accompanied by suspicions about *Free Stamp*'s backers. "The people pushing *Free Stamp* were primarily the suburban liberal crowd, what we call the wine and cheese crowd," Polensek, the representative of a primarily Eastern European constituency in Collinwood, recalled. "And a lot of Cleveland was skeptical about this, like this sculpture came only from this one group." Left out of the debate until they were expected to accept *Free Stamp* gratefully as an act of corporate benevolence, some council members felt, not surprisingly, that the sculpture was both tainted and an imposition.

Further, Kathleen Coakley, director of Cleveland's Committee for Public Art, recalls that more than a few black councillors viewed *Free Stamp* as a "white suburban kind of art that didn't fit with inner-city, downtown Cleveland." Decades of racial tension—a 1987 study ranked Cleveland the second most segregated city in the nation—only heightened hostilities black council members felt toward *Free Stamp*'s primarily white backers, who had seemingly decided among themselves what kind of art inner-city Cleveland needed.[67] Squeezed in a predominantly nonresidential downtown area filled with government buildings and corporate headquarters, Willard Park is not exactly an inner-city neighborhood. Still, Cleveland's black councillors saw the campaign to get *Free Stamp* erected there as yet another example of misguided liberal paternalism. "My constituency did not favor *Free Stamp*," Patmon recalled, adding, "If BP had really wanted to help the city of Cleveland, why not some funding for the real social problems, like drug use?"

Patmon's fundamental issue with *Free Stamp,* however, was the history of "freedom" it claimed to celebrate: "As a black man, I feel there really ought to be *chains* hanging from the top of that stamp. My experience was not the experience of Ellis Island—my family was brought to this country in chains, as slaves. I have not shared in that dream of freedom, that Ellis Island dream. It is a bitter pill to swallow to see freedom announced in that sculpture, and that experience was not mine." *Free Stamp* was for all Clevelanders, Council President Westbrook said, a symbol of "common heritage," a reminder of their "deep love of freedom." But these notions of commonality were hardly shared by Cleveland's black council members, who saw *Free Stamp* as another example of American historical amnesia. Competing versions of Cleveland's history—Eastern European versus African American, Ellis Island immigration versus slavery—all contributed to the civic debate that swarmed around *Free Stamp.*

"Why should City Council say yes to the *Free Stamp*?" asked one Cleveland journalist. "Not because it is by a famous artist and will bring prestige to the city. And not because City Council is the pawn of BP. But simply *because it is a gift,* something that rises above both politics and art."[68] But such reasoning was profoundly misinformed: As more than a few Cleveland council members recognized, the act of *giving*, especially corporate philanthropy in the public sphere, is never free from strings. The issues surrounding *Free Stamp*'s civic acceptance were permeated with "politics and art": the politics of corporate interest and the aesthetics of civic consensus. The particular manner in which *Free Stamp* was historicized to symbolize both the stamped approval of Cleveland's European immigrants and the philanthropy of the city's largest and most important corporate entity placed the public sculpture squarely at the center of local political and aesthetic concerns.

In the end, it was those interests—BP America's decision to "dump" *Free Stamp* on City Hall and thereby avoid more negative PR or a prolonged legal battle, and artistic and official determination to shape the sculpture into a symbol of Cleveland's common ground—that held sway. Wined and dined at the Cleveland Museum of Art, convinced of Oldenburg and van Bruggen's art world acclaim, and of *Free Stamp*'s potential to shape civic prestige, the majority of the City Council voted to accept the sculpture in Willard Park. Only Bill Patmon and Mike Polensek cast negative votes, Polensek joking, "I wouldn't want it in my ward, personally. . . . I'd rather see an Iraqi tank sitting there." At the sculpture's dedication ceremony, 15 November 1991, Polensek passed out T-shirts emblazoned with the same quotation.[69] Jay Westbrook wore a *Free Stamp* tie handpainted by local artist Hector Vega, and, after thanking BP for its gift, made the following comments:

> It is amazing how one piece of work with such a small four-letter word (backwards) can be so powerful. . . . We talk about Cleveland's renaissance, a rebirth of public spirit, a new day for our young, filled with rich opportunities for the future. But what is a renaissance without art? It seem to me that *this art, this gift,* captures in its simplicity the rivers and springs of spirit of our Cleveland community.

In a sense, *Free Stamp* does capture the spirit of Cleveland (Fig. 32). It is remarkably multivocal: Schoolchildren touring the city's government district like to climb on it; wedding parties take photos at the site; one homeless woman slept under the sculpture for several weeks; a "Free Mike Tyson" rally was held in front of *Free Stamp* in April 1992. At the press conference the day *Free Stamp* was dedicated, Oldenburg and van Bruggen argued that public art "has to have the capacity for surprising you and renewing itself and changing in your imagination." *Free Stamp* certainly fits their criteria—the fact that it serves newlyweds, the homeless, and city leaders much as it once was supposed to serve Sohio shows how mercurial their sculpture truly is.

But if *Free Stamp* mediates both ordinary and official interests, it cannot be said that it does not obviously privilege one over the other: "Ne-

■ 32. **Claes Oldenburg and Coosje van Bruggen,** *Free Stamp,* 1991; Cleveland, Ohio. Owner: City of Cleveland. Postcard courtesy Herman Rueger, Nu-Vista Prints, Willowick, Ohio.

gotiation and cultural mediation," John Bodnar writes, "do not preclude domination and distortion."[70] Certain personal and local interests may be sustained in *Free Stamp,* but its dominant meaning can be read as BP America's corporate privilege in Cleveland's public sphere. *Free Stamp* completely dominates Willard Park's small space, as well as the Firefighters Monument that was already there. Its scale is so large that notions of oppression and domination are more clearly read in *Free Stamp*'s presentation that those suggesting a fluid and diverse democratic culture. If *Free Stamp* is about freedom, as its makers and so many of its supporters attest, this is the freedom of the fist; its form alone speaks of physical power, of brute persuasion. It is a mighty bureaucrat indeed who has the strength to lift this stamp, and the power to use it.

But it was the *process* by which *Free Stamp* changed from being a corporate bauble in Public Square to being a public sculpture in Willard

Park that really attests to corporate privilege in Cleveland. That process was private, a closed-door conversation held between the artists and BP America that was fairly typical of the "calculated neglect of democratic communication" that occurred throughout the 1980s.[71] Neither party consulted Cleveland residents about *their* art preferences; neither grasped that public art involves considerably more than simply putting a sculpture in front of an office tower, or erecting it in a park. Both assumed that the sole act of giving was good enough for the public interest.

In 1986 a *Washington Post* journalist described Cleveland as two cities: a "new" city of "corporate headquarters, service and professional jobs, downtown construction, recreational and cultural amenities," and an "old" city of "neighborhoods struggling against decay, double-digit unemployment, racial tension, factory closings, poverty, and long-suffering schools."[72] As Jay Westbrook said in his dedication speech, *Free Stamp* symbolizes the new Cleveland, the renaissance city born of the tax abatements, deregulation, and takeovers that formed corporate culture in 1980s America. As such the *Free Stamp* story is sweeping testimony to the effect of corporate America's contemporary patronage of public culture. The public realm is reduced, in favor of the corporate sector. Private interests—profit and public relations—take precedence; public concerns, and indeed the public itself, are ignored and dismissed. History gets erased or rewritten as corporate largesse is translated into corporate rights. Cleveland's firefighters, its African American population, and the real-life dimensions of its contemporary postindustrial malaise are marginalized in favor of BP America's privilege in the public sphere.

Commissioned by one oil company CEO and axed by another, designed for Public Square and redesigned for a public park, *Free Stamp* embodies the fallibility of encouraging private interests to take complete responsibility for public culture. Giving American business free rein in the public sphere, as neoconservative politicians and intellectuals eagerly advised in the greed decade, not unexpectedly gave corporate America control in that sphere. But if the public art context of *Free Stamp* speaks to that control, it is hardly immutable. "Horton the Hatchetman" himself was toppled in a corporate coup in July 1992, when BP America executives weary of his "unpleasant," "undiplomatic," and basically "Napoleonic" behavior ousted him from the company.[73]

Time will tell whether *Free Stamp* is subjected to similar treatment—

in the world of public art and cultural democracy, nothing is constant. Writing about another monument, a Victory Arch conceived by Iraqi President Saddam Hussein in the mid-1980s, Samir al-Khalil remarked, "Cities collect objects like these, and then time transforms their meaning. Symbols of authority, somebody's victory and everybody's kitsch can turn into their opposite."[74] Whether *Free Stamp* sustains Cleveland's corporate authority or is adapted to a more democratic public sphere remains to be seen.

CHAPTER FOUR

Sculptures from Strip Mines
Contemporary Public Art and Land Reclamation

n October 1985 *Effigy Tumuli* was dedicated in Ottawa, Illinois, 124 kilometers (77 miles) southwest of Chicago's Loop (Fig. 33). Described as the "biggest public sculpture park since Gutzon Borglum's Mount Rushmore . . . which it exceeds in size," *Effigy Tumuli* is spread over a few dozen hectares of a former strip mine next to Buffalo Rock State Park, on a sandy bluff 27.4 meters (90 feet) above the Illinois River. Commissioned to reclaim the site as public art, sculptor Michael Heizer designed five gigantic earth mounds shaped as local creatures: a turtle, a water strider, a catfish, a snake, and a frog (Fig. 34). Known for megalithic sculptures such as *Complex One* (1972–74) and *Levitated Mass* (1982, see Fig. 25), Heizer retained his characteristic abstract aesthetic in the *Effigy Tumuli* mounds, which were built "not as mimetic representations of animals but as geometricized three-dimensional maps of animals."[1]

The five effigies, Heizer explained, also paid homage to the Woodland Indian earth mounds (tumuli) that once covered the central Midwest. "It's in the nature of my work that I keep in mind the environment I'm taken into," said Heizer, adding, "The native American tradition of mound building absolutely pervades the whole place, mystically and historically. . . . It's a beautiful tradition, and it's fully neglected. And it's from a group of people who were *genocided.* So, in a lot of ways, the

■ **33. Michael Heizer,** *Effigy Tumuli,* 1985; aerial view of five earth mounds in a 62.4-hectare (154-acre) site, Buffalo Rock State Park, Ottawa, Ill. This photo shows three of the mounds: the large *Water Strider* mound, the smaller *Frog* mound (seen at the top left of the *Water Strider*), and the *Catfish* mound (seen at the top left of the photo, near the banks of the Illinois River). The *Turtle* and *Snake* mounds are to the far right of the park. Aerial photo: Bob Knoedler, Streator, Ill.

Effigy Tumuli is a political and social comment. . . . It was my chance to make a statement for the native American." Transforming an abandoned strip mine into a public sculpture park featuring huge effigy mounds, Heizer seemed to suggest "that the solution for industrially induced destruction may be found in the natural practices of earlier cultures."[2]

Originally forest and farmland, the *Effigy Tumuli* site was strip-mined in the 1930s by the Osage Coal Company for a thin vein of low-grade anthracite 9.1 meters (30 feet) below the surface. "It was a grievance against the planet that didn't have to happen," says Heizer, explaining that the cheap coal mined at the mesa probably generated little profit.[3] Unregulated surface mining severely despoiled the site, as huge drag shovels gouged the ground and left it littered with 7.6-meter (25-foot)

■ **34. Michael Heizer,** *Effigy Tumuli,* 1985; aerial view of *Water Strider.* Aerial photo: Richard Hamilton Smith, St. Paul.

furrows of toxic waste overburden (pyrite and shale) and pools of contaminated water. Even after fifty years the area was virtually devoid of vegetation, an eerily empty and alien landscape surrounded by lush acres of parkland—and many more acres of similarly abandoned mines. Dirt bikers loved it: Every good-weather weekend, entire families of off-roaders came to ride the ridges at the former strip mine. But in the late 1970s the state's Abandoned Mined Lands Reclamation Council (AMLRC) discovered that acid water runoff at the site was polluting the Illinois River and nearby fields, and threatening local water supplies. Now owned by the Ottawa Silica Company, which purchased the site in the mid-1960s, the area was earmarked for reclamation.

Edmund Thornton, heir and chair of the company—and a member of the AMLRC—offered to donate the site to the state in return for a substantial tax break and as long as cleanup was combined with public art. "If this land was going to be reclaimed," Thornton, an Ottawa native, said, "I thought it should be done in a way that's creative and unique."[4] Shaped from tons of refurbished soil, Heizer's gigantic earth mounds

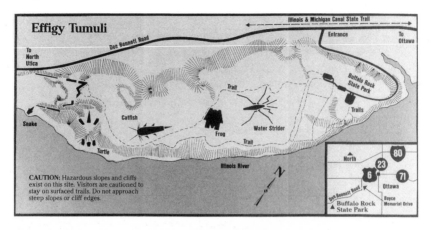

■ 35. *Effigy Tumuli* brochure, Illinois Department of Conservation.

would highlight a public sculpture park managed by the Illinois Department of Conservation, which already ran the adjacent 17.4-hectare (43-acre) Buffalo Rock State Park. Pilgrims to the site would read about the mounds in brochures and at a specially designed visitors' station staffed with tour guides doubling as groundskeepers (Figs. 35 and 36). Then they would search out the art as they walked along the *Effigy Tumuli Sculpture Trail*. A strip-mined wasteland would be reclaimed as a sort of nature preserve cum public art, planted with grasses, crisscrossed with pedestrian pathways, dotted with helpful sculpture-locator signs.

"This is the largest site sculpture ever envisioned, and will be the largest ever constructed and built," Thornton boasted, anticipating *Effigy Tumuli* as a kind of artsy tourist attraction as compelling as Buffalo Rock State Park's baseball field, picnic benches, and namesake caged wildlife. With visitors drawn to the work's sheer scale—"As long as you're going to make a sculpture, why not make one that competes with a 747, or the Empire State Building, or the Golden Gate Bridge?" Heizer asked—one writer predicted that *Effigy Tumuli* might "turn out to be one of the country's most successful public sculptures." Another said audiences would be attracted to the artwork's ecologically "positive dialogue" and "ritualization of reclamation." Heizer believed broad interest in Indian culture would bring people to the park: "I thought, this

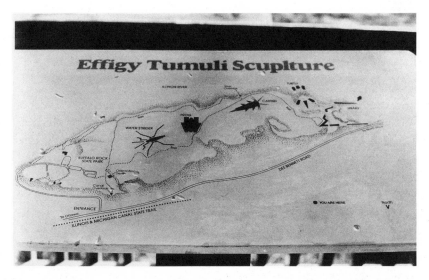

■ 36. *Effigy Tumuli* sculpture-locator sign. Note bullet holes in the sign. Photo by author, April 1993.

won't be some Disneyland looking kind of a park. It will be reminiscent of that native American history. And people out there seem proud of having those mounds. They get people excited. So, it's good material for a public work." Anticipating public accolades and admiring Heizer's artful reclamation of an industrially spoiled landscape, one writer declared *Effigy Tumuli* "a paragon of art in the '80s: a little corporate ingenuity, a dash of public/private cooperation, and a lot of artistic vision."[5]

A paragon of contemporary art *Effigy Tumuli* may well be, but more as a stellar example of misguided environmentally correct art than anything else. For all its critical acclaim, *Effigy Tumuli* is a physical and public art disaster: The mounds have largely eroded, actual reclamation is questionable, and even the most sympathetic art lovers find the sculpture park a huge disappointment. Many in Ottawa see it as a local mogul's private folly and tax dodge; some feel the park should be returned to the dirt bike paradise it once was. However laudable Heizer's goal of curing an industrially wrecked landscape with contemporary sculpture based on Indian cultural traditions, *Effigy Tumuli* raises serious questions about artistic intervention in the environment, about the links between land reclamation and public art, and about the real meaning of public culture in contemporary America.

In the past decade environmental correctness has become the Great American Crusade: Recycling is de rigueur, shoppers tote groceries in canvas bags, cars flash bumper stickers with slogans such as "Save the Whales" and "Earth First," and eco-tourism to places like the Galápagos Islands is booming. Spurred by consumer interest and potential profit, American corporations have hungrily pursued eco-marketing, changing product packaging (McDonald's switched from Styrofoam back to paper, Sure and Secret deodorants shed their cartons, the music industry banned the CD longbox), changing products (McDonald's offered a meatless burger), and adopting eco-friendly ad campaigns ("We're taking the environment personally," says Amway; "Environmental responsibility fuels our research," touts Ford; "Touch-tone the ozone," beckons Working Assets Long Distance).[6] Even Hollywood has leapt onto the green bandwagon: The animated feature *FernGully* (1992) damns the destruction of the rain forest and encourages kids to "be kind" to Mother Earth; the romantic comedy *Green Card* (1990) portrays a clandestine group of Green Guerrillas planting ghetto gardens with topsoil donated by Burger King.

Eco-aesthetics are no less fashionable. Artists describe the "healing" and "regeneration" and "transformative potential" of their earnestly environmentally sensitive sculptures and paintings. Much of this eco-art is made out of "more organic" materials, such as wood and clay and earth, possibly as a rebuff to the glitzy bloat of so much art (and architecture) in the 1980s. Recent exhibitions, such as "Revered Earth" and "Fragile Ecologies," and newly formed groups such as IFTA (International Friends of Transformative Art, dedicated to art "that goes beyond art for art's sake and really matters to people and the planet") further attest to the art world's heightened eco-awareness.[7] More telling is the art itself: the sculptures and fountains of, among others, Isamu Noguchi and Buster Simpson; the parks and gardens designed by Nancy Holt, Jody Pinto, Alan Sonfist, and Athena Tacha; the land reclamation projects developed by Herbert Bayer, Mel Chin, Stan Dolega, Michael Heizer, Andrew Leicester, and Robert Morris.

In the early 1970s Robert Smithson, land reclamation's original aesthetic overseer, called for a "dialectic" between industry and art. "Such devastated places as strip mines could be recycled in terms of earth art,"

Smithson argued. "The artist and the miner must become conscious of themselves as natural agents. . . . Art can become a resource, that mediates between the ecologist and the industrialist. . . . A lesson can be learned from the Indian cliff dwellings and earthworks mounds. Here we see nature and necessity in consort." A few of Smithson's own sculptures indirectly dealt with environmental rehabilitation. *Spiral Jetty* (1970), for instance, was designed on one level to reclaim the polluted waters of an abandoned oil mining area in Utah's Great Salt Lake; *Broken Circle* (1971) partially revamped a sand quarry outside Emmen, Holland. Tapping into that era's eco-consciousness, Smithson proposed "earth sculpture" reclamation projects to the Hanna Coal Company in Ohio and Colorado's Minerals Engineering Company. "Artists should not be cheated out of doing their work, or forced to exist in the isolation of 'art worlds,'" he wrote in 1972. "There should be artist-consultants in every major industry in America."[8]

Despite serious charges of industrial complicity—does land reclamation artwork mitigate environmental destruction by disguising it, after the fact, as art?—in the past two decades Smithson's notions have become increasingly widespread. With alchemical vision, more and more artists look upon the industrial landscape's abandoned mines, disused quarries, landfill sites, and toxic waste dumps as the stuff of art. In 1979 Robert Morris turned an abandoned gravel pit near Seattle into a terraced amphitheater; in 1981 Stan Dolega converted a Hanna, Wyoming, landfill (and former coal mine) into a dirt sculpture; in 1983 Harriet Feigenbaum made an art project out of a Lackawanna Valley strip mine by planting thousands of grapevines in a serpentine configuration; also in 1983 Mierle Laderman Ukeles started *Flow City,* "the first ever permanent public-art environment planned as an organic part of an operating waste-management facility" in New York City; in 1990 Mel Chin transformed a Superfund site outside St. Paul into a public garden. Challenging neoconservative eco-amnesia by acting as planetary shamans, contemporary artists "seek to initiate beneficial change and reverse the damages from mankind's battle with nature" by using art as a "tool for environmental healing."[9]

At the most elemental level, of course, cleaning up the earth is better than ignoring environmental destruction. Yet eco-art's good intentions are often fraught with contradictions, chief among them assumptions of aesthetic amorality, which allow eco-artists to turn industrially abused lands into gardens and sculpture parks without critically considering

■ 37. **Robert Morris,** *Untitled,* 1979; 1.6-hectare (4-acre) reclamation project for Johnson Gravel Pit No. 30, outside Kent, Wash. View facing east across earthwork looking toward Kent and Boeing plants. Photo by author, May 1991.

how and why the abuse came about—and the role their art plays in that process. Intent on reconstructing without critiquing the multifaceted political, social, economic, and cultural problematics of environmentalism, land reclamation artists tend to harbor a kind of moral innocence—they see themselves as merely artists, just making "affirmative art."

An exception might be found in Robert Morris, a fairly cogent analyst of land reclamation's "ménage-à-trois between art, government, and industry." Reflecting on his own aesthetic reworking of Johnson Pit No. 30, an overgrown 1.6-hectare (4-acre) gravel pit in Kent, Washington, which he cleared, terraced, and then "planted" with a few blackened tree stumps to remind visitors of the site's former industrial manipulation (Fig. 37), Morris warned that environmentally recuperative art could sanction further destruction:

> The most significant implication of art as land reclamation is that art can and should be used to wipe away technological guilt. Will it be a little

easier in the future to rip up the landscape for one last shovelful of a non-renewable energy source if an artist can be found—cheap, mind you—to transform the devastation into an inspiring and modern work of art?

Most eco-artists, however, are profoundly ambivalent about how their work often abets past and aids future environmental despoilation. Morris himself, for instance, cleared all the shrubs and trees at the Kent gravel pit, then steeply terraced the hillside, to make the area *look* more like a devastated industrial zone (which it didn't, at first glance). Such action dangerously disturbed the site: Significant soil destabilization and slumping (the south side of the hill simply slid away) soon followed. Yet even after interfering with the landscape to dramatize the problem of its reclamation—and situating the sculpture so that viewers look past Kent's pastoral landscape and onto Boeing's defense plants—Morris begged the question of complicity, resignedly noting that "all great monuments celebrate the leading faith of the age—or, in retrospect, the prevailing idiocy. . . . Art is always propaganda."[10]

Contemporary environmental aesthetics are further hampered by tendencies to romanticize nature. Although few follow the radical tenets of deep ecology—whereby people are subordinate to the supposedly biocentric base of "natural" law—many eco-artists adopt totalizing and sentimental views of a benign natural universe. Such views mask industrial complicity by ignoring the local, political, and economic contexts of environmental crisis. "I propose that in today's world," writes Suzi Gablik, probably the best-known eco-art critic, "the word *ecological* has replaced the word *metaphysical*, as the need for restoring awareness of our symbiotic relationship with nature becomes the most pressing spiritual and political need of our time."[11] Gablik's pronouncement regarding "our symbiotic relationship with nature" not only discounts the various roles that race, gender, ethnicity, and class play in today's world but defines "nature" on universal and reverential terms.

This myth of an abstract and apolitical nature accompanies equally stereotypical assumptions of a degraded modern humanity and an idealization of prehistoric cultures. "Other civilizations created Altamira, Stonehenge, and Borobudur; ours has produced the shopping mall, the missile silo, and the cooling tank," Gablik writes. "Modern individuals do not see the Earth as a source of spiritual renewal, but as a stockpile of raw materials to be exploited and consumed. Native Americans say that for whites, every blade of grass and spring of water has a price tag on it." Much of the eco-aesthetic critique, as Gablik's remarks suggest, is built on deep-felt disgust with the conditions of late capitalism. But such righteous disdain is the voice of privilege, the voice of those who, for whatever reason, are disillusioned with material success and seek refuge in the "ecological." It discriminates against those who haven't attained that success (much less a standard of living above poverty level) and ignores the real-life problem facing both the third and first worlds: "how to foster economic development that does not ruin the environment."[12]

Gablik's comments further reveal that the antimodernist eco-aesthetic critique is rife with New Age notions linking so-called primitive cultures with environmental ethics. Many eco-artists, for example, believe primitive art—especially American Indian art—provides a superior stylistic strategy for ecological rehabilitation: Aviva Rahmani's *Medicine Wheel Garden*, a section of a long-term reclamation project off the coast of Maine, is "based on a Native American ritual that heals the earth"; Heather McGill and John Roloff's *Isla de Umunnum* (Ohlone for "island of the hummingbirds"), a wetland reclamation project in California, features sculptural forms derived from American Indian architecture; Heizer's *Effigy Tumuli* draws on the midwestern mounds of the Adena and Hopewell Indians as the basis of its land reclamation strategy.[13] "Native American art, mythology, and beliefs have influenced the theme, content, and imagery of many ecological artworks," notes Barbara Matilsky, adding, "In indigenous cultures, nature centers the members of a group by providing necessary boundaries of behavior, as well as access to the realms of metaphysical enlightenment. The relationship of first peoples to their environment offers industrialized cultures important lessons in communication and psychological and social integration with nature." Or, as Marianna Torgovnick writes, "A significant motivation for primitivism in modernism is . . . the wish for physical, psychological, and social integrity as a birthright."[14]

In contemporary America this uncritical reverence for primitivism as a harmonious and transformative aesthetic is particularly pronounced. The huge vogue for primitive stylistics—in the consumer frenzy for pseudosacred Indian artifacts such as dream catchers and Kokopelli wind chimes, in art exhibitions such as the Museum of Modern Art's 1984 show "Primitivism in Twentieth Century Art," in eco-arts' fetishistic attention to Native American culture—is couched both in neoconservative nostalgia for a supposedly simpler and more virtuous time and in New Age notions of modern (Christian) spiritual bankruptcy. Primitivism is elevated as an eternal and universal aesthetic, above politics and beyond history. Primitive spirituality, particularly Native American spirituality, is celebrated as a kind of secular mysticism and embraced as the savior of alienated modernists—thousands of whom anted up for the "Native American Spiritual Wisdom" provided by hucksters such as Sun Bear (Vince LaDuke, a former *Bonanza* actor), who offered $50 sweat lodge sessions and $150 "vision quests" from his Vision Mountain headquarters (near Spokane) before his death in 1992.[15]

Such patronizing denies the autonomy and complexity of primitive cultures, ignores colonialist attitudes of Western superiority, and muddies the already conflicted realm of land reclamation artwork. Native American culture may be based on ethical stewardship of the land, but simply copying its stylistics is hardly an effective critique of a postindustrial world. Reducing the complexity of primitivism to a few visual bons mots and ecologically correct clichés is arrogant; reducing the complexity of environmentalism to the same is untenable.

Much as they uncritically exalt the regenerative potential of primitive art, many eco-artists are equally biased in their disdain for developing an authentic social or public art of land reclamation. Immersed, as current psychotherapeutic patois might have it, in a "hostile-dependent relationship," many contemporary artists determined to heal an all-inclusive Mother Earth also tend to despise the human factor responsible for despoiling that earth—and now demanding its repair. Eco-artists may provide solutions to environmental problems, but myopic absorption in the preservation and restoration of a romanticized nature, and, in aesthetic self-expression and design, often seems to take precedence over the equally important elements of dialogue and interaction essential to a democratic public culture.

Land reclamation is, after all, predicated on public intervention in the environment. Although the 1977 Federal Surface Mining Control and Reclamation Act set standards for getting sites "back to approximate original contour," the overall objective has been to reclaim disturbed sites for public use: nature preserves, reservoirs, subdivisions, playing fields, campgrounds, sculpture parks. A former 587.2-hectare (1,450-acre) phosphate mine near Lakeland, Florida, for instance, has become an "ambitious mixed-use development" that by the year 2001 will feature 3,500 condominiums, houses, and apartments, a shopping mall, several office parks and recreational lakes, a 300-room hotel, and a golf course.[16] The concept of land reclamation *artwork*, then, implies that such intervention goes beyond "back to contour" federal mandates by merging public utility with aesthetic possibilities. But by subordinating audiences, and nature, to autonomous visions of an ecologically recuperative aesthetic, even environmentally correct artists are remiss in terms of the necessarily public dimensions of land reclamation.

Effigy Tumuli exemplifies the conflicted state of contemporary land reclamation artwork, in which attention to an aesthetic treatment of the land more or less based on an appropriation of Indian art supersedes public stewardship. "I don't want some ditzy cornucopia of lilacs and all that stuff," Heizer said when *Effigy Tumuli* was in the planning stages, adding, "This is not a garden. The type of work I like is pure and simple and profound." Asked in 1977 how people should relate to his sculpture, Heizer replied, "You don't have to relate to it. It's not a requirement. . . . The point is, it's work of an artist."[17] A decade later, when asked about the public dimensions of the Illinois sculpture park, Heizer blasted, "I don't care how people utilize my art. I'm a sculptor." He is equally dismissive of land reclamation artwork: "I'm not for hire to go patch up mining sites. The strip-mine aspect of it is of no interest to me. I don't support reclamation-art sculpture projects. This is strictly art."[18] Perhaps unnerved by potential accusations of industrial complicity, Heizer takes as his defense artistic independence. Eager to distance his art from "entertainment"—"Look, I'm not out to entertain. So much damn art is about that!"—he sees the Ottawa public sculpture park primarily as an extension of his own personal aesthetic agenda.[19]

In the late 1960s Heizer was one of the earthworks generation, artists who journeyed to remote areas of the American Southwest to construct huge outdoor sculptures. Questioning the New York art world's narrow view of culture as commodity, as precious and portable museum object, as "entertainment," Heizer, Smithson, Walter De Maria, Nancy Holt, Charles Ross, and James Turrell worked in the deserts of Nevada, Utah, Arizona, and New Mexico making art about, of, on, and often literally in the landscape. The problem with art, Heizer said in 1969, was that it had been "subjected to thousands of years of utility (magic), justification (religion), and decoration (architecture). . . . Art fits into this environment like a subservient bauble. Utilitarian nuances still pervade the contemporary dialogue."[20]

The earthworks answer was to create site-specific sculptures rooted in the materials and topography of their environs, art such as Smithson's *Spiral Jetty* and Heizer's *Double Negative* (1969–70, Fig. 38), near

■ 38. **Michael Heizer,** *Double Negative,* 1969–70; Overton, Nev. Photo by author, August 1985.

Overton, Nevada. Aesthetic individuality was central to such enterprise: Distancing themselves from the art market's voracious appetite for collectibles, earthworks artists also distanced themselves from audience expectations of accommodation, of "utility." Yet strict autonomy was hard to maintain: Few artists could afford the costs of land purchase, labor, and heavy machinery leasing required of earthworks. Less interested, really, in art world anticapitalism than in self-expression, the earthworks generation came to rely on private underwriters such as art patron Robert Scull and gallery owners such as Virginia Dwan—who exhibited and sold pricy photographs of the outdoor sculptures.

Driven by aesthetic independence, Heizer, for one, was also determined to "be a contributor to the development of American art . . . to contribute to creating an American identity." He painted in New York for several years but felt stifled by European artistic traditions, by "paintings on canvas and sculptures that you walk around and that look like *Balzac* or *Moses*," which he considered irrelevant. "I wanted to finish off the European impulse," he said, adding, "I admire the work. I think it's incredible, but I don't think you can continue to make that kind of art and live in our society." Alienated further by the portents of apocalyptic doom ("we were coming close to the end of the world . . . living in the postnuclear age informed everything, the clock was ticking—Vietnam had threatened everybody and it was time to get to the point"), Heizer left New York and headed for a place "where one might find a simple overview of society, irrespective of epoch or identity."[21]

For Heizer, such a place was the American West. It was familiar turf—his family had lived there for three generations: His father was an anthropologist at the University of California, Berkeley; his maternal grandfather headed the California Division of Mines; his paternal grandfather, a mining engineer, ran the Nevada-Massachusetts Company's tungsten mine at the turn of the century.[22] Like them Heizer saw the West as a bonanza, an open space of physical, financial, academic, and now aesthetic possibility. Ironically, by seeing it as a simple and timeless place, Heizer made light of the American West's limited resources and discounted the complex and historically situated work of his own ancestors and the Indian cultures that have long lived there—and whose art he would come to emulate in *Complex One* and *Effigy Tumuli*.

For 1960s artists conflicted by desires for creative autonomy and dependence on art world support, the West was an amalgam of a similarly compromised American scene: a zone of individual opportunity constrained by corporate and military concerns—casinos, mining companies, and nuclear-testing sites. Visiting *Double Negative* in 1971, Virginia Dwan commented on Heizer and De Maria's cynical sense of the West, especially Nevada: "They really dig this place—no pun intended. They feel it sums up where we really are now in this country—all the materialism and vulgarity of Vegas, and the death industries outside. It's a kind of instant America—instant marriage and divorce, instant winning and losing, instant life and death . . . they like the frontier mentality."[23]

Updating the American frontier myth by becoming a progressive and independent art world pioneer (in a 1960 speech JFK had asked all Americans "to be pioneers on that New Frontier"), Heizer returned to the West.[24] Here he vowed to make uniquely *American* art, its form derived from what he considered "allowable" sources (the Indian architecture and sculpture of South America, MesoAmerica, and North America), its content from the land itself, its size on par with the grandest feats of architecture and science, and its durability a challenge to late capitalism's throwaway mind-set and atomic anxiety. The Anglo pioneer cannibalizing the culture of others, Heizer was also caught up in what Warren Susman characterized as the duality of post–World War II American culture, in which abundance and self-confidence clashed with Cold War paranoia. Describing *Complex One,* Heizer remarked, "When that final blast comes, a work like *Complex One* will be your artifact. It's going to be your art, because it's designed to last. It *will* stick and it's accurate and it's going to represent you. *Complex One* is designed to deflect enormous heat and enormous shock. It's very much about the atomic age."[25] If *The Last Whole Earth Catalog*—the bible of the early ecology movement—advocated "getting back to nature" as the answer to the malfeasance of postwar life, the earthworks movement was similarly motivated by what might be viewed as escapist self-indulgence. Shaped by Heizer's ambition of independence and his yearning to reinvent American art, *Double Negative* and *Complex One*—and their 1980s counterpart, *Effigy Tumuli*—also embodied his political alienation, social apathy, and astounding egoism.

Inseparable from its place, and the materials of that place, *Double Negative,* for example, is a prototypical site-specific sculpture. For many it is a quintessentially American art. With a crew of contractors and heavy equipment (tractors and drill rigs), Heizer blasted and bulldozed the 457.2 meters (1,500 feet) long sculpture out of the earth atop Mormon Mesa, 128.7 kilometers (80 miles) northeast of Las Vegas. Actually, *Double Negative* consists of two cuts—9.1 meters (30 feet) wide and 15.2 meters (50 feet) deep—facing each other across a deep cliff; a kilometer or so below is the Virgin River. Some 217,680 metric tons (240,000 tons) of earth and rock were "displaced" during the making of *Double Negative,* which entailed drilling into the mesa's 3-meter (10-foot) rhyolite cap, charging and exploding the rocky earth, and then "ripping and pushing" the sandstone into the escarpment between the two trenches. Virginia Dwan said the sculpture's title referred to the double zeros on Las Vegas roulette wheels, but Heizer explained that it was really an elaborate pun about making art:

> In *Double Negative* there is the implication of an object or form that is actually not there. In order to create this sculpture material was removed rather than accumulated. . . . The title *Double Negative* is a literal de-

scription of two cuts but has metaphysical implications because a double negative is impossible. There is nothing there, yet it is still a sculpture.[26]

For art world comedy, Heizer's timing was way off—the late 1960s and early 1970s were not particularly good years to make jokes at Mother Earth's expense, especially not after Congress passed the National Environmental Policy Act (1969) and established the Environmental Protection Agency (1970), and not after Earth Day (22 April 1970) helped turn ecological responsibility into a cultural crusade. After photos of *Double Negative* and other Heizer earthworks were shown at the Dwan Gallery in 1970, some critics denounced the artist's apparent environmental irresponsibility. *Double Negative* "proceeds by marring the very land, which is what we have just learned to stop doing," one wrote in 1971. "The disturbing effect such a work has had on the desert ecology—one of the most fragile ecologies on this planet—is depressingly unjustifiable," another said a few years later.[27] Edmund Thornton credits such critical blasts with stimulating Heizer's interest in *Effigy Tumuli:* "I think he felt this project was his way of making up for the harsh, environmentally disastrous works he had done in his past—like *Double Negative.* He felt *Effigy Tumuli* was a way of making a more positive, a softer kind of art."[28]

Despite its bad environmental reputation and remote location, *Double Negative* soon acquired significant art world status as a must-see Great American Thing. Criticized for its inaccessibility, *Double Negative* was (and still is) regularly (if not exactly easily) visited. "You'd be very surprised how many people have seen the *Double Negative.* People from all over the world go to see it," Heizer remarked in 1983, the same year one writer estimated that 5,000 people had visited the sculpture since its inception. (That might not seem like very many, but, as Tom Wolfe cynically observed in 1975, the art world consists of only about 10,000 culturati anyway.) Part of *Double Negative*'s attraction, of course, is its inaccessibility: The difficulty of seeing it in the flesh, which requires climbing the 182.9-meter (600-foot) mesa in four-wheel drive and then bouncing along the clifftop hunting for it with a U.S. Geological Survey map (there are no signs to point the way), definitely sets the earthworks pilgrim apart from the average art lover. Heizer scoffs at the idea that earthworks such as *Double Negative* are "too far away" to be seen: "They are not really hidden away, they are simply in their place. I make my work for people to see but they may have to go to a little trouble to get to it."[29]

"Place" accounts for a good deal of *Double Negative*'s appeal. Like the Virgin River watercolors Thomas Moran sketched a century earlier, *Double Negative* evokes the American West's mythos as a wild, untamed, boundless, and solitary place, a frontier of "freedom, opportunity, abundance, and success," the lifeblood of the nation.[30] Europeans, in particular, exclaim about the vast "open" space of *Double Negative*'s West, awed by comparison with their own fenced (and hence civilized) environs. The setting and huge physical scale of Heizer's sculpture confirm their expectations of what America is all about, as Umberto Eco describes:

> Cultivated Europeans and Europeanized Americans think of the United States as the home of the glass-and-steel skyscraper and abstract expressionism. But the United States is also the home of Superman. . . . Every now and then Superman feels a need to be alone with his memories, and he flies off to an inaccessible mountain range where, in the heart of the rock, protected by a huge steel door, is the Fortress of Solitude.

Superman's fortress, Eco writes, is a "museum of memories," a place where his life—and all America's—is recorded and preserved.[31] For some *Double Negative* is a similar sort of museum, an earthworks gallery of uniquely *American* ideals of scale (big), self (solitary), nature (redemptive *and* resourceful), and art (individualistic).

For others the pilgrimage to Mormon Mesa is inspired more by romantic notions of the American West's spiritual resonance. Earthworks such as *Double Negative,* art historian John Beardsley remarks, "are consecrated places for a willfully secular era." Milanese art collector Count Giuseppe Panza di Biumo regularly visited the sculpture because, as he explained, "it retains a relationship to the natural landscape not unlike that maintained by prehistoric cultures that made a religion of nature . . . modern civilization has lost this sensibility, so I am moved by the strength of the *Double Negative* and feel close to its existence." If tourists have trekked to the Grand Canyon for the past century in search of the American West's mythologized antithesis to the corruption and decadence of urban, industrial life, art lovers flock to *Double Negative* for similar reasons: to reaffirm their faith in a redemptive, sublime American landscape.[32]

Heizer doesn't deny that *Double Negative* engages contemporary notions of natural divinity—he once explained that he worked in the desert because it provided "that kind of unraped, peaceful, religious space artists have always tried to put into their work."[33] In 1983 he allowed that it was "interesting to build a sculpture that attempts to create an atmosphere of awe. . . . Awe is a state of mind equivalent to religious experience." Yet in the same interview he said *Double Negative* "had nothing to do with landscape or the romanticism of the West, I was looking for material. The West isn't romantic to me, I'm from there." Elsewhere he expanded on his pragmatism: "Well, you might say I'm in the construction business. . . . I have a tremendous real estate file on every available piece of property in six western states. I look for climate and material in the ground. When I find the right spot, I buy it."[34]

Great American Thing or Superman's cave, religious icon or simply art world matériel, *Double Negative* exemplifies the profoundly ambivalent attitudes Americans harbor about land, especially western lands. Viewed with reverence, they are also scanned for opportunity; celebrated for majestic grandeur, they are also treated simply as property. As historian Patricia Nelson Limerick writes, "If Hollywood wanted to capture the emotional center of Western history, its movies would be about real estate."[35]

The story of *Double Negative* might provide the perfect script. Despite Heizer's fierce anticommodity rhetoric ("I want to get rid of the parasites in art. With this thing, you can't trade it or speculate with it the way they do with traditional pieces. I would sell it, yes, but it would still make me sick to my stomach to sell it," he told a reporter in 1973), *Double Negative* is now very much a precious museum object. Commissioned by Virginia Dwan in 1969, the sculpture was deeded by her to the Los Angeles Museum of Contemporary Art in 1985. The museum now regularly arranges docent-led tours of *Double Negative* (although apparently one group recently failed to find it despite spending several hours wandering atop Mormon Mesa) and has had it appraised for insurance purposes. But then, even at the start, earthworks resistance to art world commodification was easily met. Collector Robert Scull, who financed many of Heizer's Nevada projects, said in 1969, "I've collected art for the last ten years because I love it and I want to own it. It ennobled me and my surroundings. But things have changed with the discovery of Heizer's work. My walls used to be my gallery. Now the vast open spaces have become my gallery."[36]

By the mid-1970s Heizer himself had reneged on his earlier diatribes against cultural commodification: "I was never out to destroy the gallery system or the esthetic object," he said in 1974, adding, "I'm not a radical. In fact, I'm going backward. I like to attach myself to the past."[37]

Youthful flirtation with art world anarchism aside, Heizer ingratiated himself among museums and collectors with sculptures that seemingly embodied ancient design and ritual. Indeed, much of the earthworks movement (and the reverie attached to it) was inspired by the era's romance with so-called prehistoric or primitive cultures, an attraction based on wishful thinking that they were more spiritually attuned, and more ecologically aware than contemporary culture's "civilizational malaise."[38] Like the "getting back to nature" current of the ecological counterculture—and eco-art a decade later—the earthworks movement responded to the crisis of modernism by "getting back" to primitive art.

Nancy Holt's *Sun Tunnels* (1976), for instance, was inspired by celestial observatories such as Stonehenge; the shape of Smithson's *Spiral Jetty* stemmed from life cycle imagery of Celtic and Maori cultures; Heizer's *Complex One* was based on the mastaba form originally covering the Zozer Pyramid in Saqqâra, Egypt. As a child Heizer often accompanied his anthropologist father on travels to Central America and the Middle East. His interest in revamping older architectural and sculptural forms, materials, and techniques (Robert Heizer was an authority on ancient haulage systems) in contemporary large-scale artworks such as *Double Negative* and *Effigy Tumuli* stems from this upbringing: "I attempt to maintain the venerable traditions of megalithic societies . . . which used and worked with massive pieces of material and created large structures."[39]

Despite attention to ancient art history, aesthetic individuality—the abiding tenet of late modernism—remained central to the earthworks movement; the public, whatever their reasons for seeing these desert sculptures, were never a weighty factor. Nevertheless, in the 1980s, when land reclamation became a legal necessity for American industry, many companies courted the earthworks artists as environmental saviors and public relations helpmates. Mandated to clean up its messes, corporate America turned to artists who had proved they could work on a huge physical scale and who had acquired significant art world status. Perhaps the taint of industrial malevolence and environmental irresponsibility could be softened by the primitive (read innocent) stylistics of blue-chip earth artists. Whatever the motivation, the site-specific, romantic, preindustrial, and self-referential character of the earthworks aesthetic was transferred to the public realm of land reclamation.

A few years before he began work on *Effigy Tumuli*, Heizer was hired by the Anaconda Minerals Company, a division of Atlantic Richfield.

■ 39. **Michael Heizer,** *Geometric Land Sculpture,* 1982; projected dimensions: 122 meters (400 feet) by 1,524 meters (5,000 feet) by 122 meters (400 feet), 907,000 metric tons (1 million tons) of dirt and rock, Anaconda Minerals Company, Tonopah, Nev. Courtesy Anaconda Minerals Company.

Anaconda was moving tons of earth from a site near Tonopah, Nevada, to extract molybdenum (moly), a kind of lead ore used to strengthen steel. In 1981 Heizer was contracted to use about 30 percent of the extraction overburden to build a huge sculpture at the edge of the plant site. Anticipating about 90 million metric tons (100 million tons) of waste over a five-year period, Heizer designed *Geometric Land Sculpture:* 122 meters (400 feet) tall, 1,524 meters (5,000 feet) long, and 122 meters (400 feet) wide (Fig. 39). The project's large-scale forms, like his chosen name for the sculpture, were consistent with Heizer's central preoccupation with mass and space. Despite his family's long history in Nevada—one of his grandfathers worked in Tonopah mines in 1910—*Geometric Land Sculpture* reclaimed the industrial landscape on purely formal grounds.

But reducing the social, physical, and financial realm of the Tonopah mine to an American version of the Egyptian pyramids was hardly a popular idea among the 300 workers at the moly plant.[40] When the plant opened in 1978, moly prices had already fallen from eleven to nine dollars a ton; when *Geometric Land Sculpture* was commissioned, prices had fallen to six dollars a ton. Since the project added about five cents to the cost of mining a ton of moly, workers worried that the sculpture's costs (estimated at around $2.9 million) might affect the longevity of

■ **40. Michael Heizer,** *Geometric Land Sculpture,* Anaconda Minerals Company, Tonopah, Nev. Photo by author, August 1985.

plant operations, and their jobs. Some resented the fact that a "New York artist had been hired to tell them how to dispose of the waste," especially after company engineers had begun site reclamation experiments with dunes and desert flora. In 1984, with moly at less than three dollars a ton, Atlantic Richfield closed the Nevada plant: Moly production, and work on *Geometric Land Sculpture*—only about one-third complete—came to a halt, and the workforce was reduced to eight employees (Fig. 40). As Tonopah went from boom to bust, many of the town's 4,000 residents blamed *Geometric Land Sculpture* for "bankrupting" the local economy. Plant superintendent Bert Johns argued that there was "no direct connection: the mine closed because steel prices plummeted and Atlantic Richfield was no longer interested in keeping the mine open."[41] Still, when Cyprus Tonopah Mining Corporation took over the site in 1988, their agenda did not include finishing *Geometric Land Sculpture.*

The failure of the Anaconda project did not deter Heizer, however, from accepting mining company CEO Edmund Thornton's offer to turn

Ottawa Silica's abandoned strip mine into an arty adjunct to Buffalo Rock State Park. An avid conservationist, Thornton had already used some of his vast family fortune to build Ottawa's Thornton Park and to maintain a nature preserve outside town; as a member of the AMLRC and the Illinois Nature Conservancy, he was ecologically literate. Through a relationship with New York curator Eva Pape, he was also attentive to contemporary art, often flying the company jet to East Coast art openings and museum shows. When the state demanded he clean up his company's polluted strip mine, Thornton took Pape's advice and tried to convince Isamu Noguchi to make a "spectacular sculpture park" out of the barren land.[42] After Noguchi declined he hired Heizer.

Thornton arranged financing through the Illinois AMLRC and the U.S. Department of the Interior's Office of Surface Mining (OSM), which collects fees from working coal mines to implement reclamation projects at abandoned mines across the country. In Illinois, OSM fee collection through September 1984 totaled over $96 million; a portion of this (eventually about $1 million) was allocated to reclaim the Ottawa site, considered by the AMLRC the most derelict in the state.[43] Thornton also worked out Heizer's commission—an undisclosed six-figure fee shared by a $25,000 NEA grant and Thornton's private philanthropy, the Ottawa Silica Company Foundation—and Heizer began developing sculptural plans.

Although Ottawa wasn't the West, the vast expanse of Thornton's strip mine offered the same material and magnitude as Heizer's desert projects, and he projected his mainly formalist concerns onto the midwestern site. He took thousands of photos of the area—from a helicopter, from a boat, from walking all over the 120.7-hectare (298-acre) site (of which about 62.4 hectares [150 acres] were severely polluted)—and enlarged them in his Tribeca studio, searching for a schematic conception that might link his aesthetic interests with the AMLRC's reclamation agenda. To minimize costs the council dictated that whatever sculpture was built had to be made of the same materials used to reclaim the site—limestone and grasses—and follow the contours of grading and sloping. No new topsoil (or any other material) was to be brought to the site, and successful reclamation (essentially soil stabilization) would depend on reducing soil acidity and on revegetation. Heizer's task was to turn the reclaimed soil into sculpture.

When Thornton mentioned the Indian effigy mounds that had once dotted the area, Heizer, familiar with the ancient sculptures through his

■ 41. Adena Culture, Serpent Mound, c. A.D. 900–1200; 376.1 meters (1,234 feet) long, near Locust Grove, Ohio. Photo courtesy Ohio Historical Society.

upbringing, recognized the possibilities of reworking them in the guise of reclamation artwork. Mound making—building earthen sculptures—not only fit AMLRC criteria but provided the huge scale and abstract stylistics that are Heizer's aesthetic trademarks. Surviving Indian mounds are truly gigantic: The Serpent Mound, built circa A.D. 900–1200 by the Adena and located near Locust Grove, Ohio, is 376.1 meters (1,234 feet) long (Fig. 41); the Monk's Mound, the largest of the truncated platform mounds at Cahokia, Illinois, built around A.D. 900–1100 by the Mississippi cultures, measures 320.0 meters (1,050 feet) by 240.8 meters (790 feet), and is 30.5 meters (100 feet) tall.

In Ottawa an updated form of Indian art—Heizer's revision of indigenous mound building—would be utilized at a site of industrial devastation and recalled as an instrument of ecological healing. Heizer's appropriation of Indian art followed an established American pattern of culturally co-opting anything and everything native—from land to spiritual traditions—and redefining it to fit particular needs. Buffalo Rock State Park, for instance, was so named because local Indians supposedly used to stampede buffalo over the bluffs; the fact that bison hunting had not occurred for centuries before the park's opening in the mid-1900s was disregarded in favor of an instant historical identity that romanticized the native past and ignored the area's industrial reality.

Armed with a copy of I. A. Lapham's *Antiquities of Wisconsin*, an 1854 Smithsonian publication that featured fifty sketches of now long-gone midwestern effigy mounds, Heizer extended this proprietary interest in Indian culture and designed eight sculptures for the Ottawa park: a catfish, a water strider, a turtle, a snake, a frog, a beaver, a salamander, and a hawk.[44] When engineering bids came in at more than double the original estimate (the AMLRC had predicted reclamation costs would total about $300,000, but the lowest bid was $680,000), the latter three designs were dropped. The *Water Strider* mound (see Fig. 34) was built during the start of reclamation efforts, which included treating and discharging murky pools containing over 22.7 million liters (6 million gallons) of acidic water, adding some 5,442 metric tons (6,000 tons) of limestone to reduce the soil's acidity, and excavating and grading 351,900 cubic meters (460,000 cubic yards) of material to provide proper surface drainage and stabilize the soil. The remaining four mounds were built during the second phase of reclamation, when the top-soil was seeded and covered with straw mulch and excelsior matting.[45]

Hoping to "reactivate" the Indian mound-building tradition, Heizer was nevertheless reluctant about relying on representational sculpture forms or generating a serious environmental critique:

> The hardest thing in the whole job was making the decision to go ahead and deal with that kind of effigy imagery—to deal with imagery at all. But I decided that there was no way I could come into that region and do what modern man had done since they ran the Indians out, which was to build more cities, more modern things, more abstract-looking things. So there had to be imagery; it had to be within those terms.

Although called upon to mitigate the damage caused by modern industry, Heizer initially wanted to avoid the look of abstract art—such as his own, as he called it, "modernist sculptural geometry"—because it seemed linked to the ideology he held responsible for the dissolution of the Ottawa site and Indian culture in general.[46] It was less threatening to copy the mound builders than to critique how and why they disappeared and have to confront his own personal and aesthetic relationship with the modernist context of their disappearance. Equating abstract art with

■ 42. **Michael Heizer,** *Effigy Tumuli,* 1985; aerial view of *Turtle* and *Snake* mounds, Buffalo Rock State Park, Ottawa, Ill. Aerial photo: Bob Knoedler, Streator, Ill.

modernist misuse, Heizer confounded the meaning of his own aesthetic style.

Heizer eventually did design mounds based on insect and reptile shapes, ranging in length from 103.6 to 630.9 meters (340 to 2,070 feet) and in height from 2.1 to 5.5 meters (7 to 18 feet). But the highly abstract renditions of those shapes, as well as their huge size, suggest both his ambivalence about modernism and his abiding commitment to high modern art, with its focus on avant-garde independence and aesthetic evolution, and its disdain for popular culture. Each *Effigy Tumuli* creature, for example, was rarefied to what Heizer described as its "geometric essentialization." The designs for the *Turtle* and *Snake* mounds particularly demonstrate his preference for the reductive impulse of late modernism (Fig. 42). Moreover the *Effigy Tumuli* sculptures are overwhelmingly huge; they cannot really be seen except from a helicopter or airplane. And, finally, there is this remark Heizer made to critic Douglas

McGill: "When I first drew in the beaver, I thought it looked okay. But then I started looking at it and I said 'Beaver? Walt Disney did that.' So it had to go."[47] Despite its nomenclature as public art and its grounding in the reclamation of Indian cultural traditions, *Effigy Tumuli* especially seems to embody Michael Heizer's master modern narrative: ambivalent, self-absorbed, aloof, antisocial.

Still, the dedication of the sculpture park, on 29 October 1985, was very social, attended by Illinois Lieutenant Governor George Ryan (chair of the AMLRC), Sue Massie (director of the AMLRC), Alan Cole (member of the U.S. Department of the Interior's OSM), Heizer, Thornton, and about eighty other Illinois Department of Conservation representatives, art enthusiasts, reporters, and photographers, many of whom went for rides in the lieutenant governor's helicopter to get a bird's-eye view of the mounds. During the ceremonies Ryan remarked that *Effigy Tumuli* had great potential as a "tourist attraction" and exclaimed how Heizer's reclamation of the former strip mine had cost no more than if the council had done it art-free (total costs for reclamation were approximately $1 million). Thornton called the project a "dream come true" and announced that the Ottawa Silica Company was donating the site to the state of Illinois "for public recreational use," thereby enormously expanding the smallish 17.4-hectare (43-acre) Buffalo Rock State Park complex. Cole echoed that the park was a "permanent project for public enjoyment" and exclaimed, "There's no clue here now that the land ever was used for extraction of minerals."[48]

And "Off-Road Warrior" Paul Smith, a local twenty-six-year old dirt biker, used the opportunity to crash the party and publicly demonstrate his deep disgust for *Effigy Tumuli* and its sponsors by "roosting" Ryan and his guests: "making a pass through the crowd on my dirt bike and shooting a 20-foot [6.1-meter] high rooster tail of rock, mud and clay on them." The lieutenant governor responded by sending his helicopter in pursuit of Ottawa's version of Mad Max (he escaped), and the "Shootout at Buffalo Rock," as *Chicago Tribune* journalist Wes Smith (no relation) described it, was under way (Fig. 43).[49]

Like the other public art controversies discussed in this book, Ottawa's shoot-out stemmed from a strong local sense of exclusion in the process of commissioning, making, and finally dedicating the *Effigy Tumuli* sculpture park. "A lot is done behind closed doors here," Evelyn Muffler, Smith's sister, remarks. "We were never consulted about that so-called public park."[50]

■ 43. "Off-Road Warrior" Paul Smith on a dirt bike, holding cocked gun, on land owned by his family and previously used as a toxic waste dump. Photo: Stephen Warmowski.

For many of Ottawa's 20,000 residents, the frustration of being shut out, and being ignored, is nothing new. Documentary filmmaker Carol Langer captured their civic alienation in her 1986 movie *Radium City,* the story of female employees who worked at two local factories painting luminescent clock faces. Radium Dial opened in Ottawa in 1922, offering young girls good salaries ($17.50 a week) to paint glow-in-the-dark numbers on Westclox clocks and watches. Women started dying of cancer almost immediately, and legal action ensued. The case received considerable attention from the Chicago press. But Radium Dial continued to operate in Ottawa until the late 1930s, when owner Joseph Kelly abandoned it and opened a new factory a few weeks later across town under a new name—Luminous Process. At this factory women continued to apply luminous paint to watch dials, instrument panels, theater-seat numbers, doll eyes, and fishing lures; Luminous Process also played a central role in the reprocessing of radium into polonium, an essential ingredient in atom bomb manufacturing, during the 1940s. In 1977 the factory was shut down because of repeated health and safety violations, and Joseph Kelly, Jr., abandoned the site.[51]

Radium City charts the deaths of the original Radium Dial girls ("The Legion of the Doomed" one Chicago newspaper called them), the disingenuous disclaimers made by Joseph Kelly, Sr. (he blamed the deaths on diphtheria), and the complicity between the government and the company (since 1948 the Argonne National Laboratory in southwest Chicago has repeatedly "tested" employees, conducting the largest such medical study of a group of workers in the United States, and it continues to exhume and analyze their bodies). Langer's film further details the problems of "disposing" of the two factory buildings. The original Radium Dial building was torn down in 1968, its highly radioactive remains strewn all over the city—behind the football field, by the YMCA, in landfills near the future site of *Effigy Tumuli*. When farmers and dog owners near these hot spots reported a dramatic increase in animal tumors and hunters began noticing deer with abnormal growths, residents started to worry about radium emissions at the still standing Luminous Process building. A group called RAPE (Residents Against a Polluted Environment) formed in 1980 and demanded civic action. Then Mayor Jim Thomas downplayed the picocuries that Geiger counters were ticking off at the Luminous site and called RAPE activists "obstructionists" responsible for giving Ottawa its "Death City" reputation. Finally, in 1984— just as Michael Heizer signed on to the *Effigy Tumuli* project—the state of Illinois began to tear down the factory, carefully packing its contaminated bricks and boards, and all the earth around, in steel barrels destined for a Washington State toxic waste dump. Workers wore hard hats with adages such as "Have a Happy Half-life." The decontamination process took over two years and cost the state some $6.5 million. Kelly's company pled poverty and paid nothing toward cleanup.

Langer's unrelentingly depressing film chronicles the corporate arrogance and government apathy that created Ottawa's deplorable state of radium contamination—in the water, in the food chain, in the animal population, in the high local levels of cancer, childhood leukemia, brain tumors, and abnormal births. *Radium City* also describes feelings of betrayal and abandonment in a community lied to and ignored for decades. "They didn't care about the people at work in that factory, they were just a piece of equipment," one man remarks. Another Ottawa native recalls how her mother, shortly before she died of cancer contracted while working at Radium Dial, submitted, "It's not what you know, it's who you know in this world." Comments such as "it's dangerous to live around here" and Langer's own description of Ottawa as "the town that failed to see the light," speak volumes about its current physical and psychological condition.

To counter civic resignation, RAPE has fought to see Ottawa cleaned up, waging battles against industrial pollution and further landfill development. Daphne Mitchell, one of RAPE's cofounders, says RAPE is "committed to keeping Ottawa and La Salle County as pristine as can be. We're surrounded by chemical plants and all the rest and we're just trying to keep those businesses honest."[52] Still, environmental cleansing does not look especially hopeful: Ottawa was recently targeted to become a "megadump" for the entire state of Illinois, at a site just across the road from Buffalo Rock State Park and *Effigy Tumuli*.

Platted in 1830, Ottawa is a town with a personality split between industrial exploitation of its natural resources (sandstone, silica, coal) and recreational exploitation of its natural beauty (the Illinois River and surrounding lands). Ottawa has made glass products—windows, bottles, marbles, laminated windshields—and various other industrial items (from polyvinyl sheeting to ice-cream freezers) for well over a century; over the decades the factories of Libby-Owens Ford, Union Carbide Plastics, Ottawa Silica, and of course Radium Dial and Luminous Process, have all contributed to the town's economic health and environmental degradation. The area's plentiful abandoned mine sites attest to the impact coal mining has had on Ottawa, too; it is surrounded by more than its share of the state's 4,000 former deep mine and surface mine sites.

Ottawa is only a two-hour drive from Chicago, closer yet for the city's south suburbanites. Located near two popular state parks—Buffalo Rock and the much larger 587.7-hectare (1,451-acre) Starved Rock— Ottawa is a weekend/vacation fun spot fringed by biking and hiking trails, picnic and camping grounds, swimming and fishing areas, boatdocks, golf courses, restaurants, and bars. Recently lots of new vacation homes and cabins have sprouted up near Ottawa as well: Painted Deer Run is one such development, being built only a kilometer or so from *Effigy Tumuli*, in the immediate vicinity of the numerous landfills (including the proposed megadump) and toxic waste dumps (some legal, some not) that also make use of the desolate acres formerly mined for coal and quarried for sand.

The mix of industrial waste and recreational tourism is not usually a great success, but Paul Smith's stepfather—Roger "Sparky" Fullmer—turned both to his advantage by buying up about 162 hectares (400 acres) of the more than 810 hectares (2,000 acres) of Ottawa's abandoned mines and in the late 1960s opening a gun shop (actually more of an ammunition supply and reloading outfit) and very popular shooting range. Fullmer's property was just a few kilometers from the site that would become *Effigy Tumuli* and practically in the backyard of Edmund Thornton's own expansive estate outside Ottawa. Making the most of the area's industrial offal, Fullmer's firing range became a gun lovers' happy hunting ground, where Civil War buffs blasted their cannons, U.S. Army battalions honed their shooting skills, and Chicago SWAT teams practiced operations (complete with machine guns and tear gas). For ten dollars a day, more mundane marksmen aimed at home-brought targets (old tires, broken TVs, lawn ornaments, huge stuffed animals) thrown down the 12.2-meter (40-foot) gully of a former illegal toxic waste dump. One soon-to-be divorcé carefully placed a Bang & Olufsen stereo in the ravine, took a photo, fired a .35 Magnum into it, took another photo, and, showing onlookers the before-and-after pics, said, "The bitch won't get that."

Paul Smith also made use of Ottawa's industrial wasteland: As a teenager he discovered that the region's strip-mined hills and ridges were perfect for dirt biking—free from vegetation, far from residential zones, and chockful of the gorges and gullies, banked curves, and natural whoop-de-dos that off-roaders delight in. The lands were virtually deserted, save for the trucks dumping garbage and toxic waste (in the 1960s various Chicago factories dumped some 650 gallon-size steel drums full of paint sludge at a site 0.8 kilometer [a half mile] from *Effigy Tumuli*). Ignoring potential health threats, Smith and his buddies took the land for themselves. It wasn't exactly theirs to take—the Ottawa Silica Company owned a lot of it—but in the American spirit of homesteading (or in this case bikesteading), they laid claim. And the Ottawa Silica Company didn't seem to mind—at no time were fences built or security guards posted on what most people regarded as completely worthless and uninhabitable property.

"It was a dirt bikers' paradise," Smith's friend Kelly Dempsey recalls.

It was known all over the Midwest for great off-road riding and every good weekend some sixty to eighty people would use the area to ride—more on holidays. Off-road riding isn't about drugs or drinking, you know, it's about whole families doing stuff together, and this place was famous. It was a free space for public access, and we don't have too many of those left in this country.

Seizing the abandoned zones of private enterprise, Ottawa's off-roaders reclaimed the area as public space: open, accessible, active. Their style of land reclamation was neither an aesthetic nor an ecological ameliorative, nor did it offer a critique of the local industry that had provided their dirt bike paradise. Rather, their reclamation of Ottawa's industrial wasteland was predicated on creating a free space, a common, for a community of dirt bikers. At least it was free space until the day in 1984 that Smith and Dempsey went riding and noticed a few little red flags attached to wooden stakes, the marks of surveyors. "We knew then our paradise was about to be lost," says Dempsey. "But we didn't know it was going to be turned into that so-called 'public' park."

Dempsey's comments—like Paul Smith's disruption of *Effigy Tumuli*'s grand opening—reveal how opposing definitions of public space—what it is and who it is for—are central to the controversies that surround public art. Certainly Ottawa's dirt bikers saw *Effigy Tumuli* as an example of civic elitism—"Public art for who?" asks Jim Farrell, one of Smith's closest friends. "Edmund Thornton's public or Ottawa's public?" As were other Ottawans, local dirt bikers were skeptical of *Effigy Tumuli*'s million-dollar price tag—"Pouring money down a rathole," Smith complained—and unimpressed by its modern art stylistics—"I can't see how those mounds are supposed to be insects and animals," says Evelyn Muffler. "I can't see them at all, and you can only really see them from an airplane or helicopter." But the main source of conflict regarding *Effigy Tumuli* lay with differing assumptions about the public sphere: The meaning of public space held by Edmund Thornton and Michael Heizer was not that held by Ottawa's off-roaders.

Ironically, dirt biking burgeoned at the same time as the ecology and earthworks movements, in the late 1960s. It began when scores of street bikers took the fenders off their motorcycles and modified their suspensions for off-road riding. Off-roading loosely (very loosely, some might say) related to the back-to-the-earth ideals of the day: "Dirt riders don't have to deal with speed limits or laws against sliding, jumping, or wheelying," one off-road enthusiast recently romanticized. "When I ride on the street, I don't get the same feeling of freedom that I do in the dirt."[53] Spurred by the era's *Easy Rider* lust for freedom and the daredevil machismo of Evel Knievel, thousands of adolescent males—like Paul Smith—began riding the range on one of Rokon's, Yamaha's, Honda's, Suzuki's, or Kawasaki's specially designed chrome ponies. An entire industry soon emerged, complete with magazines (*Dirt Rider, Dirt Bike*), apparel (full-face helmets, chest protectors, race pants, ergonomic boots), tournaments and rallies (the American Motorcycle Association [AMA] National Hare Scrambles, the AMA/Camel Supercross), and off-road trails and parks (such as the Perry Lake ATV [all-terrain vehicle] Area, east of Topeka, managed by the U.S. Corps of Engineers). After his stepfather's death in 1988, Smith took over the gun range and made further use of Ottawa's eco-nightmare by starting an off-road park (the Buffalo Rock Shooting and Riding Range) on several hundred hectares of an abandoned sand quarry.

As off-roading's popularity and profits have grown, so have environmentalist efforts to restrict it. Most of the Oregon Dunes, considered by dirt bikers to be some of America's best off-road haunts, are now closed to riding, and similar closures are under way in other states. The California Desert Protection Act (S.21), for example, proposes to close two-thirds (3.2 million hectares, 8 million acres) of the Mojave to dirt biking, as well as to ranching, mining, and other commercial and public uses; under the bill only recreational activities such as backpacking and horseriding would be allowed. In addition, many counties and communities have passed restrictive ordinances aimed at banning off-road ranges because of noise: Jerry Habel "faced major legal hassles" over dirt bike noise before he was able to open the Daniel Boone Motocross Park in southeastern Kentucky.[54]

Certainly the dirt biking version of "getting back to nature" is a lot louder than a quiet day hike in open space. And dirt biking has been environmentally reprehensible in more than a few instances, as when irresponsible riders go off trail to practice their full turns and double jumps. The off-road response to real and potential restriction, to what *Dirt Rider* editor Charlie Morey calls the "grossly single-interest legislation" of the "enviro/extremo public relations machine," has been to combine in-house policing with a vocal demand for continued access to the public sphere. Project Stealth, which encourages the use of quieter mufflers, and the Tread Lightly campaign, which (in conjunction with the U.S. Forest Service) pledges "driving responsibly to protect the environment and preserve opportunities to enjoy my vehicle on wild lands," are two recent off-road regulatory gestures.[55]

Even more persuasively, dirt bikers have lately joined forces with the multiple-use movement and have begun to lobby for their continued presence on public lands: Almost every issue of *Dirt Rider* over the past few years has featured editorials and articles advising off-roaders on how to shape public and political interest through letter writing, rallies, press conferences, fund-raising, and so on. Morey is an especially enthusiastic off-road activist. He says, "Our only hope for winning—for not seeing [S.21] passed this year—is to influence public opinion. The people who have innocently believed the beautiful lies told by environmental extremist groups need to hear the truth. How can a bunch of dirt riders accomplish that? It requires a strong grassroots effort (that's you!) and a lot of luck, but it is possible." Filling his columns with what he calls "the rational-thinking, multiple-use point of view," Morey urges tolerance and a "win-win situation" for all: "Somewhere in the middle there's room for all of us to live without destroying each other's ideals and needs. Somewhere in the middle, there's government by the people and for the people rather than by and for the best-funded or loudest-screaming special interest group."[56]

In Ottawa the off-road fight for the right to a more democratic public space followed a similar train of thought, if a somewhat different course of action. As does Morey, many of Ottawa's off-roaders argued for multiple use of the lands they had been using for dirt biking for over a decade. Kelly Dempsey allowed that there was plenty of room for "dirt art" and dirt biking, "but only the one is being allowed. In the 1970s there were lots of places around here for casual dirt biking. Now, because of development and environmentalism and liability insanity, it's all being shut down."

Less motivated by political activism than Charlie Morey, Ottawa's off-roaders vented their frustration about public space accessibility, about *Effigy Tumuli*'s "single-interest" utility, more like a midwestern version (though this was hardly intended) of the eco-maniacs in Edward Abbey's *The Monkey Wrench Gang,* or the "ecotage" practitioners of Earth First![57] When surveying stakes sprouted on their stomping grounds, dirt bikers pulled them out; when signs advertising the nearby housing development were erected, they changed the letters to read "Tainted" Deer Run. When *Effigy Tumuli* was being built, some of the equipment at the site was vandalized and off-road tracks were found on the mounds; Smith's family denied any involvement but agreed to pay damages. And then, when the sculpture park opened, Smith would often drive to the entrance and try to scare visitors with stories of the illegal toxic waste dump nearby that "oozed a waterfall 'colored like Kool-Aid.'" "Instead of a giant catfish, I think they should put a skull and crossbones with an arrow pointing to the toxic waste dump," Smith said in 1985, adding, "They should be cleaning up the dump instead of building a park only a couple of people will see."[58] "He would tell people that one of the mounds looked just like Elvis at the gates of Graceland if you turned the aerial photo the right way," Evelyn Muffler recalls. Smith also joked about making his own dirt art at the shooting range—"a death skull or maybe a picture of Elvis"—as a way of "flipping off" Edmund Thornton when he flew his airplane over the range to take a look at the *Effigy Tumuli* sculpture park next door.

If *Effigy Tumuli* tourists weren't deterred by Smith's tales of toxic contamination and Elvisiana, they did worry when they saw bullet holes in the sculpture-locator signs (see Fig. 36), found shell casings littered around the mounds, and heard guns being fired at what seemed to be "awfully close" quarters. And after more than a few swore they were actually being shot at—"Mostly it was people saying they heard bullets flying over their heads, but some said they actually saw them hit the ground," park superintendent Mark McConnaughhay was quoted as saying—the Department of Conservation shut the park down in December 1990. Edmund Thornton was outraged by this affront to his notion of the public sphere: "A lot of public and private money went into this, and to have it closed and unavailable I think is a travesty."[59] Convinced that potshots from the nearby Buffalo Rock Shooting and Riding Range were the source of the problem, the state threatened to close Smith's business unless he built a higher revetment to catch stray bullets. Smith eventually complied with court orders, and *Effigy Tumuli* opened again in mid-August 1992. About a week later Paul Smith died of head injuries suffered in a motorcycle accident.

Shortly before he died Smith said the following about the *Effigy Tumuli* sculpture park:

> They might reopen it, but nobody is going to come to see it anyway. There is still nothing to it but a few dirt hills. You can't tell what it is unless you read their little signs. The conservationists call what we do on our dirt bikes "land abuse" but we call it "land use." We took a wasteland and we used it. They ruined it so nobody uses it. And I say if you can't use the land, it's abused.[60]

Indeed, *Effigy Tumuli* is open but often completely deserted. It has never become the viable "tourist attraction" predicted by Lieutenant Governor

■ 44. **Michael Heizer,** *Effigy Tumuli,* 1985; Buffalo Rock State Park, Ottawa, Ill.
View showing eroded mounds. Photo by author, April 1993.

Ryan. Visitors to Buffalo Rock State Park take pictures of the site's two
caged animals, have family picnics, play baseball, and climb the bluffs.
But, according to Department of Conservation employee and *Effigy Tumuli* tour guide Judy Schoenenberger, few of the park's 78,000 or so annual visitors "spend much time" in the sculpture park. "It's kind of hard
for even me to comprehend," she remarks. "I know Heizer wanted us to
get on top of these figurines and experience the art, but that's hard considering the state of reclamation here."[61]

Effigy Tumuli's "state of reclamation" is abysmal. While Heizer and
the sculpture park's engineering crew followed all the rules for surface
mine reclamation—grading, soil neutralization, mulching, seeding—the
site retains the ambience of a lunar landscape. Despite careful study of
soil mechanics and slope permeability, the strong winds that whip across
the mesa have badly eroded the precisely rendered mounds, which have
been further damaged by several summers of drought (Fig. 44). There is
some speculation about how reclaimed the site really is: Sheets of excelsior matting applied to the tumuli to promote seed growth are clearly

visible; vegetation is sparse; soil erosion and water impoundment remain a serious problem. "We could probably put limestone down for hundreds of years and the soil still wouldn't be sweet enough for grass to grow," says Schoenenberger.

Land reclamation is a relatively new endeavor, and standards and methods for stabilizing disturbed lands vary widely. It is generally agreed, however, that the key to long-term rather than quick-fix reclamation is revegetation to prevent soil erosion and slow water runoff. Healthy plants need healthy dirt, but the soil acidity at the *Effigy Tumuli* site is so severe that seed growth—even preceded by large doses of pH balancing minerals and fertilizers—has been minimal. (On a scale of 1 to 14, healthy soil has a pH of around 7. The soil at the Ottawa site measured around pH 2 before reclamation. Even at successfully reclaimed sites, the pH balance generally improves by only about 75 percent.) The AMLRC understandably refused to import topsoil to the site—the cost would have been outrageous. Instead, thousands of tons of powdered limestone were blown onto the site, as were large amounts of nutrients and mulch. Unfortunately, the silty, clayey strip-mined soil proved impenetrable to plant roots.

Another problem at the *Effigy Tumuli* site was that the actual depth of soil reclamation was only a few centimeters. This is not unusual: Land reclamation typically involves stabilizing only the first 15.2 centimeters (6 inches) of a surface. But as revegetation has failed, overburden and mine soils continue to precipitate to the surface, forming a nasty slurry similar to quicksand. This muck is so potent it destroys shoes and can burn skin—this is, after all, acidic soil. Schoenenberger often tells potential sculpture park visitors to wear "sturdy boots, like waders" that can withstand site conditions.[62] It is not surprising that more than a few opt for other forms of art appreciation and recreation.

If reclamation of the *Effigy Tumuli* site is one issue, another is that of park management and maintenance. The Illinois Department of Conservation was assigned the task of taking care of the *Effigy Tumuli* sculpture park when it opened in 1985. The site needs a lot of care, from mowing the mounds and removing debris to testing hardier seed stock, but overall maintenance has been minimal. Drought, budget cuts, and overwork (just four Department of Conservation employees are responsible for maintenance of more than 445.5 hectares [1,100 acres], including Buffalo Rock State Park, the sculpture park, and the nearby Illinois & Michigan Canal State Trail) have all affected *Effigy Tumuli*'s physical state. During the years of litigation between the state and Paul Smith, the park was closed and maintenance virtually ceased.

Conditions at *Effigy Tumuli* have especially been affected by in-house feeling that the mounds are a costly, high-maintenance, and incomprehensible corporate tax dodge. One Department of Conservation official told Edmund Thornton, "We've never been responsible for a sculpture park before. We really haven't known what to do with it." As JoAnn Hustis, longtime reporter for the *Ottawa Daily News,* notes, "The Department of Conservation has never taken care of that area. As soon as *Effigy Tumuli* was done it started to erode, and the Department of Conservation didn't seem to care. In this area, *Effigy Tumuli* is a laughing-stock, it's considered a real boondoggle. All the money the state spent on those mounds, and they don't even spend a dime more to keep them up."[63]

Such comments suggest that beyond its unfortunate physical condition, *Effigy Tumuli* is also a public art disaster. Conceived as clear-cut forms covered by 15.2- to 20.3-centimeter (6- to 8-inch) grasses, the mounds are so completely disparate from the images portrayed in park brochures (see Fig. 35), on the visitors' station plaques, and on the sculpture-locator signs (see Fig. 36), that visitors cannot recognize them. "People have this thing about immediate gratification. If they can't get it right away, they don't like it," says Heizer.[64] But the problem with *Effigy Tumuli* is that viewers can't "get" the mounds at all—they have so severely eroded they are practically invisible. This is hardly the case with sculpture mounds where maintenance (amid admittedly less hostile environmental conditions) is regularly undertaken: The Serpent Mound is as long as one of Heizer's effigies (although not as tall) and easily perceived by earthbound visitors.

Of course, audience interest in the Serpent Mound probably has a lot to do with its authentic Indian origins, and the fact that it was not built on top of toxic waste. Well-meaning eco-artists fail to anticipate public reaction to the environmental danger zones—the dumps, landfills, and abandoned mines—that they choose to turn into art. Especially in the last few decades, thousands of Americans have joined grassroots activists fighting power lines, power plants, substations, landfills, and other industrial accoutrements from appearing in their neighborhoods. If that public was aware of the abiding toxicity at the *Effigy Tumuli* sculpture park, or of the noxious toxic waste dump less than 0.8 kilometer (0.5 mile) away, they probably would not visit the site at all. As it is,

Ottawa residents tend to stay clear of the area—their local history has taught them that. Out-of-towners who tour *Effigy Tumuli*, however, have not been so privileged to the real facts of Ottawa's industrial heritage.

Promised public sculpture, these visitors bring expectations of visual surprise and aesthetic stimulation to *Effigy Tumuli*. Promised effigy mounds, they anticipate contemporary versions of the Serpent Mound or perhaps some sort of a New Age artpark with "Native American Spiritual Wisdom." Promised a park, they anticipate benches and maybe an observation tower—accessible spaces where they can reflect on the sculpture and the site. Promised "the largest site sculpture ever envisioned," they expect art world grandiloquence.[65] But visiting *Effigy Tumuli* is more a journey of endurance than one of pleasure and reward. Trudging through the clayey muck from one eroded effigy to the next, looking in vain for areas that allow contemplation (except for the platform at the sculpture park entrance, there are no benches in the 1.6 kilometers [1 mile] long site, and Heizer was adamantly opposed to building an observation tower), visitors denied *Effigy Tumuli*'s public sculpture park promises rather resignedly concentrate on "getting through" the site.

The Department of Conservation, says Schoenenberger, tends to use *Effigy Tumuli* "as a great vehicle to talk about ecology and environmental destruction" to local high school and college biology classes. "I get groups of ten or twenty who come over to my booth and say, 'Hey, what was that all about?' and then I take them back through it all and explain it. It's an area that definitely needs someone to interpret it." Pointing out blackened coal patches and piles of overburden and describing the wildlife in the area (deer, coyotes, Eastern meadowlarks), Schoenenberger's tour of *Effigy Tumuli* concentrates on the problems of land reclamation and environmental responsibility. "I know that's probably not what the artist wants people to think about," she says, "but people can't see the art, and when I talk about how the area is being reclaimed they really respond, they really seem to understand what it's all about."

Despite Department of Conservation efforts to cast *Effigy Tumuli* in environmentally correct terms, hardly anyone in Ottawa has much particularly charitable to say about the sculpture park. Ottawa's off-roaders, of course, want the site born again as a dirt-biking paradise. Activist groups such as RAPE say they appreciate the reclamation Band-Aid but point to the toxic waste dumps and landfills nearby, and the threat of the new megadump. More cynical residents call *Effigy Tumuli* a "taxpayer rip-off," some saying that the overextended department

■ 45. **Ken Indermark,** *Billboard/Shrine,* 1992; billboard on Highway 122, near Danville, Ill. (destroyed). Photo: Ken Indermark.

should concentrate on opening more playing fields and expanding the bike paths along the I & M Canal State Trail. Even Edmund Thornton admits that many Ottawans consider *Effigy Tumuli* a joke: "I think people around here view it with bemusement, sort of as a folly. They felt it was a corporate folly, my folly. They have no sense of the artistic statement that was made, how they are modern-day sculptures." But by failing to establish civic participation and trust with *Effigy Tumuli,* Thornton virtually guaranteed such reaction. In a town spooked by corporate dishonesty and environmental irresponsibility, it is hardly surprising that the pet project of a local tycoon is greeted skeptically.

If *Effigy Tumuli* glossed over Ottawa's environmental and human abuse, an eco-conscious artwork an hour's drive away did not (Fig. 45). In 1992 Chicago artist Ken Indermark constructed a billboard/shrine on Illinois Highway 122 outside Danville, where in 1989 a tanker carrying 15,140 liters (4,000 gallons) of Treflan herbicide overturned on a curve. The driver was killed, and the toxic spill contaminated a huge section of Tom Korn's rural property. Korn hired Indermark to memorialize the

■ 46. **Andrew Leicester,** *Prospect V-III,* 1982; wood, mixed-media sculpture, 38.7 meters (127 feet) long by 9.8 meters (32 feet) high by 5.5 meters (18 feet) wide, Frostburg, Md. Photo: Andrew Leicester.

site—and protest the chemical company's reluctance to accept blame and clean it up (a process that eventually took over two years and cost hundreds of thousands of dollars).[66] The sculpture consisted of bicycle parts, plastic flowers, toys, and whirligigs attached to a brightly painted billboard featuring the artist's home phone number and the message "See! Sacred Land on Rt. 122 at Curve." Indermark's shrine spoke to junk culture and roadside attractions; unlike *Effigy Tumuli,* references to a "sacred" American landscape were critically couched in real-life detail. Too real for some, the billboard was torched in late 1992—an action straight out of *The Monkey Wrench Gang*—but Indermark and Korn promise to see it revived in the near future.

Perhaps a more applicable comparison with the specific land reclamation context of *Effigy Tumuli* is *Prospect V-III,* a 1982 monument to coal miners in Frostburg, Maryland (Fig. 46). Hired by the state's art council, Minneapolis artist Andrew Leicester built a sculpture on the reclaimed site of several abandoned deep mines (whose depressions are

■ 47. **Andrew Leicester,** *Prospect V-III,* 1982; detail, Infant Miner's Room. Photo: Andrew Leicester.

called prospects) and a former strip mine. Over 38.0 meters (127 feet) long and 9.8 meters (32 feet) high, *Prospect V-III* is a structural montage of past coal-mining architecture: tipples, conveyor belts, shafts, furnaces, company town cottages. The sculpture's walkway overlooks the Georges Creek Basin, where George Washington discovered coal during a 1782 survey; its interior includes a mine shaft and several rooms (Fig. 47). The "Infant Miner's Room" features a blue cradle cum coal cart, set on one-way tracks leading to the mine shaft; on the walls of the small room are brightly colored Maryland butterflies, whose metamorphosis into black lungs further symbolizes the fate of male children born into coal-mining communities a century ago.

If the sculpture works on one level to reclaim the area's rapidly disappearing vernacular architecture, it works on another to reclaim this industrially abused site as public art. Leicester made *Prospect V-III* public by using regionally familiar forms, by locating it on the accessible grounds of Frostburg State College, and by using interactive elements such as walkways; Leicester, as does Heizer, encourages audiences to experience his art physically. But *Prospect V-III* is also grounded in Frostburg's social and political specifics: "To make public art that means something to the public," says Leicester, "you need to work with historical themes and with the community, in addition to working with the formal, sculptural, and architectural aspects of place and environment." Conducting extensive interviews with area miners, Leicester incorporated many of the objects they gave him—picks, shovels, lunch pails, union posters, photographs—directly into the sculpture. "The longer I worked on the project," says Leicester, "the deeper grew my understanding of the mining community. There was a real interaction between my work and the people, even to the point where I changed some of my concepts on account of things miners told me."[67]

But Leicester also maintained his critical point of view. When arts council members objected to his inclusion of black lung imagery, he refused to remove it. The conflict was resolved when members of the community backed him, as Leicester recalls:

> I refused to take out the imagery and the committee told me I had to.
> Then what happened was the coal mining community rallied to my defense. The miners and their families stood up [at a specially arranged meeting] and defended the imagery as part of the realism of coal mining.
> The good thing is that the conflict helped to create a bond between the community and the piece more than ever.[68]

Prospect V-III is clearly site- and community-specific public art; local enthusiasm is so strong that a citizens' group conducts tours of the site and provides for its maintenance.

Ostensibly a memorial to coal miners, *Prospect V-III* is also critical of coal mining and environmental abuse. The destructive facts of mining—such as black lung disease and union battles—are clearly pronounced, as is the sense of a landscape lost to slag heaps and mine spoils. Leicester's sculpture celebrates miners but also condemns their unnecessarily difficult lives by contextualizing corporate greed. Similarly, the walkway overlooks the natural beauty of the Georges Creek Basin but then reverses to show that landscape dug and despoiled. *Prospect V-III* is an outstanding example of land reclamation artwork that revamps an industrially abused environment, engages an audience, and initiates a critical dialogue about the factors that affected that environment and its public. Despite the urgency suggested by the recent flurry of artistic intervention in blighted spaces, this sort of critical edge seems largely absent among today's "Gaea Pioneers." Yet if eco-art is to be more than the servant of industry, it must critique the circumstances of its necessity. Land reclamation artwork must move beyond self-serving tributes to so-called primitive cultures and address the eroding circumstances of public space.

The story of *Effigy Tumuli* is the story of those circumstances, the story of several groups fighting over a piece of public space pie. Dirt bikers, environmental activists, and the land reclamation artpark crowd—Thornton, Heizer, and the AMLRC—all laid claim to around a hundred hectares of a polluted wasteland. Ultimately, claims for an artpark—actually a corporate tax dodge contemptuously disguised as modern sculpture and disingenuously posed as public art—won out. Aesthetic complicity, industrial irresponsibility, environmental crisis, and, especially, public access, were all but ignored at *Effigy Tumuli* in deference to Michael Heizer's master modern art narrative and Edmund Thornton's notions of corporate philanthropy and land reclamation. But then *Effigy Tumuli* is largely ignored by any sort of audience—it may exceed Mount Rushmore in size, but aggrandizement alone rarely translates into public trust. While this may be of little concern to those who created *Effigy Tumuli,* it is central to the sustenance of a genuine public culture. Given that Ottawa's land reclamation artpark was predicated on public intervention in the environment, Paul Smith was right: "If you can't use the land, it's abused."

CHAPTER FIVE

Raising Community Consciousness with Public Art
The *Guadalupe Mural* Project

Guadalupe, California, is a small rural town, located at the northernmost tip of Santa Barbara County. Drivers zipping along Highway 1, aiming for the surf at Pismo Beach or the Mission architecture in San Luis Obispo some 72 kilometers (45 miles) away, can cruise through Guadalupe in about ten seconds flat. After they cross the county line right outside town, they're usually surprised that the place they've just passed through is even a part of rich, Republican Santa Barbara County.

Many Guadalupe residents (approximately 5,479 in the 1990 census) want to change those impressions.[1] They anticipate the day when all those fleeting cars and RVs will slow down, take a left at LeRoy Park, and spend some time savoring one of the best things that their town has to offer: a four-panel mural depicting the histories and hopes of this primarily agricultural, and mostly Mexican American community (Figs. 48 and 49). Designed and painted by Los Angeles artist Judy Baca from 1988 to 1989, in collaboration with literally hundreds of the town's inhabitants, the *Guadalupe Mural* seems to testify to the possibilities of public art and cultural democracy in contemporary America.

Baca spent months in Guadalupe, scoping out its streets and psyche. Headquartered on Main Street in the abandoned auditorium of the United Ancient Order of Druids (a defunct fraternal club dating to

■ 48. **Judy Baca,** *Guadalupe Mural,* Panel 1: "The Founders of Guadalupe," 1988–89; acrylic/panel, 2.4 meters (8 feet) by 2.1 meters (7 feet), Guadalupe, Calif. Copyright Judy Baca.

1884), she sought out public interest and input as the essential ingredients in Guadalupe's first public artwork. "Successful integration of a public artwork requires the people envisioning what a monument should be in their town," remarks Baca.[2] To find out what that was in Guadalupe, Baca talked with everyone, with Guadalupe's movers and shakers (the postmistress, the mayor, the public health officer) and with migrant laborers and civil rights activists. "I went into the fields and took Polaroids and gave them to the farmworkers," Baca recalls (Fig. 50). "They got interested in what I was doing with the mural project and would come visit me at the Druid Temple, right down the street from all the restaurants where they ate their lunches and dinners."[3]

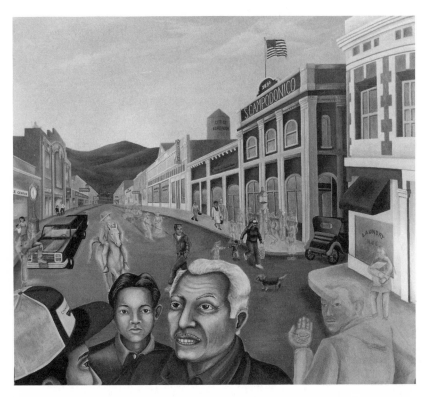

■ 49. **Judy Baca,** *Guadalupe Mural,* Panel 2: "The Ethnic Contributions," 1988–89; acrylic/panel, 2.4 meters (8 feet) by 2.1 meters (7 feet), Guadalupe, Calif. Copyright Judy Baca.

She ate her meals at those restaurants, too, in the Imperial Cafe and the Far Western Tavern and the Taco Loco. She hired teenagers from several Chicano and Filipino farm families to help collect historical information and make a town time line. She rephotographed thousands of pictures culled from local scrapbooks and school yearbooks, all loaned to the project by interested citizens and arts enthusiasts. Finally she called a town meeting and drew on the insights of a diverse audience to choose the imagery for each of the 2.4- by 2.1-meter (8- by 7-foot) panels. Hired by the Santa Barbara County Arts Commission simply to paint a mural, Baca turned Guadalupe's public art project into community consciousness-raising. "The processes of coming into, understand-

■ 50. Judy Baca in fields with farmworkers, Fall 1988. Copyright Judy Baca.

ing, and successfully mobilizing an entire community," writes critic and artist Suzanne Lacy, "are intrinsic aspects of a complex artwork, all parts of which clearly bear the stamp of Baca's socio-aesthetic intention."[4]

But in the process of creating community through public art, Baca did not anticipate how a symbol of civic pride and solidarity would also become so highly prized as an art object. Meant for LeRoy Park, in a specially designed gazebo in front of the town's community center, the *Guadalupe Mural* is currently installed at City Hall. Many Guadalupeans say that that's just temporary, until enough money is raised to build the mural shelter in the park; funds from the Santa Barbara County Parks Department to aid with the park's rehabilitation were withdrawn midproject, and residents are now raising the money completely on their own. Others feel that the mural should stay at City Hall. "A lot of people are worried that it might get damaged, vandalized, if it goes into that park," Mayor Renaldo (Rennie) Pili remarks. "They say it is so beautiful that they want it to stay here, at City Hall, where it can be protected."

Issues of agency, of how people make and remake their lives, their identities, and their sociocultural and political environments, are central to contemporary debates surrounding public art. If artists, government arts agencies, and corporate sponsors tend to devalue the dialogue and debate necessary in the development of public art, the model that Judy Baca followed with the *Guadalupe Mural* was clearly that of community engagement. Still, while she treated Guadalupe's public art process as a forum for civic dialogue, the town's focus on the mural's preciousness may have tempered its own political and public agency.

The *Guadalupe Mural* project started in 1987, when El Comité Cívico Mexicano de Guadalupe (known locally as the Comité) took on a twenty-year lease to manage and maintain LeRoy Park, a 1.2-hectare (3-acre) park and community center at the western edge of town. Located about a block off Main Street (most of Guadalupe, in fact, is concentrated in a square kilometer and a half [1 square mile] along Main Street), the park was officially under the jurisdiction of the Santa Barbara County Parks Department. Rife with spray paint and broken glass, viewed as "an eyesore and a disgrace to the county park system," the park had been more or less abandoned by both the county and the city.[5]

LeRoy Park was a teen hot spot, the place where local kids liked to socialize, drink beer, and tag some graffiti. Aside from school and church functions, there was little organized activity for Guadalupe's kids; except for the bars along Main Street and the weekly bingo game at City Hall, there weren't many places besides LeRoy Park where they could hang out. Some outsiders (especially those in Santa Barbara) suspiciously viewed LeRoy Park's youthful habitués as crack-selling, gun-toting gang members; in contemporary America, it seems, any group of kids larger than two hysterically gets labeled a gang. Most Guadalupeans laughed at the idea of local gang activity (Guadalupe has never seen any drive-by shootings or Uzi fusillades), and many rightfully bristled at racist accusations likening their Mexican American community to a rural outpost for juvenile terrorism. They knew that LeRoy Park was teen central in Guadalupe, and that some teens had contributed to its vandalism. They also knew not to confuse teen angst with gang warfare.

Members of the Comité, a nonprofit group that started in 1923 with the goal of promoting Mexican American culture and recreation, were eager to refurbish the park and the community center (built in 1955), and to provide some outlets for Guadalupe's kids. In 1980 Guadalupe's population was three-quarters Mexican, and LeRoy Park was their primary public space: the site of frequent quincenedas (traditional "coming out" celebrations for teenage girls), Sunday tardeadas (social gatherings with live music and food booths), and, especially, Fiestas Patrias (three-day festivals with parades held every year around September 16, commemorating Mexican Independence Day). Basketball games, wrestling matches, wedding receptions, and family reunions had once been common at LeRoy Park's community center, but by the mid-1980s the vandalized and deteriorating building was deemed unsafe and unusable.

The Comité aimed at cleaning up the park and building a better community center, adding an auditorium and theater, rest rooms, and dining and day-care facilities. They also wanted to have some sort of mural, a history of Guadalupe, displayed at the park in an outdoor gazebo or colonnade covering the sidewalk to the community center's front door. Seeking funds for LeRoy Park's rejuvenation, the Comité turned to two county agencies—the Santa Barbara County Arts Commission and the Parks Department. To their surprise, both pledged substantial financial support for the mural project: $20,056 from the Arts Commission and about $25,000 from the Parks Department, which also promised to subsidize LeRoy Park's predicted $400,000 refurbishment costs.

Santa Barbara County prevailed throughout the 1980s as one of America's wealthiest districts, although almost all its money was concentrated in the south—in Santa Barbara, an upscale oceanside resort with a population of about 75,000, some 104 kilometers (65 miles) south of Guadalupe. Self-proclaimed birthplace of the hot tub and the Egg McMuffin, center stage for one of daytime TV's most popular—and glitziest—soaps, host to Nancy and Ronald Reagan (whose Rancho del Cielo was just 46.7 kilometers [29 miles] away), and chockful of affluent retirees, in the 1980s Santa Barbara embodied Reagan-era prosperity and privilege. "There is little or no industry here," wrote one resident-journalist, "and everyone seems to be working, full-time, on his life-style." Not exactly everyone's lifestyle: In the 1980s Santa Barbara was also the site of one of America's "most poisonous" battles over homelessness. When the city took aggressive measures to ban outdoor camping and sleeping for the town's 3,000 or so "vagrants" and tried to deny voting rights to those without an address, homeless activists reacted by marching on the Reagan ranch and taking their case to the U.S. Supreme Court.[6] Santa Barbara's Shangri-la-la image was further tarnished by the huge Chevron derricks that were erected in the early 1980s only a thousand meters offshore, and their attendant oil spills.

Guadalupe was—and remains—Santa Barbara's antithesis. Situated in the fertile Santa Maria Valley along California's central coast, Guadalupe revolves almost entirely around agriculture. Multiple crops of lettuce, cauliflower, artichokes, and strawberries are grown annually, and the town prides itself on being "the broccoli capital of the world." In 1980 city statistics claimed a median income of $14,424, but a majority of Guadalupeans are farmworkers, and in 1988 the average annual income for a farmworker household (approximately 5.3 persons, with one primary wage earner) in Guadalupe was $13,416, or about $1,000 less than the federal guidelines that year for an impoverished household. Moreover, as anthropologist Victor Garcia discovered, in the 1980s resident farmworkers in Guadalupe (as those in California's other Chicano/Mexican agricultural enclaves) were largely displaced by migrant laborers who were contracted at much lower wages and whose numbers—and annual household incomes—were not the stuff of official statistics.[7]

Simply in terms of 1980s economics, the contrast between the two towns could not have been greater: Santa Barbara brashly embodied Reagan-era wealth and arrogance; Guadalupe—where hundreds of farmworkers tried to survive underemployment, unemployment, and low wages—showed the broader impact of the so-called Reagan Revolution. Before the *Guadalupe Mural* project, little of Santa Barbara County's wealth ever reached this northernmost part of the district; indeed, LeRoy Park's planned restoration was the first time in years that county agencies had even expressed any interest in Guadalupe's public and cultural welfare.

Guadalupe had not always been so impoverished or insignificant, as Baca and the townspeople found when they sifted through local history searching for stories and themes that might shape the mural. Located just 8 kilometers (5 miles) from the Pacific Ocean, the area was once flush with Chumash Indians, whose shell middens can still be found along the Nipomo Dunes, a 29-kilometer (18-mile) stretch of stunning coastline (with the highest beach dunes in the western United States) now managed by the Nature Conservancy. The background of the mural's initial panel shows the local dunes and features a large portrait of a Chumash hunter wearing an elaborate abalone necklace (see Fig. 48). "The Indian is an apparition," Baca notes. "You can't paint him solid, or he'll stop looking like a spirit and more like a mud monster."[8] Similarly ghostlike, a brown bear—the Chumash totem—peeks from behind. Brown bears were once plentiful in the dunes and hills fringing Guadalupe; locally they are commemorated at Oso Flaco ("skinny bear") Lake outside town, which Baca painted on the picture's right side.

The remainder of the first panel, called "The Founders of Guadalupe," concentrates on the town's Hispanic roots—and quite literally: Evoking historical links and relationships, plantlike forms leech from the lettuce fields and the adobe house in the panel's center and reach for the Chumash Indian on the left and the vaqueros (cattle handlers) on the right. Named after Mexico's patron saint (Nuestra Señora la Virgen de Guadalupe), Rancho Guadalupe was a 13,125-hectare (32,408-acre) land grant given in 1840 to Teodoro Arellanes and Don Diego Olivera, who introduced cattle to the region; Arellanes can be seen roping steers at the right. The redwood shingle–roofed adobe houses they built near the site of today's LeRoy Park were among the earliest in California, and Baca highlighted their significance in the middle of the panel. Here she also captured the local legend of two lovers—an Anglo soldier and an Indian woman—so passionately romantic they burst into flames. Baca thinks the tale probably stems from memories of John Frémont's 1846 expedition into the area, which left the Guadalupe adobes razed and the Chumash population decimated. The Arellanes and Olivera families rebuilt, but in the 1870s the ranch was sold to Teodore LeRoy, a French trader and bank agent who founded the town of Guadalupe around the original adobes and subdivided the ranch into farming plots.

In 1881 LeRoy donated 1.6 hectares (3.9 acres) of his land "for the use and enjoyment of the inhabitants of the Village of Guadalupe for recreation and healthful amusements." The deed further stipulated that the park's trustees were responsible for preventing and excluding "all riotous and disorderly persons and all conflicts and dissention."[9] Despite such provisos LeRoy Park, not unlike Guadalupe itself, was occasionally the site of violent, usually racially motivated, outbursts. One of the park's larger oaks, for instance, was called the "hanging tree" and was used to lynch several Chinese workers brought into the area in the 1890s to build the Southern Pacific Railroad. Banned from residential areas of the community, those Chinese laborers who remained in Guadalupe opened shops along Main Street and lived above or in back of their businesses.

The second panel of the *Guadalupe Mural* (see Fig. 49) tells the story of the town's diverse ethnicity and its long history of racial conflict. During the Gilded Age, Guadalupe's fertile soil attracted Chilean, English, Italian, Peruvian, Portuguese, Scotch, and Swiss-Italian immigrants who operated family farms and dairies. The railroad opened in 1901, and Guadalupe became a major center for vegetable shipping, although it was always overshadowed by Santa Maria, a town 12.8 kilometers (8 miles) away and more in the middle of the valley's numerous farms. Packing sheds and ice docks were built close to Guadalupe's rail yards, employing hundreds of farmworkers and shipping thousands of carloads of produce annually to metropolitan markets. Beet production for Union Sugar (now Holly Sugar), a large factory established in nearby Betteravia in 1897, was met by Japanese farmers who, within a few decades, dominated area agriculture.

Circumventing antialien landownership laws by purchasing property under the names of their American-born children, Japanese workers owned more than half Guadalupe's farmland and constituted more than 51 percent of the city's population by 1940. Many left farm labor and set up businesses along Main Street: H. Y. Katayama owned a successful jewelry store; Harold Shimizu managed the city's Chevrolet franchise. Setsuo Aratani (aka "The Boss") was the era's most prominent grower, and Tani Vegetables were once a dietary staple throughout California. Guadalupe's richest resident, Aratani donated several hectares of his own land in the late 1920s to the Guadalupe Joint Union Grammar School to build a baseball diamond, then sponsored a local team's tour of Asia. "Marvelous has been the sense of responsibility of our Japanese friends," boasted the priest of Our Lady of Guadalupe, the town's Catholic church, in 1936. "Towards their fellow citizens, they have been fair, honest, and sincere."[10] Yet by March 1942 most of Guadalupe's Japanese population were incarcerated at internment camps in California and Utah. Few returned to Guadalupe after the war, especially after learning that much of their property had been seized by other local growers and merchants.

Framed by a view down Guadalupe's Main Street, the second mural panel shows the Druid Temple and the Community Service Center on the left, and the City of Guadalupe water tower, Neto's Bakery, the Imperial Cafe, and the 1894 S. Campodonico building, once the town's largest general store, on the right. In the background another view of the dunes shows how they were used when silent film directors shot desert scenes for movies such as *The Ten Commandments* (1923), *The Thief of Baghdad* (1924), and *Son of the Sheik* (1926). The "City of the Pharaoh" set for Cecil B. De Mille's *The Ten Commandments*, the largest silent movie set ever constructed, was built and buried in the sands of Guadalupe; currently a Hollywood group is trying to raise funds for an archaeological excavation of the site, now littered with the remains of twenty or so giant sphinxes and several 10.7-meter (35-foot) statues of Pharaoh Ramses.[11] Fixing Guadalupe's moments of movie fame in the back of the mural panel, Baca filled the foreground with portraits of contemporary Chicano and Filipino Guadalupeans.

This second panel, called "The Ethnic Contributions," is further filled with blue-green ghosts—figures from Guadalupe's past intermingling with the town's present-day residents. The ghost of a small Chinese girl reaches out to grab the hand of a Mexican child being tugged down the street by her farmworker mom—identified by a gimme cap with a United Farm Workers (UFW) logo (Fig. 51). The ghost of a G.I. rests his foot on a red Toyota pickup. The ghost of Teodoro Arellanes rides a horse down the main street of the town he helped found. The ghost of a Druid peeks from his former temple rooftop, while next door John Perry stands in front of the NAPA auto parts store he manages. The ghost of Setsuo Aratani, holding a stopwatch dated "1942" and with a tag on his back reading "Manzanar" and "Topaz" (the two internment camps where most of Guadalupe's Japanese citizens, including Aratani, were imprisoned during World War II) gazes at the figures commanding the panel's foreground: Manuel Magana (the Comité's current head), a youthful portrait of Ariston Julian (Guadalupe's director of public health), and a farmworker (also wearing a UFW gimme cap). Other ghosts of Filipino, Mexican, and Okie descent—all of whom found farm work in Guadalupe in the 1920s and 1930s, when large-scale vegetable growing intensified—stand on street corners watching contemporary field workers, lunch boxes in hand, and Jinnie Ponce, Guadalupe's postmistress, stride to work. Mixing the blue-green ghosts of the past with figures from the present, Baca illustrated Guadalupe's racially diverse yet interlinked history, reminding viewers that yesterday's racial conflicts continue to shape attitudes and behaviors.

The elimination of Japanese workers in 1942 created a huge labor shortage, remedied for several decades by the Bracero Program (1942–1964), an "emergency" bilateral labor agreement between Mexico and the United States that brought thousands of Mexican migrants into California agriculture on six-month visas. Guadalupe's agroindustrial economy boomed in the postwar years, and thousands of braceros were employed in the fields and packing sheds, as well as in the fifteen or so area agribusinesses ranging from flower and vegetable seed processing plants to fertilizer factories. Even after the program was terminated, Guadalupe's Mexican population climbed—from 18.6 percent in 1960 to 75.0

■ 51. **Judy Baca,** *Guadalupe Mural,* detail Panel 2: "The Ethnic Contributions."
Copyright Judy Baca.

percent in 1980 and 83.0 percent in 1990—as farmworkers flowed into the area in search of jobs. During the bracero era they had often lived in labor camps provided by the growers; when the program ended the city of Guadalupe saw massive Mexican settlement, and white flight to newer housing developments in nearby Santa Maria. With only a handful of growers and agribusinesses owning most of the farmland, Guadalupe in a sense became a bedroom community for the region's farm laborers. The mural's third panel, "The Farmworkers of Guadalupe" (Fig. 52), focuses on the Mexicans—and also the numerous Filipinos—who came to work in the vegetable fields and remained to live in town.

It shows a typical cauliflower harvest crew organized around a mobile field apparatus—a gigantic machine that facilitates the cutting, bagging, packing, and loading of vegetables. Starting in the 1950s growers had turned to field packing, a process of harvesting and packing vegetables in the field, which eliminates the need for packing sheds and their crews. Each season huge field-packing apparatuses enter the Santa Maria

■ 52. **Judy Baca,** *Guadalupe Mural,* Panel 3: "The Farmworkers of Guadalupe," 1988–89; acrylic/panel, 2.4 meters (8 feet) by 2.1 meters (7 feet), Guadalupe, Calif. Copyright Judy Baca.

Valley. Cutters—mostly men—walk in back of an apparatus, which is pulled across the fields by a tractor. They cut, trim, and toss cauliflower heads onto the conveyor belt, where baggers—mostly female—wrap them in plastic bags marked with company logos. They usually bag twenty to twenty-five heads per minute. Packers behind them grab the plastic-wrapped heads and place them in cartons, assembled by one worker and loaded onto pallets by another. In this panel the packers and loaders, and the tractor, are obscured by the rows of cauliflower cartons, often stacked twelve high.

In the picture's background lush acres of harvest-ready vegetables bump up against Guadalupe's hills, while farmworkers up front place cauliflower heads onto an endless blue belt. A female worker on the right wears a red bandanna decorated with symbols of the Virgin of Guadalupe. Above these views Baca painted an enormous orange arch, a rolling conveyor with six old-style wooden crates (replaced in today's fields by waterproof cardboard cartons). Each crate has a colorful picture postcard–like label with a typical scene from a Guadalupe farmworker's daily life. Each has a cheerful "greeting," the visualization, says Baca, of the "Mexican radio voice," the booming, cheesy speech that bellows from the border radio stations that many field workers tune in to when they get off work.

"Bienvenidos" ("Welcome") shows the typical farmworker's arrival in town after hopping a freight, bedroll and belongings in tow; "Vivienda" ("Accommodations") shows the overcrowded and unsanitary conditions of migrant housing; "El Sueldo" (loosely translated as "Wages") shows a picker sweating pennies from a handful of freshly harvested strawberries; "Neblina Peligrosa" ("Dangerous Fog") shows the toxic pesticides and fertilizers that helped generate Guadalupe's agricultural bonanza but now dangerously affect the health of farmworkers—and of the whole town; "Dolor de la Espalda" ("Back Pain") shows the backbreaking stoop-and-cut labor of lettuce picking; and "Ayuda Extranjera" (literally translated as "Foreign Aid") shows the farmworker writing a letter and sending a money order—probably most of his wages—to his family in Mexico. Most of Guadalupe's cauliflower and broccoli crews are resident farmworkers, but lettuce, strawberry, and artichoke crews consist of migrants who move from one harvest site to the next throughout Central California and claim Mexico as their home.

Despite local grumbling today that Cesar Chavez "just couldn't organize farm labor" in Guadalupe, in the 1970s resident farmworkers saw better pay and improved working conditions as a result of UFW activism in the area. In the recessionary 1980s, however, growers fought the financial (and political) impact of such union success with agribusiness contractors, who organized migratory crews of undocumented, minimum-wage, workers. This, and the total shift to field packing (the last of Guadalupe's packing sheds was torn down in the early 1980s) so dramatically affected the local economy that by the mid-1980s the once flourishing City of Guadalupe was suffering serious economic blight. Today more crops than ever are harvested in the Santa Maria Valley, but less agricultural work has become available for resident farmworkers, Guadalupe's majority population. Dependent on, yet displaced from

■ 53. **Judy Baca**, *Guadalupe Mural*, Panel 4: "The Future of Guadalupe," 1988–89; acrylic/panel, 2.4 meters (8 feet) by 2.1 meters (7 feet), Guadalupe, Calif. Copyright Judy Baca.

farm labor, Guadalupe's resident farmworkers now work sporadically, and for significantly lower wages than a decade ago, as "reserve labor" when contractor-hired migrants are unavailable. Still committed to the value and integrity of "hard work," they supplement their incomes at area fast-food restaurants and Wal-Marts and speak harshly of those "who can work but prefer to go on government-relief."[12] Still committed to American promises of opportunity and equality, they dream of a better future for their families and their community.

The *Guadalupe Mural*'s fourth panel (Fig. 53), titled "The Future of Guadalupe," depicts those dreams. It is dominated by a female angel, copied from one of the large nineteenth-century marble tombstones still

■ 54. **Rod Rolle,** *Strawberry Field of Dreams,* 1988. Photo of female farmworker with baby in field. Photo: Rod Rolle.

standing in the Guadalupe Cemetery. Perched amid that cemetery, her body is circled by symbols of plenty and privation, by scenes of Guadalupe's lush fields and its dilapidated shacks—rough wooden huts built for migrant laborers in the 1920s and still inhabited. Her real-life counterpart, a female farmworker with a baby firmly snuggled to her back, is seen at the left of the panel, stooping and cutting an infinite loop of verdant crops. Field conditions are extremely dangerous—workers tell of losing fingers and limbs, of being dusted by pesticides and getting bad headaches and rashes—but, without adequate day-care opportunities or the money to pay for sitters, many women must bring their babies to the fields (Fig. 54). Making direct eye contact with the viewer, the angel beckons us into Guadalupe's world. Her hands spill an inviting stream of unpolluted water, a symbol of nourishment indicative of Guadalupe's bounty and potential.

Guadalupe's angel spreads her wings over the town, its seemingly endless and unchanging cycle of harvest, farm work, and poor housing at her feet. Her ancillary wings picture the dreams of the female farm-worker, dreams shared by all Guadalupeans: affordable health care, improved living conditions, better schools, a healthy environment. Each wing shows a specific scene: a doctor listening to the heartbeat of a farm-worker; a planned residential community; a boy kicking a soccer ball at a new high school; a tern and several otters—some of the area's rare and endangered animals—thriving at the Nipomo Dunes. Like the other panels, the mural's final picture features specific local details—Guadalupe's hills in the background, its cemetery in the center, its fields and shacks—that ground those dreams in the reality of local circumstances. Guadalupe's future is not, in other words, Baca's vision of a utopian ideal but a hopeful possibility stimulated by personal and public desires for civic revitalization and community agency.

In each of the mural's four panels, Baca drew on specific formal devices that help the audience become hooked into her social and political agenda. Each panel is large and brightly colored, with a central compositional focus that draws viewers into scenes of Guadalupe past, present, and future. Three of the four panels are structured with dominant foreground figures (the Chumash Indian, Manuel Magana, the female farm-worker) who help guide viewers to look deeper in. The final panel is missing that foregrounded formal element (the angel occupies a middle-ground position), perhaps because Baca wanted to encourage viewers to guide themselves through the picture and personally consider the social and political action required to create Guadalupe's future.

Colored, of course, by public input, the fourth mural panel was also shaped by Baca's analysis of Guadalupe's recent history. In 1970 Mexicans and Mexican Americans made up over 66 percent of Guadalupe's population, yet the police force, city government, and school board were primarily Anglo. Racial tensions heated up as angry parents confronted the school board about the segregation of Mexican and Anglo pupils, the excessive use of corporal punishment for Mexican students, the paucity of Spanish-speaking teachers and bilingual education, and the fact that 100 percent of the students in special education classes were of Mexican ancestry. Ariston Julian, who went to Guadalupe's junior high in the 1960s, recalls teachers telling the children of local growers "to sit up front and lead the rest of the class, because they would lead the community when they grew up."

Anger boiled over in 1972, when students walked out of school protesting conditions and when, at a PTA meeting a few months later, ten people were arrested for "disturbing a public meeting." Police reports reveal that the arrests were motivated by fears that "radical" UFW and Brown Beret activists had linked arms with Mexican parents to take over the school, and maybe the town. Eventually, while seven of the Guadalupe Ten were found guilty and served time in jail, the California State Advisory Committee to the U.S. Commission on Civil Rights, in a lengthy monograph titled *The Schools of Guadalupe . . . A Legacy of Educational Oppression,* concluded that the school district had indeed grossly violated Mexican American civil rights, and superintendent Kermit McKenzie resigned (after forty-two years in the district).[13] Ironically, in the 1980s Guadalupe's Junior High School was named after McKenzie.

The case of the Guadalupe Ten was a turning point in the town's life. Encouraged by the success of the UFW and the growing political power of the Chicano movement, Guadalupeans pressed for significant institutional changes; by 1975 bilingual teachers and classes, for example, had been added to the district. The case pushed the town (or at least the school board) to confront its racism. It also stimulated outsider views of Guadalupe as deeply divided and debased. A "three-year investigation into alleged prostitution, drug trafficking and public corruption" led to the infamous Guadalupe Raid of 1983, when more than 130 police officers, Santa Barbara County sheriff's deputies, and DEA and FBI agents —in seventy police cars and several helicopters—stormed the town in search of whores, dope, and political payoffs. While some prostitutes and pot were uncovered, the sting of the century came off as a scene out of *Police Academy* when only eighteen arrests were made (two on outstanding traffic warrants), and most charges were later dismissed. Another raid, in 1986, led to forty-six arrests—most for illegal immigration.[14] Still, media appetites through the 1980s continued to exaggerate Guadalupe as the Vice Capital of Central California in hysterical headlines and exposés.

"Guadalupe is like other small towns," comments Julian. "Its bad reputation was enhanced by its minority reputation. There was lots of unrest because Mexicans were the new presence in an older community." Some reacted to Mexican demands for equality by reasserting their own authority—naming the junior high after McKenzie, for example. Other xenophobes alarmed by Guadalupe's swelling minority population automatically equated Mexicans with marijuana and money laundering and used those popular racist stereotypes to their own advantage; it is interesting how Guadalupe's raids always seemed to occur during the county sheriff's reelection campaign. Likewise, overstated accounts of a Guadalupe Cartel came primarily from newspapers in Santa Maria—the town's economic rival since the turn of the century. Equally sensationalized reports of Guadalupe's guerrilla gangs stemmed from outsider octogenarians chilled by glimpses of Mexican American teens "hanging out in LeRoy Park and doing god knows what." By 1988, when Judy Baca arrived, Guadalupe, once described as "the most progressive little town in Santa Barbara County," was widely considered a cesspool of criminality.[15] Worse, it couldn't seem to shake its new mean streets image: Stricken by the avarice of agribusiness and the consequences of racial struggles and racism, Guadalupe seemed to have succumbed to historical amnesia and forgotten the labor and education gains made only a few years earlier.

El Comité Cívico Mexicano de Guadalupe hoped to revive the town's civic spirit with their refurbishment of LeRoy Park, and they turned to Baca for help. Well known as a "muralist, activist, and spokesperson for the Hispanic community," Baca has utilized public art as a means to community engagement since the late 1960s, when she began painting murals in East Los Angeles. A second-generation Mexican American, born (in 1949) and raised in Southern California, Baca had experiences not unlike those of Guadalupe's resident farmworkers: "When I went into the school system, I was *forbidden* to speak Spanish. . . . In elementary school, most of the Spanish-speaking kids were treated like they were retarded and held back. I thought to myself, they're not going to be able to do this to me. I'm going to learn what they're saying." Her mother encouraged her: "Like a lot of immigrant people, she felt that education was the key if I was to avoid suffering the kind of things that she had suffered." She also encouraged Baca's pursuit of a pragmatic, socially responsible art: "My family didn't want me to be an artist because it was a crazy thing to be. What impact does your art have on real life? I think a lot of the ethic seeped into me: it's not good enough just to be an artist. . . . What does it mean to the people you live around? So in college I also minored in history and in education."[16]

Graduating from California State University, Northridge, in 1969, Baca taught school and then headed the Citywide Mural Project, a Los Angeles City Council–funded outfit that eventually produced more than 250 murals in various L.A. neighborhoods (Baca herself directed more than 150 of them). Citywide was advised by SPARC (the Social and Public Art Resource Center), which broke off in 1976 to become a multicul-

■ 55. **Judy Baca,** *Great Wall of Los Angeles,* 1976–83; overview of 762 meters (2,500 feet) long mural in Tujunga Wash Flood Control Channel, Van Nuys, Calif. Copyright Judy Baca.

tural arts center committed to "producing, exhibiting, distributing, and preserving" public art. Under Baca's direction SPARC has involved hundreds of artists and community groups in public art projects ranging from AIDS awareness exhibits to multimedia programs on drug treatment. The Great Walls Unlimited: Neighborhood Pride program of SPARC has produced 50 murals in locales from Venice Beach and Little Tokyo to Hollywood and South-Central. As testimony to the "grassroots process of public involvement" that shapes these murals, not one was damaged during the L.A. Uprising of 1992.[17]

The largest project SPARC has undertaken, and the work for which Judy Baca is probably best known, is the *Great Wall of Los Angeles,* a mammoth mural in Van Nuys (Fig. 55). In the mid-1970s Baca was approached by the U.S. Army Corps of Engineers at the outset of their reclamation of the Tujunga Wash Flood Control Channel in the San Fernando Valley. In the 1930s the corps had channelized the Los Angeles River, lining the riverbed with concrete and constructing flood-control ditches some 4.6 meters (15 feet) deep and 22.9 meters (75 feet) wide. This hardening of the river's arteries actually caused more flooding, left unusable dirt belts on each side of the channels, and divided the city into distinct ethnic neighborhoods—Chicano, African American, Asian, and Anglo. Fifty years later, blending land preservation with civic improvement, the corps began turning these channel grounds into recreation areas with small parks and bike paths. Because of her success with City-wide, Baca was hired to paint what would become the world's largest mural—4.3 meters (14 feet) tall and 762.0 meters (2,500 feet) long in the flood control channel.

The *Great Wall* is a "monumentally scaled history painting depicting the panorama of events that contributed to Los Angeles' distinctive profile."[18] A visual history of California, the mural emphasizes the role of racial minorities. Baca conceived the epic wall as a painting describing the diverse communities of Los Angeles: "When I first saw the wall, I envisioned a long narrative of another history of California; one which included ethnic peoples, women and minorities who were so invisible in conventional textbook accounts. The discovery of California's multicultured peoples was a revelation to me."[19] The San Fernando Valley, home of "Valley Girls" and a fierce antibusing coalition, was the destination of Anglos fleeing inner-city Los Angeles in the 1950s. With the *Great Wall,* Baca, who grew up in nearby Pacoima, proposed to restore to public consciousness the area's diverse ethnic and cultural history.

The content of the mural easily conveys that history. Viewed by walking or biking along a path parallel to the wash channel or by driving along adjacent Coldwater Canyon Avenue, the mural opens with scenes of prehistoric creatures in the La Brea tar pits and currently closes with pictures of African American and Chicano Olympic champions from 1948 to 1964. Chumash theology and industry dominate early mural panels, and the destruction of Native American culture is depicted in scenes of the arrival of the Spanish; a detail shows a huge white hand uprooting a native during the Spanish conquest. Colonization, Mexican rule, and the presence of Catholic missionaries continue the story. The Treaty of Guadalupe Hidalgo, by which Mexico ceded Southern California to the United States in 1848, is followed by statehood, the gold rush, massive immigration from Europe and Asia, the building of the railroad with Chinese labor, and the beginnings of woman suffrage.

Twentieth-century scenes trace the early years of the aviation and movie industries, Prohibition, and the impact of the Great Depression on

■ 56. **Judy Baca,** *Great Wall,* 1976–83, detail: "Deportation of Mexican-Americans." Copyright Judy Baca.

various ethnic groups: blacks segregated in South-Central, Indians selling their land for forty-five cents an acre, and the 350,000 Mexican Americans deported to make room for Dust Bowl refugees (Fig. 56). The 1940s are demarcated by scenes of the Japanese Fighting 442nd, the most decorated infantry division of the U.S. Army during World War II (Fig. 57), and of their families exiled to California internment camps in Manzanar and Tule Lake. Women working in factories are juxtaposed with the helmets of dead soldiers. Other 1940s panels include Jeannette Rankin, the only member of Congress to vote in opposition to a declaration of war against Japan, and the building of the California Aqueduct, which aided developers by transporting water from north to south but created a desert in the Owens Valley. The mural's final sections range from the baby boom and white flight to McCarthyism and the civil rights movement, with cultural referents to Elvis, Charlie Parker, and Big Mama Thornton. The *Great Wall* currently ends with positive pictures of opportunities found and rights gained by minorities in the 1950s and

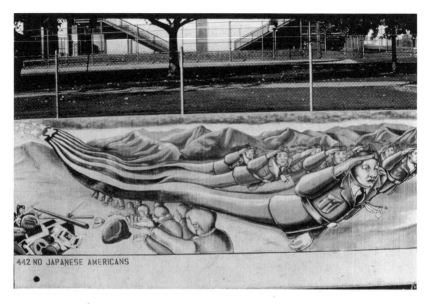

442 ND JAPANESE AMERICANS

■ 57. **Judy Baca,** *Great Wall,* 1976–83, detail: "Japanese American Fighting 442nd Regimental Combat Team." Copyright Judy Baca.

1960s, and Baca hopes eventually to include Los Angeles's recent history and project its image in the next millennium.

Scattered throughout the *Great Wall* are the names of those who helped plan and paint it. Although Baca is often given sole artistic credit for the Van Nuys mural, hundreds aided in determining its narrative structure and overall aesthetic. In addition to a handful of arts professionals and consultants, Baca recruited 215 teenagers to work on the wall during the summer months of 1976, 1978, 1980, 1981, and 1983. Treating the *Great Wall* as an educational project and a vehicle for "the rehabilitation of self-esteem," she hired kids ranging in age from fourteen to twenty-one as artistic contributors and collaborators.[20] Their ethnic and racial backgrounds varied; many were gang members or on probation. The Mural Makers, as they called themselves, received instruction in drawing and painting and were taught math skills oriented to grid making and design. Job counseling and drug therapy were also provided. Mondays through Thursdays the crews worked on the mural, completing almost 305 meters (1,000 feet) during the first summer. On

Fridays Baca arranged for university teachers and community activists to discuss ethnic history, economics, and politics with the kids. Combining their art training with ideas about cultural self-determination, the Mural Makers researched and designed much of the *Great Wall*.

Baca insisted that they be paid for their work, knowing "it not only gives them sorely needed income but also tells them their work is valuable to the community."[21] Initially a Los Angeles youth counseling group called Project HEAVY (Human Efforts at Vitalizing Youth) made its CETA (Comprehensive Employment and Training Act) monies available to Baca's teams. But in the 1980s, when neoconservative politics dominated and social service dollars were axed nationwide, salaries were paid with grants from the National Endowment for the Arts, the California Council for the Humanities, and the Los Angeles Olympic Organizing Committee and donations from local businesses. However, because of prohibitive insurance rates and a lack of dependable financing, work on the *Great Wall* came to a halt in 1983—about the same time that a similar sort of antipublic, antiethnic backlash occurred in Guadalupe.

Involvement with the *Great Wall* provided youths with summer jobs, and, equally important, as Mural Maker Todd Ableser wrote in 1983, it generated "feelings of identity and pride": "After my first year on the mural, I left with a sense of who I was and what I could do that was unlike anything I'd ever felt before. The feeling came from . . . seeing what I was personally capable of at a time in my life when my self-confidence had been extremely low." Baca is proud to tell the success stories of the Mural Makers she has guided through the *Great Wall*, which transformed not only the Tujunga Wash Flood Control Channel but also the lives of hundreds of former juvenile delinquents. Like Tim Rollins's collaboration with K.O.S. (Kids of Survival) in the Bronx, Baca's work with the *Great Wall*'s Mural Makers helped unleash potential and empower a group that many had declared irredeemable.[22]

The *Great Wall* catalyzed a tremendous feeling of group consciousness, of community, among the Mural Makers, many of whom returned year after year to work on the project. As seventeen-year-old Nancy June Avila recalled in 1983, after her first summer on the project, "There's one way to describe the worksite of people and that is we're one *Big Family* and I hope when the public comes to admire our mural they'll share the magic and emotion that our crew shared with one another."[23]

Baca's basic intention in persuading teenagers such as Ableser and Avila to revisualize California's history was to push them to confront their own racism. "The black, Asian, and Chicano communities are miles apart," notes Baca. "There's terrific geographical and cultural isolation; the people just can't read each other at all."[24] Such separatism contributes to ignorance and stereotyping, the main components of racism. To combat racism, Baca organized racially diverse crews, arranged the Friday history lessons, and used role playing and improvisational theater to unmask the dangers of racist behavior. One young Chicana started a summer declaring, "I ain't *never* gonna work with them niggers!" After working with Baca on the *Great Wall* for three months, she had changed so much that she was promoted to head an all–African American crew that was videotaping portions of the mural, an assignment she enthusiastically accepted.[25] Brought together in multicultural awareness and respect, the *Great Wall's* Mural Makers became a family, a community.

The collectivity inherent in the *Great Wall,* and in subsequent works such as the *Guadalupe Mural,* stems from Baca's insistence that a socially committed art can "break down the divisions among . . . people, give them information and change their environment." Her convictions stem from her identity as a Chicana artist and feminist. She says,

> I have been called a Spanish-speaking artist, a Spanish-surname artist, a Mexican artist (in the early '60s), a Mexican-American artist, a cultural worker (in the late '60s), a Chicano artist, a Chicana artist (during the discovery of gender), a Latino artist, a Latina artist (during the discovery of women in Latin America), an "other" (as in check one), an ethnic artist, a folk artist, a Hispanic artist, a barrio artist, a primitive artist, a neighborhood artist, a street artist, an urban artist, a multicultural artist. . . . All these terms have been coined, in essence, to define my relationship to a border my grandparents came across during the revolution in Mexico.[26]

Reclaiming the forgotten history of that bordered relationship was a central component of the Chicano movement in the 1960s and 1970s, which focused on the construction of a moral community based on collectivism and cultural empowerment. Many Chicano activists sought inspiration in a "heroic Aztec past [that] emphasized the virility of warriors and the exercise of brute force." Many Chicano artists symbolized that past in murals resonant with images of powerful Pre-Columbian deities such as Quetzalcoatl and with slogans such as "Viva la Raza," creating a gendered vision of masculine authority, writes historian Ramón Gutiérrez, that "rarely extends to women."[27]

Baca's art, as the *Great Wall* and the *Guadalupe Mural* attest, is an encompassing analysis of power and possibility based on a feminist critique of class and racial oppression. No less committed to *El Movimiento*'s vision of cultural nationalism, Baca's aesthetic employs narrative structures and social critiques to envision a broadly defined community free from both racism and sexism.[28] She follows neither an assimilationist nor an oppositional model but creates public art that addresses collectivity, honors difference, and encourages dialogue. In both the Van Nuys and Guadalupe murals, from one scene to the next, Baca offers images of diverse cultural realities and models of social change, images that "bind together disparate histories and adversarial constituencies." This is not to suggest that her public art projects emphasize a kind of broad unity that absorbs diversity. Rather they encourage a kind of multicultural tolerance. As she remarks, "In the case of *The Great Wall* the metaphor really is the bridge. It's about the interrelationship between ethnic and racial groups, the development of interracial harmony . . . there are really two products—the mural and another product which is invisible, the interracial harmony between the people who have been involved."[29]

The *Great Wall* actually engages several communities: the kids who painted it and the residents of the San Fernando Valley who see it every day. The bright coloration of the panels, the dynamic and fluid style, and the easily recognizable and evocative images demand attention. Baca studied at the Taller Siqueiros in Cuernavaca in 1977 and incorporated the painting styles of Los Tres Grandes (José Clemente Orozco, Diego Rivera, and David Alfaro Siqueiros) in the *Great Wall* and subsequent public art projects. Like the subjects of their murals, the *Great Wall*'s images are *big,* and purposely so; says Baca, "By taking a small object and transforming it into a giant image, you teach people to look at it in a different way. Claes Oldenburg knew about that. When your whole body fits into the eye of a monumentally rendered head, you are going to look at it in a way you never looked at the eye before. The same thing is true of the issues included in the mural."[30] The *Great Wall*'s style, in other words, is the principal tool used to engage and raise the consciousness of its audience.

The *process* of creating the *Great Wall* was instrumental to that consciousness-raising. Throughout the project Baca and the crews interacted with the community: giving numerous talks, conducting open forums on the mural, posting the designs in public places. Researchers tracing the history of California's minorities interviewed Van Nuys residents and presented their stories at the Friday lectures; these reclaimed

■ 58. **Judy Baca,** *Great Wall,* 1976–83, detail: "Laundry Lines." Copyright Judy Baca.

memories often worked their way into the *Great Wall.* Trying to visualize California's migration patterns in the early 1940s, especially those of Dust Bowl refugees and Japanese American deportees, Baca asked her assistants, "What did the Okies and the Nisei have in common?" One response, stemming from community conversations, was an image of laundry, and, as a result, long clotheslines of pants and shirts were symbolically used to link several mural segments (Fig. 58). Donations of paint, brushes, tools, scaffolds, portable toilets, food, and other supplies were also solicited from the community, from local schools and neighborhood groups. Baca knew that most of these materials could have been purchased, but asking the community to contribute to the project gave residents a sense of ownership in the *Great Wall* as substantial as that of the kids who painted it.

At first some Van Nuys residents feared the presence of "hoodlums" in the wash channel and attributed neighborhood crime to the Mural Makers; at one point "narcotics agents watched with binoculars to catch the marijuana smokers they were sure were there."[31] But because of Baca's insistence on collaboration between community residents and the kids in the development of the *Great Wall*, the former have come to embrace the mural as an emblem of collective identity. Local high school teachers use it to supplement (or replace) textbooks, and an informal survey reveals that those who walk along the mural or drive past it on a daily basis consider the *Great Wall* "their story, their history." The mural has had an impact, then, in raising community consciousness about the changing historical role, from dispossession to empowerment, of California's ethnic minorities. But, more significant, it has truly succeeded as Baca intended, as a "catalyst for the regeneration of the community."[32]

This is precisely what Baca intended in Guadalupe. In late 1987 the Comité asked Santa Barbara County's Arts Commission and Parks Department to help finance an original mural painting by Baca at LeRoy Park, and in January 1988 Baca made her first visit to the town. Her presentation in the gym of the park's community center, a slide-lecture on public art, was well attended by members of the Comité and county agencies, the junior high school principal, the postmistress, the head of the Guadalupe Chamber of Commerce, several city council members, and representatives from the American Legion, the Senior Citizens Center, and the Community Service Center. Convinced of civic interest, the Arts Commission and Parks Department agreed to help fund a mural project, and contract negotiations began over salary, assistance, materials, insurance, maintenance, and copyright. The problem of where to house the project was resolved when John Perry, a Guadalupe history buff, loaned the Druid Temple, a deserted building with a cavernous second-floor auditorium next door to his auto parts store. Finally, in August 1988, Baca accepted a salary of $20,056 from the Arts Commission and signed a contract promising to produce a mural for LeRoy Park. She retained copyright on the mural, and the county Parks Department agreed to pay for project assistants, materials, and maintenance. They also agreed to help with LeRoy Park's overall refurbishment—the park, after all, was an official county entity. Baca took a sabbatical from the University of California, Irvine, where she has taught since 1981, and moved to Guadalupe, where she lived (on and off) for the next year.

"What I found when I arrived in this town only three hours from Los Angeles," Baca recalls, "was amazing. . . . Guadalupe's history paralleled the history of California that I had depicted in *The Great Wall* of Los Angeles." It is not surprising, then, that Baca followed this public art model in Guadalupe, first organizing crews of teenagers to help and then orienting the project toward an examination of Guadalupe's racial attitudes and behaviors. "I'm very attached to young people," she says, "because I identify with their rebellion, the struggle they're going through. I believe that they have a future, that they are the gauge of what the society is doing . . . they are the barometer of racism."[33]

More specifically, Baca works with teenagers because she views public art as an educational enterprise, a critical forum for discussions of race, ethnicity, gender, and class. She works with kids because they are often the public sphere's largest audience: They hang out in the parks and streets where so much public art winds up, and sometimes they get in trouble in those parks and streets. In Guadalupe, Baca worked with four high school students: Mila Castro, Gabriel Estubillo, Alejandro Pereira, and Adriana Quezada. All were the children of resident farmworkers, and a few had contributed to LeRoy Park's graffiti "problem." "It is interesting working with kids who get in trouble with the law," says Baca, "because they'll know who the powers are and maybe how to beat the bureaucratic system." Relying on them as liaisons between herself and Guadalupe's figures of authority, Baca offered the kids salaries and art training. She also offered an education in empowerment.

The Santa Barbara County Arts Commission and the Parks Department were interested in Guadalupe's teens, and the entire *Guadalupe Mural* project, for somewhat different reasons. After newspapers ran upbeat articles on the *Great Wall* with headlines such as "Teenage Gangs Put Down Knives for Brushes," arts agencies around the country flocked to Baca and begged her to "bottle" her formula for deflating juvenile delinquency and cleaning up graffiti. Thinking that Guadalupe was under siege by "fierce" gangs and seeing LeRoy Park's graffiti as a sign of "alienated youth trying to take possession of its community" (which, in a sense, they were), county agencies asked Baca to redirect the town's teen spirit in a more constructive manner.[34] They saw the *Guadalupe Mural* project as an answer to vandalism and Baca as an orchestrator of graffiti abatement.

But Baca's intentions are ultimately much more revolutionary than curtailing property damage. She encourages the kids she works with, and everyone else, quite literally to take possession of their community. If arts agencies treat her mural projects (and those of other artists) as social Band-Aids, she views them as instruments of social reform. "Should public art and public good be equated? My answer has always been 'Why not?'" says Baca.

Adamantly opposed to the artist-knows-best syndrome of much public art, Baca and her student assistants began the *Guadalupe Mural* project with a critical study of the town's social context. Having spent twenty years in the public sphere, she knows the failure of imposed styles and sensibilities:

> The notion that we can impose ideas of beauty in neighborhoods, for example, could be as "colonizing" as any previous conquest of our ancestors. For inherent in this idea of Great Art from the powers that be is the belief that the people—the indigenous people—do not have a culture or traditions of their own. It is precisely this idea that made the burning of the Meso-American codexes possible 500 years ago.

Cultural imposition is hardly an Anglo monopoly: While directing the Citywide Mural Project, Baca saw some artists doing "*awful* things," such as "coming into an ethnically mixed community and, because the artist was Chicano, painting a Chicano piece with only Chicano kids." Baca's version of public art, in contrast, is that of cultural democracy, the product of a long and involved process of civic dialogue and participation.[35] Determined to avoid accusations of personal or aesthetic bias and to discover Guadalupe's own cultural autonomy, Baca spent months in town simply talking with people, collecting information and ideas.

Attending community meetings, going to church, visiting school classrooms, hanging out at dance halls on Saturday nights, spending time in local diners, watching workers jump off freight trains, frequenting the vegetable fields, calling on growers, showing up at swap meets, walking door to door, and roaming the streets, Baca met most of Guadalupe. She posted signs all over town inviting people to the Druid Temple, where she and the students conducted oral interviews and amassed historical material: old newspaper clippings, photographs, family albums, postcards, police reports. The temple itself proved a treasure trove, full of the Druids' costumes (lots of robes and paste-on beards), correspondence (terse letters about membership and dues), and the stuff of their monthly rituals (mysterious pictures of fraternal handshakes and initiation protocol). Once it had been the site of the secret ceremonies of Guadalupe's elite, a place where grown-ups played dress-up. Now the Druid Temple became the clearinghouse for a broader and more democratic consideration of Guadalupe's history and identity.

Community response was overwhelming. Asked to participate in Guadalupe's Christmas Parade in December 1988, Baca and the students decorated her car with ornaments and pinecones (Fig. 59) and rode

■ 59. Float entered by Judy Baca and students in Guadalupe Christmas Parade, December 1988. Copyright Judy Baca.

behind the fertilizer truck ("a place of prestige," she says, laughing). As the *Guadalupe Mural* project grew, Santa Barbara photographer Rod Rolle was hired to reshoot loaned materials; eventually an archive of 3,000 slides was established from the pictures that Guadalupe residents eagerly shared. In April 1989 hundreds turned out for a community portrait (Fig. 60) that Rolle shot from a cherry picker in the middle of Main Street ("Es invitado para asistir LA GRAN FOTO GUADALUPE, Sea parte de la historia," announced the posters that the mural crew distributed all over town).

After spending months without lifting a paintbrush, Baca called a town meeting and invited everyone to contribute to the mural project. More than 100 people came to the Druid Temple that night, each speaking for five minutes about their memories, experiences, and hopes for the future of Guadalupe. Older residents recalled pageants and parades, May Day picnics at LeRoy Park and fireworks on July Fourth (a holiday

■ 60. **Rod Rolle,** *Guadalupe Town Photo,* 1989. Photo: Rod Rolle.

mostly replaced in today's Guadalupe by Fiestas Patrias). They spoke of the Swiss Celebration, when thousands of Swiss Guadalupeans gathered to commemorate the founding of the Republic of Switzerland, and of the Lady of Fatima Celebration observed by Guadalupe's Filipino population each December. They told of their membership in long defunct Guadalupe clubs—the United Ancient Order of Druids, the Sons of Italy, the Japanese Association. Their stories were of Guadalupe's rich history, and much of what they remembered wound up in the first two panels of the mural.

But the dominant story that emerged that night, and in all the months of the *Guadalupe Mural* project, was of a city hemmed in on all four sides by agricultural concerns with little interest in community welfare. Guadalupeans told stories of their town's lack of housing, of families living in buses and garages, on back porches and in the fields. They talked about health care, about how farmworkers sought medical service in

Mexico because they could not afford treatment in the United States. They shared their worries about pesticides and pollution, and recalled pre-UFW labor conditions when toilets and drinking water were unavailable and work with the cortito (short hoe) caused serious back injuries. They spoke of the town's need for a high school (teens are currently bused to Santa Maria schools) and expressed their concerns about educational and recreational opportunities for Guadalupe's kids.

Careful to avoid favoritism, Baca made a point of moving "between all the factions of the city" and listened to everyone's story. She heard landowners boast of growing crops from seed to full flower in seventy days and of harvesting four to five full crops a year. She heard anthropologist Victor Garcia call Guadalupe a "farm labor camp" and explain the enormous profits growers were making, especially with the incorporation of contract labor. She heard people who harvest food tell of not having enough to eat, a story especially honed on a day near Christmas when her student crew begged off work and she discovered they had all gone to get holiday food baskets for their families from the Community Service Center. After listening to all these stories, Baca and her crew began to shape the *Guadalupe Mural*'s story.

Central to that story was Guadalupe's history of racial diversity—and animosity. As the mural project progressed, Baca discovered the town's complex caste system, driven by the relationship between grower and farmworker and further measured by the length of a farmworker's stay in the United States. As is typical of American immigration patterns, each of Guadalupe's ethnic groups encountered an entrenched political structure and bigotry; eventually most infiltrated that structure and undercut racism. Today in Guadalupe, despite the appearance of racial homogeneity in a dominant Mexican population, ethnic relationships are hardly smooth. The authority of Anglo growers, of course, has the most ubiquitous impact on that relationship, but bigotry is prevalent among farmworkers themselves. Mexican immigrants and Chicanos slur new migrants as *frijoledos* (bean eaters) and *mojados* (wetbacks), and migrants retort with labels such as *agrigando* (Mexican gringo) and *pocho* (culturally dispossessed individual).

Eschewing the polemics of blame or a condemnatory visual style that might turn audiences off, the *Guadalupe Mural*, like the *Great Wall*, focuses on the resolution of racial conflict as a step toward civic empowerment. As Baca comments:

The deep-seated social issues and problems in Guadalupe are historic, and once one understands this history it is clear how they are derived. California—not just Guadalupe—has a history, a long history, of interracial struggle. It is essentially the American problem: How do people from very different places come together, and develop some kind of respect for one another's cultures and their differences? Perhaps this has been the central theme of my work forever, and maybe will be until it's over.[36]

Clearly committed to social reform, and pinpointing racism as Guadalupe's (and America's) outstanding social problem, Baca shaped the town's public art project around that problem. Carefully illustrating Guadalupe's complex history of ethnic diversity and agricultural labor, she went beyond mere narration to critique the race, class, and gender dimensions of that history and to imagine (in the ancillary wings of the fourth panel) Guadalupe's redefined future.

A few townspeople accused her of neglecting what they considered Guadalupe's "real" history. John Perry complained that the mural "focuses so much on the race thing instead of the history of Guadalupe. The dairy industry, you know, is completely left out, and there were a lot of dairy farms around here." Hank Lawrence, Guadalupe's fire chief, objected to the seeming paucity of Portuguese and Swiss-Italian historical referents. Ken Rosene, Guadalupe's public defender and the head of the chamber of commerce, commented that some residents wondered why "so many Mexicans" were depicted in the *Guadalupe Mural*. "I didn't assume that the mural was just for the mostly Mexican population," counters Baca. "I think there's a fair presentation of all the people in Guadalupe—look at Panel 2, for instance." She also points out that "the race thing" *is* Guadalupe's history and that to assume that history and race (or history and class) are separate is to ignore the realities of American identity.

Likewise, a few people questioned the *Guadalupe Mural*'s focus on farmworkers, but Baca argues that agricultural labor has been Guadalupe's defining experience. "I got a tremendous amount of material related to the problems of the farmworkers," she says, noting that the field workers were some of the mural project's most responsive participants: "I remember one evening when a Filipino broccoli crew came after a long day's work in the fields to demonstrate the differences between historical and contemporary techniques for cutting lettuce and broccoli . . . ten Filipino workmen in my studio, gesturing while squatting on the floor, as historical slides projected in the background." Moreover, many of the Comité members who had initiated and supported the *Guadalupe Mural* project were or had been farmworkers; Manuel Magana, the Comité's president, immigrated from Mexico in 1963 and worked in the fields for several decades until an injury forced him to retire on disability. Guadalupe's resident farmworkers are, and always have been, the town's majority population, and it made sense that their stories dominate the *Guadalupe Mural.*

Mostly, though, community reaction to the *Guadalupe Mural* was (and remains) overwhelmingly enthusiastic. Baca worked toward that civic acceptance with a well-orchestrated campaign that concentrated on gaining community access and integrating the art and the process with grassroots concerns. "Be prepared, be a good citizen, and know how the power structures work," Baca advises. "And *no surprises.* Always give advance warning of what you're up to, so that people don't feel imposed upon." One reporter suggested that the Arts Commission supported the *Guadalupe Mural* because they wanted to reach out to "a small community with a multi-cultural art project that will serve people not usually touched by mainstream art programming."[37] But the impetus for the *Guadalupe Mural* came from Guadalupe itself, not from Santa Barbara County agencies that had ignored the town for decades. And this is central to the mural's local success: People in Guadalupe are proud of the mural they helped create. Concomitant with that pride is a sense of ownership and responsibility.

That doesn't mean that the *Guadalupe Mural* is typical of the upbeat, feel-good, PIM (Positive Image Mentality) placebos that account for a lot of contemporary public art—such as the cutesy bronzes that Glenna Goodacre churns out (see *Pledge Allegiance,* Fig. 6) or the colorful turds in the civic/corporate plaza created by George Sugarman and Alexander Calder (see *La Grande Vitesse,* Fig. 17). Author Nelson George writes that a lot of public culture consists of civic cheerleading rather than critical debate about public needs.[38] Baca's public art cannot, obviously, be described as art world or even civic boosterism—it raises questions and concerns rather than mouths platitudes, and it is ultimately absorbed less with itself than with its audience. Enthusiasm for the *Guadalupe Mural* can be attributed to Baca's serious and intelligent treatment of both local history and the locals: The mural doesn't gloss Guadalupe's history, and it doesn't treat Guadalupeans as one-dimensional dolts. It doesn't exaggerate or romanticize the ability of "the people" to outsmart "the system," and it doesn't underplay the very real problems of race, class, and gender in Guadalupe. It is, rather, purposely complicated by layers of visual references and social possibilities.

"If I do my job right," says Baca, "the guy walking down the street with little or no education can read it. If I do it really well, it will also appeal to the more educated person, who will see references to Los Tres Grandes, to film, and to contemporary art. And if I do it even better, the work will stand without the product—without the physical mural." The strength of the *Guadalupe Mural,* like that of the *Great Wall* and other examples of Baca's public art, lies in its ability to communicate on different levels to different people without losing its "liberatory vision."[39] School kids, resident farmworkers, migrants, growers, and art critics may all respond to the mural differently, seeing it as painting, as local history, as a visual pun, as art, as a call to action. The crates in Panel 3, for instance, show real-life minidramas and also provide biting critiques of the conditions of agricultural labor; similarly, their double-entendre labels can be read either straight or as farmworker (and grower) injokes. Yet the mural's metaphor of interracial and class struggle, and community ethos, remains embedded in all those readings. Beyond, or perhaps over and above the *Guadalupe Mural*'s compelling story and visual appeal, is, as Baca says, "the work" that went into it—the work of community building and the complicated process of cultural democracy that embodies her definition of public art.

Beyond its large scale, its beautiful jewel-like colors, and its familiar scenes, beyond its art style and subject, the *Guadalupe Mural* has been embraced in Guadalupe because it is plausibly prescriptive. Through the medium of public art, Baca convinces audiences of the possibilities of social change. She says,

> I want to convey the beauty of the farm workers . . . while at the same time revealing the harsh conditions that this surface beauty belies—the low wages, health problems, substandard living conditions. Caught up in the immediacy of their material crisis, it is often difficult for these farm workers to articulate the issues that are of concern to them, to make connections that will allow them to organize their thoughts. I am hoping that the murals will help them to do this.[40]

Baca treats public art as civic construction: "I believe public art is about inspiring. If you just go to people and give them something or make something for them, you have much less of a dialogue or a participatory

public art project. You need to inspire them, not simply give them art."
With some degree of bitterness, she also makes the comment that contemporary public art is increasingly used in ethnic and minority communities as a "colonizing device." "Public art agencies talk a lot about
multiculturalism," she remarks, "but when it comes right down to it,
they're most interested in silencing the people and keeping them quiet."
Clearly, Baca imagines a more complex public art of community engagement and civic agency. Employing "mechanisms of personal agency"
that encourage people to think and act politically, Baca tried to convince
Guadalupeans to think of themselves as active citizens—not just passive
spectators.[41]

Mayor Rennie Pili concurs that the *Guadalupe Mural* project stimulated civic dialogue, noting, "There was a lot of energy here when the
mural was being made." Ariston Julian adds that it "generated a lot of
internal thinking" and "created a new sense of community." As Baca intended, the process of creating the *Guadalupe Mural* fired public imagi-
nations. A proposal was made to develop 81 hectares (200 acres) on the
town's south side for low- and middle-income housing. Guadalupe's first
historical society was formed to house the thousands of slides that were
taken for the project and the numerous other artifacts that were collected. Several of the teens involved with the project went on to college;
one former graffiti writer is now studying architecture. Baca talked
about setting up a permanent public art studio in the Druid Temple for
future projects. People discussed selling T-shirts and postcards of the
four panels, conducting mural tours, and starting a silk-screen business
to print scarves with the Virgin of Guadalupe on them—like the one
worn by the female farmworker in their third panel. And recently other
public murals have sprouted in Guadalupe: Teacher Liz Dominguez instigated a mural painted by her students at the Mary Buren Elementary
School, and a long row of colorful scenes of local history covers a fence
at the edge of town.

Local optimism was infectious, and Guadalupe's former notoriety was
undercut by outsiders who now found the place appealing. The Nature
Conservancy proposed a youth hostel and ecology center in one of
Guadalupe's vacant buildings, and linking the town more with its activi-
ties at the Nipomo Dunes. Various Los Angeles outfits became interested
in Guadalupe's small-town scenery: GTE filmed a phone ad on Main
Street in September 1993, and Ken Rosene notes that the California Film
Council has scouted the area more than a few times—and that the 1992

movie *Of Mice and Men* was "almost" filmed in Guadalupe instead of nearby Santa Ynez. From insider conversations to outsider perceptions, the *Guadalupe Mural* project certainly reshaped the mind-set and image of the community.

If the stories of contemporary public art in Concord, Cleveland, and Ottawa (and elsewhere in America) seem to substantiate Jürgen Habermas's sense of an alienated and victimized citizenry concomitant with the model of the passive and detached public sphere, Guadalupe's public art story is that of an active citizenry engaged in a longtime, ongoing, and unfinished conversation. Indeed, Mikhail Bakhtin's concept of the "dialogic imagination" can certainly be applied to an analysis of the *Guadalupe Mural* project, which clearly demonstrated a dialogue between history, affect, and agency.[42] Baca recovered and reframed symbols and stories from Guadalupe's past (from Chumash Indians to Japanese American deportees) to make contemporary discourse about the town's interracial struggle comprehensible and legitimate. Utilizing these symbols in a particularly accessible and appealing (and often humorous) visual language, she shaped Guadalupe's public art process around a civic dialogue that encouraged townspeople to remember their past and imagine their future. Ultimately the product of innumerable (and even contradictory) conversations, the *Guadalupe Mural* mediated between the town's past history, its present circumstances, and its future possibilities.

"One of the most dangerous, condescending assumptions" about public art, writes Michael Kimmelman, "is ghettoization under the guise of public outreach—that art for lower-income communities, immigrant communities, must take the form of social activism, that the history of Western culture as presented in museums is irrelevant to such people."[43] Separating "art" (real art, the art of museums) from "social activism," Kimmelman argues that aesthetics and social change are distinct and that "art" is primarily property—the painted or sculpted products of solitary artists.

However, the real issue for the public artist committed to social reform is making an *art* of social activism that goes beyond commodification and into the realm of social change—which is exactly what Baca aimed to do with the *Guadalupe Mural*. Moving beyond the "colonizing" level at which many arts agencies treat inner-city public art—as an antigraffiti, barrio beautification device, a sort of picture-making social service that keeps juvenile delinquents off the streets—Baca created a visually compelling, finely crafted, work of "art" that embodies issues of social agency. Certainly, people in Guadalupe are entitled to "art" as much as those in Manhattan. Perhaps the more significant issue is why art world critics tend to ignore what Baca and other activist artists are up to in the public sphere. The Social and Public Art Resource Center unveils dozens of murals each year in Los Angeles, and similar arts groups do the same across the country. They are rarely reviewed in the art press. When they show up in newspapers, it's usually as the stuff of local color; when they're analyzed with any depth it's usually by urban sociologists looking for ways to quantify social change. The "ghettoization" of an art world committed mainly to issues of artistic property (such as style, quality, and, ultimately, cost) seems to prohibit the serious aesthetic attention that these public artworks deserve.

After the process of making the *Guadalupe Mural* ended, in 1990, a number of issues came into play. The first was the mural's location. In September 1993 over 5,000 people turned out in LeRoy Park for Fiestas Patrias, the largest crowd the three-day festival had ever seen. Manuel Magana and other Comité members proudly showed off the community center's new kitchen and rest room facilities, and the new bleachers and retractable basketball hoops in the gym. But festival goers didn't see the *Guadalupe Mural* in LeRoy Park. Despite the fact that Baca's contract with the Santa Barbara County Arts Commission specifically called for "a visual representation of the interracial diversity and history of the city of Guadalupe for the LeRoy Park," the mural was installed at City Hall in 1990.

Baca and architect Paul Libowicki had proposed housing the mural in a plaza in front of LeRoy Park's community center, in a semicircular adobe building with several windows. Standing in the center of the gazebolike structure, the viewer could compare the scenes illustrated in the *Guadalupe Mural*'s four panels with those outside the windows. Although their proposal was moderately priced at around $10,000, the Santa Barbara County Parks Department refused to fund it. The Parks Department had generously endorsed the *Guadalupe Mural* project by paying for materials and student salaries. But, apparently in a show of strength over park jurisdiction as the project was drawing to an end, the department withdrew funding to house the mural or to help with the park's refurbishment. Currently, funds to build LeRoy Park's intended gazebo have yet to be secured; the Comité have concentrated on raising money for the rest of the community center's restoration. "The mural wasn't made for City Hall," says Guadalupe postmistress Jinnie Ponce.

"It was intended for LeRoy Park, and that's where it should go." Baca adds that, on aesthetic grounds alone, City Hall is "definitely the wrong place" for the mural. "There is a shadow that runs across the panels there," she complains. "If they were *meant* for that place, I would have designed them for that space. But they were meant for LeRoy Park."

Most Guadalupeans agree. A few, however, look upon the four panels of the *Guadalupe Mural* as valuable art objects that need to be protected on the secure walls of City Hall. Hand in hand with the issue of where the mural should be placed has arisen the issue of its worth, or its place within a "hierarchy of preciousness," as Baca describes it. The mural itself, in other words, may now outweigh the collaborative process of cultural democracy that created it, or the community revitalization it embodies. Some of those who had heralded it as a vital symbol of grassroots Guadalupe now express grave concern for its "safety" when talk of moving it comes up. Objections have been raised about putting the mural in LeRoy Park because it might "get damaged" there by graffiti writers or vandals. Conscious or not, such sentiments reveal the depth of the town's abiding racial tensions: The few who say they want to see the mural stay at City Hall are older and more established residents; those who want to see the mural placed in LeRoy Park include Guadalupe's newer Mexican immigrants and migrant workers.

During the process of making the mural, Guadalupe's historical baggage was dragged out of the closet and dusted off. Townspeople analyzed their social and political histories and confronted Guadalupe's legacy of interracial struggle. Newly attentive to issues of race and class, they openly discussed the dynamics of their past, present, and future relationships. The mural project clearly raised civic consciousness about Guadalupe's deep-seated racial problems—which became the driving metaphor in each of the mural's four panels. But, when the process of making public art in Guadalupe came to an end, civic dialogue about race was supplanted by talk about art and about protecting valuable community property. The town's sense of personal and political agency, in other words, became stalled at a level of commodification that, writes critic David Trend, "frustrates community ethos by encouraging competitive acquisition" and demonstrations of authority.[44]

"It's ironic," says Baca, reflecting on the community's struggle to define the mural experience and find an appropriate place for the mural itself: "My dream was to have them in the park, where the people are. But they've got them in a place of protection—not the park, but City Hall. I made a mistake in making them mobile. Now they are open to appropriation by City Hall and the like because they can be moved around." Baca had hoped the process of making the *Guadalupe Mural* would inspire Guadalupeans to work toward social change ("If I do my job . . . even better, the work will stand without the product—without the physical mural"). But to chastise the people of Guadalupe for their desire to protect the physical object, the mural, that brought them together and inspired levels of personal and civic revision is perhaps unfair. The reason that the *Guadalupe Mural* currently bedecks the walls of City Hall, of course, is that the Santa Barbara County Parks Department withdrew funding to construct the LeRoy Park gazebo intended to house it—not any malevolent Guadalupe City Hall authoritarianism. Mayor Pili, as do most city officials, avidly supports putting the *Guadalupe Mural* in LeRoy Park, "where it belongs," once the gazebo has been built. And, by trying to protect the mural, the citizens of Guadalupe show they are attempting to preserve and sustain the memories of the collaborative process of community revitalization and social agency that it embodies.

Indeed, beyond the issues of placement and property value that seem lately to have dominated Guadalupe's thinking about the mural, the fact is that the process of making it provided Guadalupeans with a glimpse of their social possibilities. In *The New Populism*, community activist Harry C. Boyte asserts that a progressive and democratic public culture can reawaken "generous and hopeful instincts among the people."[45] The story of the *Guadalupe Mural* project, with its emphasis on collaborative activity, its reclamation of historical memory, and its inspiration toward civic dialogue and (re)construction, certainly substantiates this. Judy Baca helped raise consciousness and helped re-create a sense of community through the public art process of making the mural. Although it is ultimately up to the citizens of Guadalupe to sustain that newly raised consciousness and actually create the democratic and egalitarian society pictured in that public art, the *Guadalupe Mural* may well be the catalyst to that transformation.

CHAPTER SIX

Public Art and Flying Pigs
The *Cincinnati Gateway* Story

If smoke proves fire, the Western Queen will stand
First may be 'mong the cities of the land;
If human gasbags are of greatest measure,
The Western city has enormous treasure.[1]

I n April 1987 Minneapolis artist Andrew Leicester won a public art competition sponsored by the Greater Cincinnati Bicentennial Commission (Fig. 61). Leicester was selected to produce a sculptural entrance to Bicentennial Commons, an 8.9-hectare (22-acre) recreational complex being built along the banks of the Ohio River, at Sawyer Point, near central downtown Cincinnati. Scheduled for completion in June 1988, just in time to celebrate the Queen City of the West's two-hundredth birthday, the entire Bicentennial Commons project—including the Procter & Gamble Performance Pavilion, the Elijah Scott Fishing Pier, skating rinks, tennis courts, and the proposed public art gateway—was part of a $14 million overhaul and expansion of Cincinnati's riverfront park system. Built on the site of a former junk heap, an abandoned railroad yard, and the leftovers of an old canal, the winning public artwork was expected to play an especially important role as the physical and symbolic gateway to the newly refurbished park.

Members of the city-appointed Greater Cincinnati Bicentennial Commission (GCBC) insisted that the public sculpture be a lasting legacy to Cincinnati's history, and especially to her two-hundredth birthday. "They had a Centennial celebration in 1888," recalled Joseph Stern, chair of the GCBC, "and they had a great crowd, an exposition, great parties, a great show; but when it was all over they had nothing to show

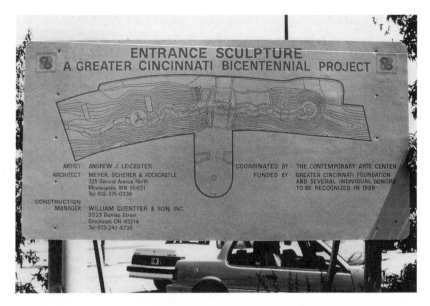

■ 61. **Andrew Leicester,** *Cincinnati Gateway,* 1988; design for Bicentennial Commons, entryway, Cincinnati, Ohio. Photo: Andrew Leicester.

for it. It was all torn down and there was a big debt. It was very important to all of us to do something permanent, so that 100 years from now it will be here for people to see." In their public art mandate, the GCBC listed the details they wanted the winning work to take into account, including "the importance of the Ohio River to the city—past, present, and future," "the importance of Sawyer Point as a site for civic renewal," and "the need to engage and entice the public into visiting Sawyer Point."[2]

Leicester's design fit like a glove. It was specifically sited to its waterfront locale and thoroughly drenched in local history, with references from Cincinnati's geological structure to the "floating palaces" that enhanced her Queen City prominence, from reminders of the city's great floods to her mid-nineteenth-century reputation as both America's hog-butchering capital and an antebellum Athens. More, in making his 146.3 meters (480 feet) long by 44.2 meters (145 feet) wide by 30.5 meters (100 feet) tall gateway, which covered about 0.6 hectare (1.5 acres), Leicester promised to incorporate the insights and hands-on expertise of

Cincinnati's citizenry, from art students to senior citizens. "The proposed work provides an emblem for the city; a gathering place and a site from which to view the river," Leicester explained. "It involves the community in its development and seeks to interact with the visitor through its use of symbols. . . . It seeks to intrigue and in doing so to impart knowledge about the city." In the concluding paragraph of his lengthy prospectus, he added, "Perhaps the most important objective of this project is to establish an interaction with the community and the individual visitor, for it is through this interaction that the work will acquire the special meaning and acceptance accorded to a true public place."

Impressed with the manner in which Leicester wove symbols of Cincinnati history into a contemporary public art design—using a reconstruction of a Miami-Erie Canal lock as the sculptural doorway to the park, for example—an eleven-member jury chose him for the Bicentennial Commons competition. Members of the GCBC supported their decision and added that they especially liked Leicester's plan to collaborate with Cincinnati's citizens. Part history lesson, part urban renewal, part civic boosterism, and part community interaction, the proposed project, eventually called *Cincinnati Gateway,* seemed the perfect public art birthday present.

Just a few months before the project was to be dedicated, however, Cincinnati went hog-wild—and all because of a quartet of life-size bronze pigs, sprouting wings. In his proposal Leicester had made it clear that his design would elaborate on several of the themes suggested in the official *Bicentennial Design Guide:* riverboats, barrels, crowns, and pigs. The sculpture's central supporting columns, for example, were made up to look like riverboat smokestacks and were linked with crown cutouts recalling Cincinnati's nineteenth-century reign as the West's Queen City. Perched high atop the tall stacks were flying pigs, reminders of the product that gave Cincinnati much of its early growth and prosperity—and its nickname Porkopolis. "I've created a 'myth of Pigasus,'" Leicester joked during a *Cincinnati Enquirer* interview in November 1987.[3]

For some Cincinnatians, however, the joke wasn't all that funny, and during the next several months the city chewed the fat over whether or not to enshrine swine at Bicentennial Commons. Local newspaper editors had a field day writing juicy headlines such as "Pig in a Poke or a Work of Art?" and "In the Sty of the Beholder," and "They Wax Po(rk)etic in Praise of Flying Pigs." Talk-show hosts spent hours pitting pig opponents and pig supporters; letter writers flooded the media;

politicians went "on record" with their personal opinions about public art and pigs. Federal magistrate J. Vincent Aug, Jr., wrote the verse "Ode to Pigasus," which included the following lines:

I've heard a recent nasty rumor

Cincinnati has no sense of humor

Now the question's grown so big

Shall we adopt the flying pig?

Is creator Andrew Leicester

Master artist or mere jester?

Certainly referencing Cincinnati's long-standing reputation as the most staid and superconservative of American cities (this is the city, after all, where *Hustler* is banned, where a Mapplethorpe exhibition was raided by the vice squad, and where Hostess Ding Dongs have been relabeled "King Dons" because of the apparent obscene overtones of their original name), Judge Aug was clearly urging his Hamilton County neighbors to lighten up.[4]

Finally, a plebiscite on pig art was held at City Hall. Largely because of the care Leicester took to invent a public space out of a devalued place, and his insistence on broad public participation in the design, development, and maintenance of *Cincinnati Gateway,* a volatile civic controversy over public art was transformed into a meaningful episode in community mobilization and participatory democracy. As an amusing, interactive, and historically informed sculpture, *Cincinnati Gateway* emerged as one public art model of a dynamic and democratic culture.

For more than a century after its civic beginnings in the 1780s, Cincinnati remained fixed along a flat, 18.1-square-kilometer (7-square-mile) basin bordered by the Ohio River 18.3 meters (60 feet) below on the south side, Mill Creek on the west, and steep hills climbing to 243.8 meters (800 feet) above sea level on the north and east. Not until the late 1800s and early 1900s, with the advent of inclined highways, electric trolleys, and cars, did Cincinnati's population flee the flats for the city's seven suburban hills. The city's industry, especially its breweries and slaughterhouses, remained crowded in the basin along Mill Creek and the riverfront, although as railroads replaced shipping, waterfront activity declined and the area became a warren of warehouses and junkyards.

Revitalizing Cincinnati's central riverfront first became an issue in 1948, when the city adopted a master plan aimed at urban renewal and public recreation. While the former quickly happened (displacing the West End's African American population to create expressways, for example), waterfront refurbishment was basically ignored until the 1960s. In that decade Cincinnati decided to "save its core" and pumped millions into downtown development, especially around Fountain Square, site of a gigantic public fountain donated to the city in 1871. Soon urban (and eventually suburban) citizens demanded downtown recreational venues, and city parents turned to the public lands along the central riverfront, building Cincinnati's Stadium and Coliseum there in 1970 and 1975. A grassy area with a serpentine wall and a concert podium, named Yeatman's Cove Park after the site where some of Cincinnati's first Anglo settlers had built a tavern, was dedicated in 1976.

Farther east remained an unsightly area of old warehouses and industrial debris, the unofficial dumping ground for more than a few downtown factories and government agencies. In the early 1970s citizens pressured the city to buy the property, clean it up, and turn it into a waterfront park and showplace; in 1972, after local philanthropist Charles Sawyer, secretary of commerce under President Truman, donated $1 million toward such a project, the city purchased the site. Arts and environmentalist groups immediately recognized the area's enormous public possibilities, and in 1977, with the aid of an NEA grant, the city's Contemporary Arts Center (CAC) displayed the designs six artists proposed for the revitalization of Sawyer Point. Ruth Meyer, CAC curator and interim director at the time, explained that the exhibition was designed "to call to the attention of the people of Cincinnati both the potential of the site itself and the potential contribution which contemporary artists can make to the design of public spaces."[5] It is interesting that the artists included Gary Rieveschl (who proposed a gigantic mound sculpture for the site), Robert Morris (who considered a rock wall design), and Andrew Leicester (who offered to screen off the "ugly jumble" of Sawyer Point's junkyard with "a visually quiet oasis"). Certainly site-specific but mostly oriented toward then current stylistic vogues (especially earthworks and minimalism), the proposals stirred some discussion but weren't taken very seriously. Sawyer Point languished through the rest of the decade.

Finally acknowledging the real appeal of the riverfront, especially as more and more Cincinnatians were turning out for Reds and Bengals games at the stadium and concerts at the coliseum (such as the ill-fated concert by The Who in 1979), the city decided to do something with the Sawyer Point site. In 1983, looking ahead to the bicentennial, the city appointed the GCBC and charged the group with turning Sawyer Point into a sports and entertainment complex with tennis courts, concert halls, playgrounds, and so on. The city agreed to invest $5.7 million in the project if matching funds could be found. Within a few years the GCBC had been promised more than $8.0 million in private donations (most of them from Cincinnati companies), including a $2.9 million trust for park operations and maintenance. When Bicentennial Commons was dedicated in July 1988, it featured, among the host of public amenities sponsored by Cincinnati's private sector, the Procter & Gamble Performance Pavilion, the Kroger Company Promenade, the Lazarus Skating Pavilion, the First National Bank of Cincinnati Skating Rink, the Josephine Schnell Russell Charitable Trust Fitness Area, the Merrell Dow Pharmaceuticals River Overlook, the Jacob G. Schmidlapp/Fifth Third Bank Adventure Play Area, the Thriftway Food-Drug Arches Overlook, and two volleyball courts gifted by United Dairy Farmers. Access to them all was gained via *Cincinnati Gateway,* initially funded in 1986 with a $300,000 grant from the Greater Cincinnati Foundation, a private organization.

Cincinnati Gateway's story actually started in 1985, when a group of landscape architects, designers, artists, and historians met in town under the aegis of the American Society of Landscape Architects and began considering ways to redesign Cincinnati's waterfront. Their agenda was to create improved pedestrian access, and simply a better visual transition, from the city's downtown core to the waterfront, somehow dealing with the two gigantic freeways (I-75 and I-71) severing the areas. Their plan called for converting Eggleston Avenue into Eggleston Esplanade, a tree-lined parkway leading from Cincinnati's Justice Center to Sawyer Point. It also called for public art—a gateway to Sawyer Point. In 1986 the $3 million urban redevelopment project (called the Eggleston Plan) was adopted by the city and included as part of Cincinnati's bicentennial revitalization package, and the GCBC were charged with commissioning an entrance sculpture.

The GCBC began by securing project funds from the Greater Cincinnati Foundation. Next, in July 1986, the Contemporary Arts Center was asked to help coordinate the public art selection process, which CAC director Dennis Barrie enthusiastically agreed to do. "I'm very much a believer in institutions such as ours being activists for public art and community," Barrie remarked, calling CAC involvement with Sawyer Point a great "public service gesture" and a terrific way for the arts center to participate in the bicentennial.[6] A contract was drawn up between the CAC and the GCBC, with the arts center receiving $18,000 of the project budget for coordination compensation.

Basically following what Barrie would later call "the tried-and-true method of the National Endowment for the Arts" approach to public art, the CAC wrote and received a $25,000 NEA grant to help with the Sawyer Point sculpture project selection process. Next Barrie put an eleven-person selection panel together ("real heavyweights," he recalled), including himself, Robert Dorsey (head of the Department of Construction Science, University of Cincinnati, and member of the GCBC), Robert Fitzpatrick (Procter & Gamble, and member of the Central Riverfront Development Committee), William Friedlander (Bartlett & Company, and chair of the Board of Governors of the Greater Cincinnati Foundation), Stewart Goldman (artist, and director of the Cincinnati Sculpture Commission), Gary Meisner (landscape architect and principal partner in Bentley Meisner & Associates, and Ohio National Trustee of the American Society of Landscape Architects), Suzanne Mitolo (director of the Miami Valley Arts Council, Dayton), Neil Porterfield (chair of the Landscape Architecture Program, Pennsylvania State University, and vice president of the American Society of Landscape Architects), Hideo Sasaki (former principal of Sasaki Associates, and former chair of the Urban Design Department, Harvard University), Robert Westheimer (associate director of the Greater Cincinnati Foundation), and Martha Winans (director of the Evanston Art Center).[7] Staff at CAC gathered information on public artists, and the selection committee nominated a diverse group of seventy-five candidates, including Vito Acconci, Agnes Denes, Jim Dine, Lauren Ewing, Nancy Holt, Robert Irwin, Andrew Leicester, Mary Miss, Robert Morris, Beverly Pepper, Jody Pinto, Martin Puryear, Gary Rieveschl, and Athena Tacha. About fifty nominees responded to the call for proposals, and the selection committee narrowed that group to nineteen; after further deliberation six semifinalists were chosen and invited to visit the Sawyer Point site. Because of the scale and the physical demands of the multihectare site, the semifinalists were encouraged to work in tandem with architects and landscape architects as they developed their ideas.

In April 1987 they presented their proposals to the selection committee, and their models and drawings were put on display at the CAC. As they made their deliberations, the selection panel members were instructed to "consider the artists' aesthetics, use of materials, experience with site projects and philosophy of the development of public space as applicable to the possibilities and limits of the Sawyer Point site." The final project was expected to "enjoy the support of the community," "require low maintenance," and be realized with the commission dollars available. Given this mandate, as well as the fact that both the GCBC and the CAC insisted that the Sawyer Point sculpture reference local history and the city's bicentennial, the selection of Leicester's design, which he developed in collaboration with the Minneapolis architectural firm of Meyer, Scherr, and Rockcastle, was no surprise. "Everyone was overwhelmingly for Andrew Leicester's proposal," Barrie noted. "We selected Lauren Ewing's proposal as second choice, but it was clearly second. The others didn't score at all."[8]

The other proposals ranged from Ewing's plan to construct a painted aluminum screen with Cincinnati scenes cut into it, to Michael Van Valkenburgh's idea of building two steel-mesh towers cum fountains. Site, Inc., proposed an entrance arch built of glass, steel, and rock ("representing the geological layers of Cincinnati") with a garden at the top. The firms of Johnson, Johnson and Roy and Scopia designed a mound bridged with a steel-mesh sculpture. And Jackie Ferrara and Paul Friedberg offered to build two wedge-shaped structures of brick and wood. Most of the proposals skirted the project mandates and, while attentive to the specifics of Sawyer Point's waterfront site, largely ignored the historical—and public—context of the commission. "The proposals were interchangeable in many cases—it could have been for Denver as easily as for Cincinnati," Barrie commented. Leicester's, by contrast, was comprehensive, creative, and quirky, completely focused on Cincinnati's riverfront history and on community participation in making and using the proposed park. "He showed us a notebook he kept of ideas and information, symbols of the city and historical subject matter, such as riverboat stacks," Barrie recalled. "The panel only had to look at the notebook to know that he understood who we are."[9] Awarded the commission in April 1987, Leicester saw his proposal undergo the scrutiny of various city agencies for six months. In October of that year, the city passed Ordinance 314, accepting the gift of an entrance sculpture to Sawyer Point whose design had met the approval of Cincinnati's Recreation Commission and the Urban Design Review Board.

■ 62. **Andrew Leicester,** *Cincinnati Gateway,* 1988; brick, steel, concrete, ceramic, bronze, water sculpture/fountain, 146.3 meters (480 feet) long by 44.2 meters (145 feet) wide by 30.5 meters (100 feet) high, entryway to Bicentennial Commons, Sawyer Point Park, Cincinnati, Ohio. Photo: Andrew Leicester.

Leicester's gateway design, like the public art project that emerged, involved the community in a number of ways and featured more than seventeen salient elements referencing Cincinnati's diverse history. *Cincinnati Gateway*'s entire structure, for example, was an enormous earthen mound, 146.3 meters (480 feet) long and on several levels (Fig. 62). From about A.D. 200 to 600, the mound builders of the Adena and Hopewell cultures made thousands of earthworks and effigies along the Ohio River, including several near the Sawyer Point site and more among Cincinnati's hills. They built a particularly large mound near Fourth Street in the West End, which pioneer Cincinnatians liked to climb for a good river view and which years later (after being flattened) was commemorated as Mound Street. Farther east, about 80 kilometers (50 miles) from Cincinnati, the Serpent Mound was built between A.D. 900 and 1200 (see Fig. 41).

Although the mound builders abandoned the region long before white

■ 63. **Andrew Leicester,**
Cincinnati Gateway, 1988; detail
of ceramic fountainhead masks
and wading pool. Photo:
Andrew Leicester.

traders and settlers arrived in the 1700s, and the mounds and artifacts they left were cut down and dug up, Leicester referenced their material culture in *Cincinnati Gateway* for several reasons. The lozenge mound shape, for example, provided a design large enough and dramatic enough to draw people to the site and channel them through Bicentennial Commons. It was also used because people standing on the ground at the terminus of Eggleston Avenue facing the entrance to Sawyer Point couldn't see the Ohio River. By fixing the sculpture on several levels, Leicester's design provided visual access to the waterfront.

Decorative embellishments on the retaining walls of the mound sculpture were inspired by the pottery and textile designs of Ohio Indians. Bronze and ceramic fountainhead masks—whose waters trickle into a small wading pool at the base of the sculpture's exterior wall—were derived from the designs on mound builder artifacts found in the Cincinnati area (Fig. 63). Several stairways make their way up and down the

■ 64. **Andrew Leicester,** *Cincinnati Gateway,* 1988; detail of serpentine stairway. Photo: Andrew Leicester.

moundlike configuration of the sculpture, their banisters recalling the curvilinear shape of the Serpent Mound (Fig. 64).

Reminders of Cincinnati's Indian cultures, these iconographic details also provided an opportunity for community input: Students at the University of Cincinnati's School of Art helped research and fabricate the masks and other ceramic models seen throughout the gateway. They were paid with project funds, and some received university credit. Throughout the project Leicester encouraged the students to experiment—to expand on their own ideas rather than simply copy found Indian objects. One student, Daniel Oates, explained: "Andrew doesn't actually make the work. Other people do that, but he's like a conductor or a director of a film. He organizes all these people and tells them how he wants it. It's a very, very different way of making art." Derek Woodham, director of the School of Art, recalls that "it was quite a good exchange. The students felt they were involved in a significant and important project." Margot Gotoff, one of seven students who collaborated with

■ 65. **Andrew Leicester,**
Cincinnati Gateway, 1988; detail of
exterior wall showing Cincinnati
Arch, wading pool, ceramic
fountainhead masks, bronze
masks. Photo: Andrew Leicester.

Leicester on *Cincinnati Gateway,* added that she considered the project "a great experience." She said, "It is nice to have something that will be there for public display."[10]

While Leicester might be accused of fraudulently appropriating and exploiting Ohio's Indian cultures, he did not pretend to replicate any of the spiritual import of the original art in the Bicentennial Commons sculpture. Nor did he try to cover up modern-day industrial detritus in a blanket of patronizing New Age "Indian" symbols. Rather he aimed to remind contemporary Cincinnatians that their history extended further than the Anglo settlements of the late 1700s by extracting visual details from Ohio's Indian cultures. He explains that he wanted to invest the waterfront public art project more completely in its historical context: "The sculpture's emphasis was supposed to be about Cincinnati over the past two hundred years; hence the bicentennial celebration. I expanded that narrow view of history by recalling the real social and cultural roots of the riverfront."[11]

Actually Leicester's analysis of local history was even more expansive: *Cincinnati Gateway*'s exterior wall, perpendicular to Bicentennial Commons, describes the city's geological structure with a design somewhat similar to that proposed by Site, Inc. (Fig. 65). The city sits on the crest of the Cincinnati Arch, an anticline of sedimentary rock. Leicester literally depicted that arch in an undulating brick wall patterned to show a cross section of the downturned strata, then dotted the wall with ceramic replicas of Pliocene-era remains and weird "fantasy fossils" that look like props from the movie *Journey to the Center of the Earth*. Again Cincinnati art students actually made these sculptural details, expanding beyond mere stylistic imitation by painting the ceramics with brilliant pigments and glazes. Beneath the brick wall, the fountainhead masks, and the fossils, Leicester designed a small seating area by the wading pool, a dropoff and pickup point for those waiting to enter or leave Sawyer Point.

Entrance into Bicentennial Commons is gained between massive, curvilinear gates 3.7 meters (12 feet) tall made of steel and concrete and covered with ceramic brick, whose scale and structure replicate the locks of the Miami-Erie Canal (Fig. 66). In the 1820s and 1830s Ohio politicians, businessmen, and real estate entrepreneurs eagerly pursued an ambitious scheme of canal projects, which would transport goods from Ohio farms to cities and link the state in a national market network. The Miami-Erie Canal concentrated shipments of goods through Cincinnati and bolstered its prominence as a mercantile exchange center, where trade in grain and hogs promoted the city's development of milling, meat processing, and brewing. First dug in Cincinnati in 1825, the canal reached Toledo (some 320 kilometers [200 miles] north) by 1840, becoming the first waterway to unite the Ohio River and the Great Lakes. Lined with slaughterhouses and other factories, Cincinnati's section of the canal extended from Eggleston Avenue to the Ohio River, a decline of 33.5 meters (110 feet), which required a flight of ten continuous locks to slow the rapid downstream flow of water. *Cincinnati Gateway*'s entryway is an accurately scaled reproduction of one of the Eggleston Avenue locks (Fig. 67), intended, Leicester wrote, "to provide a realistic feeling of the monumentality of these structures as well as dramatizing the entry into the park." The left wall of the entryway shows the route of the Miami-Erie Canal as it flowed from Lake Erie to the Miami and Ohio rivers, dropping 156 meters (512 feet) en route. Communities along the canal are listed as well. The right entrance wall delineates

■ 66. **Andrew Leicester,** *Cincinnati Gateway,* 1988; detail of entryway. Photo: Andrew Leicester.

■ 67. Miami-Erie Canal Lock doors, copied for *Cincinnati Gateway.* Photo: Andrew Leicester.

■ **68. Andrew Leicester,**
Cincinnati Gateway, 1988; detail
of Flood Column, showing high-
water marks of Cincinnati's
three major twentieth-century
floods, and ark on top. Photo:
Andrew Leicester.

Cincinnati's seven hills—Mount Adams, Mount Auburn, Walnut Hills,
College Hill, Price Hill, Fairmount, and Fairview Heights; it also serves
as a recognition wall, listing the numerous private and corporate patrons
who contributed to the Bicentennial Commons project.

The entryway leads to a circular plaza marking the end of Eggleston
Avenue and the edge of Sawyer Point. In the center of the plaza, which
was already circled with eight granite light poles and landscaping when
Leicester began the sculpture project, was placed the 30.5-meter (100-
foot) Flood Column (Fig. 68). It acts as a sort of time capsule by record-
ing the high-water marks from Cincinnati's last three major floods, when
the Ohio River crested at 21.6 meters (71.0 feet) in 1884, 19.8 meters
(65.0 feet) in 1911, and 24.0 meters (79.9 feet) in 1937, the last flood
covering over one-sixth of the city. A sculpted branch attached to the
column marks the height of the 1937 floodwaters, and atop the column
sits a miniature golden ark, a reminder of the river's significance in deter-

■ 69. **Andrew Leicester,**
Cincinnati Gateway, 1988; detail
of bridge over entryway.
Photo: Andrew Leicester.

mining Cincinnati's commercial and settlement patterns. Leicester redesigned the light poles surrounding the Flood Column, topping each
with a distinctive smokestack to illustrate the variety of riverboats that
once steamed up and down the Ohio River.

That riverfront history is further represented in the walkway above
the entrance gate. Here a bridge over the canal lock entryway resem-
bles—albeit in miniature—the bridges that river pilots once had to negotiate, including the nine especially difficult ones in the Cincinnati area
(Fig. 69). West of Bicentennial Commons, near Riverfront Stadium, is
the Cincinnati-Covington Suspension Bridge (built 1857–67), designed
by John A. Roebling and an early prototype for the Brooklyn Bridge
(1869–83). Leicester paid homage to Roebling's Cincinnati bridge (the
first to cross the Ohio River) by repeating the design of its steel cable
span in the railing of the bridge overpass. He also played with the look
of the bridge's suspension by stringing tension wires from the support

■ 70. **Andrew Leicester,**
Cincinnati Gateway, 1988; detail
of tall stacks, crown cutouts,
and fish holding tension wires
on bridge over entryway.
Photo: Andrew Leicester.

columns to huge bronze fish at the base of the columns—making it look as if the fish are being reeled in by the bridge cables extending from their mouths (Fig. 70).

The 6.7-meter (22-foot) supporting columns of *Cincinnati Gateway*'s bridge resemble the tall stacks of the typical nineteenth-century riverboat and are topped with golden crowns—and the 1.2-meter (4-foot) flying pigs that caused such a fuss. The columns are connected by colorful blue and red crown cutouts, similar to the steamship logos that were displayed on the braces linking the smokestacks on the hundreds of packets, side-wheelers, and other sorts of steamers that helped generate Cincinnati's tremendous commercial growth. These jewel-like crowns also allude to Cincinnati's nineteenth-century reputation as the Queen City of the West, an appellation coined by newspaper editor Edward Deering Mansfield and his partner in civic boosterism, Benjamin Drake, in their 1827 history of Cincinnati.[12]

The city's geographic location made it a logical convention site, and its numerous publishing firms, schools, public and private libraries, scientific clubs, literary societies, music and art academies, and bookstores made mid-nineteenth-century Cincinnati appear to be a fountain of culture amid the rough-and-tumble West. As a showcase for the arts, however, Cincinnati had a particularly pragmatic cultural edge (it still does) not untypical of the rest of Jacksonian America, which more aristocratic citizens and visitors (such as Mrs. Trollope) found boorish and graceless. Sculptor Hiram Powers, of *Greek Slave* (1843) fame, for example, got his start in Cincinnati making wax statues for Joseph Dorfeuille's Western Museum. His lifelike figures of the dying Marat and the ermine-robed empress of Russia, and his work with a larger tableau called "The Infernal Regions," which featured mechanical snakes, imps, and electrical shocks for those who deigned to touch the realistic-looking sculptures, attracted throngs to the museum throughout the 1820s and 1830s. Dorfeuille's popularity was not without its detractors: One newspaper writer, disturbed that the "enlightened people of Cincinnati delight in the horrible," commented: "Seriously, the Western Museum is a disgrace to Cincinnati, and the whole West. Such exhibitions are fit only for the barbarous ages, and it appears strange that the proprietor should find support or countenance in a city of the reputed high character of Cincinnati, for intelligence, refinement and morality." Even in the nineteenth century, in other words, Cincinnati demonstrated a certain uneasiness about its image—and about public expression and popular taste. When Dorfeuille was forced out of the Western Museum in the fall of 1838, the *Cincinnati Chronicle* heralded his departure and hoped that the museum would now become a venue of "fashionable recreation and pleasant instruction."[13]

Dollars spent on culture came from commerce: Cincinnati became a leading center for boatbuilding in the early 1800s, such that, by 1819, 25 percent of all western steamships were being built in the city. Steamboats were the primary factor in Cincinnati's reputation as the "Western Emporium," the commercial metropolis of the Ohio River Valley; by 1830 Cincinnati was the country's sixth largest city; by 1860 its industrial production was exceeded only by that of New York and Philadelphia. The central wharf—now the site of Sawyer Point—became crowded with carpenters, blacksmiths, and boilermakers; Public Landing—where the Stadium and Coliseum are now located—saw thousands of steamboat arrivals and departures every year (in 1852 alone more

than 8,000 steamers docked there). As competition increased boat owners and captains lured customers to their floating palaces with elaborate
visual come-ons and onboard amenities. Steamboats became ever more
ostentatious: high-stacked, triple-decked, gingerbread-trimmed, gaudily
colored, and often spruced up with some of the best dining rooms
(including appointments and cuisine) and musical offerings (from orchestras to calliopes) in America. Situated midway on the Ohio River,
nineteenth-century Cincinnati owed its growth to steamships and deified
them as much as Philadelphia exalted the Liberty Bell and Milwaukee
canonized beer.[14] From its tall stacks to its cutout crowns, numerous elements in *Cincinnati Gateway* celebrate all this boat-loving bravado, this
civic love of steamships that obsessed nineteenth-century Cincinnatians—and that continues to draw contemporary Hamilton County
crowds to the Showboat Majestic, a floating amusement park near
Riverfront Coliseum.

Along *Cincinnati Gateway*'s upper walkway, Leicester expanded on
this riverfront love fest with a veritable miniature golf course layout of
images and objects relevant to Cincinnati's history. At the top of one set
of steps leading to the upper walkway, a three-cornered, stepped pavilion
was constructed to symbolize the source of the Ohio River: the conflu-
ence of the Monongahela and Allegheny rivers at Pittsburgh (Fig. 71).
The triangular canopy above it represents the warning buoys used to
mark the navigable limits of the river channel. The narrow, 61 meters
(200 feet) long stream of water along the upper walkway—which itself
parallels the Ohio River—is a model of the 1,578 kilometers (981 miles)
long river and the twenty-eight dams and locks that lie between its source
in Pittsburgh and its terminus in the Mississippi River in Cairo, Illinois.
The midpoint of the river—the site of Cincinnati itself—is indicated on
the bridge above the canal lock entrance in a plaque depicting the city's
1988 boundaries and those of five northern Kentucky communities.

Along the other set of stairs, Leicester switched symbolic gears and
shifted to depictions of the actual product that endowed Cincinnati with
much of its early and mid-nineteenth-century prosperity, and with its
other appellation, Porkopolis. Here, in computer-generated imagery, or
what Leicester called a "cross between an ancient cave drawing and a
video game," was depicted a row of pigs meeting their maker along a
slaughterhouse assembly line (Fig. 72).

Hogs had been a dietary and market staple since Cincinnati's Anglo
beginnings, in part because of the abundance of acorns and nuts on

■ **71. Andrew Leicester,**
Cincinnati Gateway, 1988; detail of
upper walkway with three-
cornered stepped pavilion and
61-meter (200-foot) miniature of
Ohio River and twenty-eight
river dams and locks. Photo:
Andrew Leicester.

which they fed in nearby hills. As river transportation surged with the
advent of the steamship, larger and larger droves of hogs could be found
oinking through Cincinnati's streets on their way to the city's burgeoning
slaughterhouses. The Miami-Erie Canal along Eggleston Avenue, and
much of Sawyer Point, was lined with pig plants, which dumped so
much offal into the Ohio River that it was nicknamed Blood River.
Frances Trollope, living in Cincinnati from 1828 to 1831, spent pages
describing her "Cincinnati enemies, the pigs" in her hugely successful
1832 tract, *Domestic Manners of the Americans.* "It seems hardly fair to
quarrel with a place because its staple commodity is not pretty, but I am
sure I should have liked Cincinnati much better if the people had not
dealt so very largely in hogs," she wrote.

> The immense quantity of business done in this line would hardly be be-
> lieved by those who had not witnessed it. . . . if I determined upon a walk

■ **72. Andrew Leicester,** *Cincinnati Gateway,* 1988; detail of side wall showing pig on slaughterhouse assembly line and drawings of William Procter and James Gamble. Photo: Andrew Leicester.

up Main Street, the chances were five hundred to one against my reaching the shady side without brushing by a snout fresh dripping from the kennel; when we had screwed our courage to the enterprise of mounting a certain noble-looking sugar-loaf hill, that promised pure air and a fine view, we found the brook we had to cross, at its foot, red with the stream from a pig slaughter-house; while our noses, instead of meeting "the thyme that loves the green hill's breast," were greeted by odours that I will not describe. . . . our feet, that on leaving the city had expected to press the flowery sod, literally got entangled in pigs' tails and jawbones.[15]

Despite Trollope's disgust the number of hogs processed in Eggleston Avenue and Sawyer Point slaughterhouses increased (from 25,000 in the early 1820s to 199,000 in 1839 and 400,000 by the 1850s), and Cincinnati became the country's leading pork packer, shipping salt pork throughout the United States, Europe, and Central and South America. Porkopolis annually produced so much sausage, one 1840s visitor calcu-

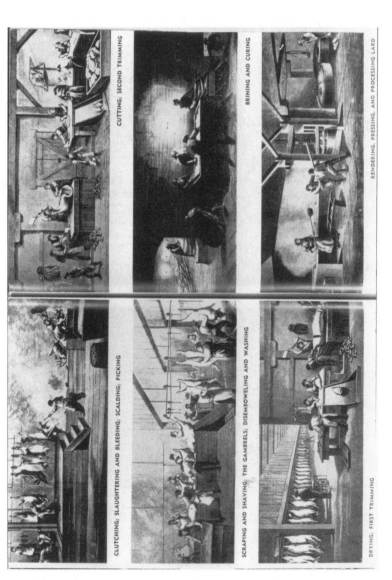

CLUTCHING; SLAUGHTERING AND BLEEDING; SCALDING; PICKING

SCRAPING AND SHAVING; THE GAMBRELS; DISEMBOWELING AND WASHING

CUTTING, SECOND TRIMMING

BRINING AND CURING

DRYING, FIRST TRIMMING

RENDERING, PRESSING, AND PROCESSING LARD

■ 73. Porkopolis pork processing, nineteenth century. Photo: Andrew Leicester.

lated, that it could "make a girdle long enough to encompass the whole globe along the line of the equator."[16]

Cincinnati's meat-processing industry employed more workers and produced more goods for export than any other in the city, with the largest forty-eight meatpacking plants employing 1,220 workers and turning out an annual product worth $3.1 million. As historian Steven J. Ross observes, the first widespread use of assembly-line and mass-production techniques in the United States occurred in Cincinnati's "swinish workshops." After being plumped up in the hills, the hogs were driven through the city's streets and into the slaughterhouses, where they were knocked unconscious, had their throats cut, and then had their bodies "disassembled" (bled, scalded, scraped, shaved, disemboweled, washed, dried, trimmed, cut, brined, cured, rendered, pressed, and processed) along well-organized and continuous production lines that made efficient use of the division of labor—and of every pig part possible (Fig. 73). Frederick Law Olmsted, whose landscape architecture firm (and then that of his sons) consulted with the Cincinnati park system from 1874 to 1915, was especially intrigued by how pigs became pork in one Cincinnati slaughterhouse:

> Walking down to the vanishing point we found there a sort of human chopping machine where the hogs were converted into commercial pork. A plank table, two men to lift and turn, two to wield the cleavers, were its component parts. . . . Plump falls the hog upon the table, chop, chop, chop, chop, chop, chop fall the cleavers. All is over . . . we took out our watches and counted thirty-five seconds from the moment one hog touched the table until the next occupied its place.[17]

Researching Cincinnati's history while developing his public art project for Bicentennial Commons, Leicester discovered that the pig and these pork-processing plants also provided the city with another source of prosperity: soap. In their first factory at upper Central Avenue—near the Miami-Erie Canal—William Procter and James Gamble rendered pig fat and grease into their earliest commercial products—candles, soaps, and cleansers, all of which made them instant profits. During the second half of the nineteenth century, Procter & Gamble led the nation in soap production, especially after introducing Ivory in 1879. The product was marketed with the slogan "It Floats" after a batch of white soap was accidentally made with extra air beaten into it and the resulting bars floated in water. Or perhaps the slogan stemmed from in-house ac-

219

knowledgment of Procter & Gamble's debt to the tons of pig parts that once floated down the Miami-Erie Canal and gave the company its start. In *Cincinnati Gateway,* Leicester honored this thrifty practicality by posing Procter & Gamble next to a few pig carcasses (see Fig. 72).

Celebrating the pragmatism of local industry and capitalizing on American culture's fascination with anthropomorphic imagery, Leicester made the pig the centerpiece of *Cincinnati Gateway* (Fig. 74). Cast in bronze and adorned with wings, placed high atop the central supporting columns of the Bicentennial Commons sculpture, stands Pigasus, symbol of Cincinnati. Like the Roman general after whom Cincinnati was named, who gave his all when asked to leave his farm and serve his country, Pigasus represents the millions of hogs after whom Cincinnati was nicknamed and who, likewise, gave their all.

Resonant with historical motifs (both humorous and more mundane) and a hands-on sensibility, *Cincinnati Gateway* is clearly an upbeat example of public art. Its visually appealing and interactive form, its amusement park atmosphere, and its archival reclamation of local history speak specifically to the Cincinnati community and more than fulfill the Sawyer Point sculpture project mandates of the Greater Cincinnati Bicentennial Commission. As he was working on the Cincinnati project, Leicester explained his view of public art: "*Contextual art* is a more appropriate term for contemporary public art. It embraces all creative works that respond sensitively to their environment. The greater the breadth of sources, the more likely a work will resonate positively within its context."[18] In order to determine and refine those sources for the *Cincinnati Gateway* project, Leicester turned to Cincinnati's public.

"I came [to Cincinnati] with no preconceptions," he remarked to a newspaper reporter in early 1988. "I let the city and its history determine the form of my work. You can't say that about the Tyler Davidson Fountain (on Fountain Square). It was made for a city in Germany." By contrast, *Cincinnati Gateway,* like the *Great Wall of Los Angeles* and the *Guadalupe Mural,* was initiated as a collaborative public art project centered on the development of community identity. "The artist chooses to make his work public by involving the public in its creation, *not* by simply putting it in a public place and observing its Pavlovian effects," Leicester says.[19] Public debate and participation are essential to his public art—a point revealed simply by contrasting the reception given his 1982 public art project *Prospect V-III,* his Maryland memorial to coal miners, with that given his 1986 sculpture *Paradise,* the Colorado prison

■ 74. **Andrew Leicester,** *Cincinnati Gateway,* 1988; detail of Pigasus. Photo: Andrew Leicester.

project that was allowed to deteriorate and was finally dismantled. With the former ongoing public participation was and remains instrumental to the sculpture's lasting civic significance; with the latter Leicester's inability to generate public participation (by being prevented from working with the inmates of the Canon City prison) created an alienating situation that led to the sculpture's actual physical demise.

Although he had made a specific project proposal to the GCBC, and had had that proposal accepted, Leicester did not develop, let alone build *Cincinnati Gateway* until after a long and involved process of collaborative research and civic debate, all of it oriented toward determining the sculpture's final look and local significance. As he explains,

> In the research period before construction, I use the media to solicit information from the general public. Besides inviting the public to be contributors towards the work's realization, this also serves to garner interest in the development of the project well in advance of the construction phase. This kind of visibility on the part of the artist helps to demystify many preconceptions that exist about artists and about public art.[20]

He began Cincinnati's public art process by conducting civic forums, describing the project and asking for feedback at library gatherings, Rotary Club luncheons, and city council meetings. He asked school groups and individuals to contribute civic and historical information, to volunteer their labor, and to donate to the project financially. Eventually, University of Cincinnati art students, senior citizens, and local designers and contractors became involved in the project. Like that of Judy Baca with the *Guadalupe Mural,* Leicester's approach throughout the *Cincinnati Gateway* project was to orchestrate the kind of public art that emerges from direct civic engagement, from democratic participation and debate in the public sphere.

An analogy can certainly be drawn between Leicester and Christo, who waged a similarly lengthy and elaborate campaign to involve the residents of Gorman and LeBec, California, and those who live in the rural communities along the Ibaraki Prefecture outside Tokyo, in his large-scale, outdoor project called *The Umbrellas* in October 1991, a campaign and a project indicative of Christo's lifework and overall goal of creating collaborative, community-based public art (Fig. 75). Yet Christo's public art projects seem especially driven by his aesthetic ideals and, while visually stunning, often bear little critical understanding of the complex historical circumstances of their locations. The 29-kilometer

■ 75. **Christo,** *The Umbrellas,* October 1991; outdoor sculpture project near Gorman and LeBec, Calif.

(18-mile) stretch of California canyon called El Tejon Pass, for instance, the stateside site of *The Umbrellas,* is near Fort Tejon in the Tehachapi Mountains, where California Indians were rounded up and imprisoned during the later nineteenth century. Millions of dollars were generated during the three weeks that *The Umbrellas* graced this terrain, as tens of thousands of tourists came to look at the temporary project, to buy T-shirts, postcards, videos, coffee cups, posters, and baseball caps emblazoned with umbrella symbols, and to think about what Christo and crew had done to the landscape. But few moments were probably spent considering what had been done in that landscape, and to whom, one hundred years earlier.

With its critical attention to local history and its emphasis on civic dialogue, *Cincinnati Gateway* is a complete contrast to *The Umbrellas.* Leicester's piece is permeated by specific historical details, and not simply for their narrative and/or visual value but because the recovery of local legends and civic deeds spurred public dialogue about the city of Cincinnati itself—its historical significance, its contemporary identity.

As a public artist Leicester is recognized for preferring multifaceted and often controversial subjects. As he says, "A kind of complexity is important to me; it gives me a chance to deal with disparity, to present a variety of sides or aspects of an event or issue." If previous public art projects, such as *Prospect V-III,* revealed Leicester's preference for iconographic intricacy, so did *Cincinnati Gateway.* The inclusion of Native American cultural details, for example, reminded Cincinnatians that their history had more depth than that suggested in a bicentennial moment. And the pig references, while not exactly motivated by animal liberation or vegan sympathies, urged contemporary audiences to contemplate the physical and psychological results of an earlier culture's fixation on profit and prosperity.

There is also, as with the *Guadalupe Mural,* a Bakhtinian sense of dialogic interconnectedness and multivalency within Cincinnati's public art project; there is "something for everyone" in *Cincinnati Gateway,* and there are multiple ways of understanding and interpreting it all. This doesn't mean the sculpture is some sort of art world version of Wal-Mart, however. It denies the pseudopopulism implied in that kind of commercial enterprise because of its authentic collaborative nature, its specific local history sensibility, and its open-ended character: Whatever *Cincinnnati Gateway* means, at any given time, is dependent upon the meaning that audiences bring to it and construct for it. Although a solid, fixed mass of brick, bronze, steel, and soil shaped into specific material culture details, as public art *Cincinnati Gateway* is constantly in flux—just as Cincinnati's public sphere is.

Leicester's efforts to engage the Cincinnati community in the development of their public art project paid off, but only after considerable brouhaha, first over project costs and second over the meaning of certain iconographic details—notably the flying pigs. Notice of his selection for the Bicentennial Commons sculpture project in April 1987 was given perfunctory local press coverage. He returned to Cincinnati in October and spent the next month or so organizing project participants, soliciting civic interest in the project, and reworking his proposal. The gateway was scheduled to be built from October through December, the slow months in the construction business, when costs are lowest. Just as groundwork was to start, however, several roadblocks went up. When it was discovered that the site rested on a 140-year-old sewer, the Cincinnati Recreation Commission and the Metropolitan Sewer District halted construction and demanded that Leicester revise his design. In order to keep the weight of *Cincinnati Gateway* off the sewer (to prevent its collapse), Leicester was told to raise the sculpture higher onto a platform built on concrete pilings. Eager to comply, Leicester learned that these revisions would add at least $75,000 to project costs. A few weeks later, when he and project contractor Bill Guentter realized that the revisions would also shift construction time to the high-cost months of spring 1988, expenses rose even further. Having signed a contract to develop *Cincinnati Gateway* for $300,000, Leicester did not want the added costs to come out of his pocket, and he asked the GCBC for help. Within a few weeks that problem was solved; Guentter solicited the donation of materials and labor from other Cincinnati tradesmen—testimony of their support for the project.[21]

These added costs prohibited a few of the project's original design elements, including a canal barge that would have been plunked down in the middle of Eggleston Avenue. Also axed was Leicester's original scheme to have a single giant pig centerpiece the sculpture. The city's Urban Design Review Board rejected this idea, claiming it would hog the view, and accepted instead Leicester's plan to put four smaller pigs atop the sculpture's support columns. On 1 November 1987, the Sunday *Cincinnati Enquirer* published a front-page interview with Leicester in which he described the revised proposal. Headlined "A Sculptor's-eye View of 'Porkopolis,'" the article featured the word *pig* over twenty times and intimated that Sawyer Point's public art project was really just the deranged joke of a demented swineherd.[22] And thus flared the public art controversy that shook Cincinnati for the next several months.

Cincinnati is, of course, no stranger to controversy—especially that involving sex and sexuality. The city's nationally known (and nationally ridiculed) reputation for moral crusading got started, critic Cynthia Carr points out, in the 1950s, when local businessman Charles Keating (later "the indicted S & L king") started Citizens for Decent Literature (later Citizens for Decency Through Law) and declared "holy war" on *Playboy*. In the 1970s the city remained gripped by antiporn hysteria as county prosecutor Simon Leis exerted his moral authority in Cincinnati's public sphere and closed down every adult bookstore and massage parlor, shut out every X-rated play (such as *Oh, Calcutta!*) and movie (such as *Last Tango in Paris*), and, winning a conviction against publisher Larry Flynt, got every copy of *Hustler* banned from Hamilton County. (Of course, Cincinnati being a river city, those who really want *Hustler* and so on can simply go across the John Roebling Bridge to "Sin City"—

Newport, Kentucky.) In the past decade Cincinnati's war on smut continued with vice squad seizures of 2 Live Crew records, right-wing religious opposition to local screening of *The Last Temptation of Christ* (which wasn't shown in Cincinnati until fourteen months after its release), and, of course, the deliberately orchestrated campaign by the Citizens for Community Values and the sheriff's department to seize and censor an exhibition of Robert Mapplethorpe's photographs at the CAC in 1990.[23] Although Leicester's sculpture didn't embody any of the sexual dynamics that have so obviously preoccupied Cincinnati for the past four decades, his satiric play with Cincinnati's civic image and historical identity and his open invitation to local citizens to become involved with the sculpture project were both at odds in a community where freedom of expression and cultural democracy have been hotly contested for so long.

Committed to community engagement, Leicester did not shrink from the controversy that the *Cincinnati Gateway* project stirred up. Rather, the civic debate spent over the flying pigs became an essential ingredient in determining what the sculpture (and Bicentennial Commons) meant to the people of Cincinnati. His immediate response to the outcry was to remark, "It's an awful indictment of a creative act to have no response." From the letter-writing campaign that ensued, it was clear that Leicester's sculpture proposal had made a pretty significant public impression. "Surely you jest!" Sue Cunningham wrote to the *Cincinnati Enquirer*'s editors. "This is a mockery of the city!" said Anne Wittekind. "Cincinnati wake up! This is an ethnic slur to me and to many others," Michael R. Patrick wrote to the *Cincinnati Post*. "I am expecting out-of-state guests in 1988 and was looking forward to showing them this lovely park. . . . But this is an embarrassment to the entire area and will make us the laughing stock of the whole country," said Marian Benz. "Pigs are not appropriate to Sawyer Point or to our image, much less a progressive image to live with in the next century," complained Milton Bortz, local hypnotist and cousin of city councilman Arn Bortz. He added, "We've got trouble! Right here in River City! Yes sir, that's trouble with a capital 'T,' and that rhymes with 'p' and that stands for *pigs*."[24]

Other Cincinnatians offered helpful suggestions about what should be seen at Sawyer Point. "Two jeweled crowns, memorializing the Queen City of the West, would be more appropriate capstones for the Sawyer Point Bicentennial sculpture—although I have seen some pigs around town from time to time," wrote William Smith. "Why not a replica of a bar of Ivory soap?" asked Henry Gill. "Why not use a sculpture of Cincinnatus and the beautiful hills," Rose Thome proposed. "Let's have flags flying—not pigs," Mary West suggested. And Gloria Orlando wrote, "If it has to be some animal atop these poles, I would much rather see the white Bengal tigers [featured at the Cincinnati Zoo]. Also, since Cincinnati is the home of professional baseball, I wouldn't mind four baseball figures atop these poles."[25]

Still others made a plea to retain the flying pigs. Joseph Stern, chair of the GCBC, reassured readers of the *Cincinnati Enquirer* that he was "confident that all aspects of our past will be embodied in the entrance sculpture in an educational and interesting manner." Elaine Reynolds said she also supported the pigs, writing, "Pigs are as noble an animal as horses, lions, elephants, etc. I am proud of our agricultural [*sic*] heritage." Paul Freshwater said, "Paris is famous for its flying buttresses, Mainz is famous for its Flying Wallendas. Cincinnati might as well be famous for its flying pigs." E. Pike Levine seconded him, noting, "The National Park Service has Smokey the Bear, the state of Michigan has its wolverine, the federal government has its eagle, Texas is known for its cattle. I see nothing wrong with Cincinnati having its pigs. P.S.: Pigs have done more for mankind than the wolverine or the bear." And Frank W. Heitmann produced this ditty for the *Cincinnati Post:*

Don't desire to hog the limelight

in this piggish Cincy plight

of porkers flying from the stacks

along the river's streaming . . . smacks

of urban flights of fancy

that really could be chancy.

Let the piglets fly on high

lest they end in a pork pie.[26]

Heitmann's porcine-inspired verse wasn't all that unique: Cincinnati's debate over the flying pigs fired up hundreds to write poems, make points with city administrators, perform scientific experiments, suggest recipes, and record songs—all about pigs. Judge Vincent Aug, Jr., wrote his eighteen-line "Ode to Pigasus." Hendrik D. Gideonse wrote the fourteen-line "Sonnet to Pigasus." Cynthia Osborne Hoskin wrote the forty-eight-line "Ode to Andrew Leicester, Porcine Elements, and Human Triumph Despite Itself." Some residents, decrying Leicester's supposed "in-swine-uation" of Cincinnati, reacted by calling City Hall, oinking into the phone, and hanging up. James Wade, a professor of aerospace engineering at the University of Cincinnati, asked students to calculate the wingspan of flying pigs. Sara Pearce, the *Cincinnati Enquirer*'s food critic, recommended a variety of pork dishes that were part of Cincinnati's culinary heritage, from braunschweiger (pork and pork liver) to cottage ham and string beans ("a most popular one-pot meal"). Bandleader Bill Walters recorded pig grunts on the B side of his single "The Blue Chip City" (yet another appellation for Cincinnati); Scott MacLarty wrote the song "When Pigs Fly" (featuring lyrics such as "No more bound by gravitation/pigs indulge in aviation") for the GCBC's New Year's Eve bash.

Political participation in Cincinnati's public art brouhaha was equally creative. Local politicos were quick to damn the "swine image" the sculpture could create for Cincinnati: Mayor Charles Luken wrote that while he recognized that part of "Cincinnati's history involved the slaughter of pigs resulting in the nickname 'Porkopolis,'" he did not "want that fact to be a highlighted portion of our history." Calling the flying pigs "inappropriate," Luken recommended that the Greater Cincinnati Bicentennial Commission "reconsider" their inclusion in the Sawyer Point sculpture. In a newspaper interview, he explained, "At first, I was willing to be patriotic and let it go because it was part of the bicentennial and I didn't want to be critical. But I think we risk a lot of embarrassment from people who come here from outside the city and see this as a symbol of the city. . . . I think most people will wonder, 'Why did Cincinnati put Porky Pig on a piece of sculpture?'"[27]

City Councilman Steve Chabot (rhymes with *habit*) got even more PO'd about the possibility of pigs at Sawyer Point. "I'm not pro-pig or anti-pig," claimed Chabot, whose previous civic cause célèbre had been the licensing of local garage sales, but his office had received "a flood of angry mail" and "an overwhelming number of phone calls" "against the pigs." (One disgruntled citizen had written, "The Cincinnati skyline is beautiful. Don't spoil it with a wino's nightmare.") Posing as the Great Populist, Chabot called a press conference at the Bicentennial Commons site and said, "This isn't something that is going in someone's private art gallery. This is going in a public place where every resident and their grandchild will have to look at it. The people should have a say on

"LEAVE THIS MATTER TO US EXPERTS..."

■ **76. Jim Borgman,** cartoon from *Cincinnati Enquirer,* 11 January 1988, showing Steve Chabot as "publicity hog" during debate over *Cincinnati Gateway.* Courtesy Jim Borgman.

whether it goes there or not." Seemingly an admirable champion of the folk, and of their right to be included in a cultural conversation of the magnitude of *Cincinnati Gateway,* Chabot probably acquired his sudden interest in public art more because of his longtime interest in Mayor Luken's seat. As Leicester observed in a January 1988 newspaper interview, "It's easy for a politician who is being criticized for pollution and unemployment—vast problems that he is probably scared to deal with—to make a platform and raise concern by picking on a defenseless pig."[28]

Of course, much of this Great Pig Debate was media driven. When Leicester defended his *Cincinnati Gateway* design by saying, "I think for me to change the pigs there would have to be a major Gallup Poll on the matter," the press was quick to oblige. Local papers, radio and TV stations, and city councilmen such as Chabot (ridiculed as a "publicity hog" in several newspaper cartoons) escalated the debate by constantly conducting public opinion polls assessing whether Cincinnatians were pro- or anti-flying pigs (Fig. 76). One hundred readers responded to the

Cincinnati Post's pig poll: 51 voting no and 49 voting yes to the inclusion of flying pigs in the Bicentennial Commons sculpture. Channel 12's on-air poll had the pigs triumphing 91 to 82. Chabot's office said "80% to 90%" of callers were "dead set against the statues." In addition to all this pulse-of-the-people attention, the local media saturated the papers and the airwaves with innumerable swine-related stories: interviewing the livestock operations manager at Kahn's, Ohio's largest meatpacker; debating the art historical origins (and copyright) of the winged pig motif; listing major pig breeds; discussing the dietary virtues of the "new white meat" being promoted by the Pork Producers Council. Soon Cincinnati's pork problem had captured national attention, with *Today* show host Bryant Gumbel asking, "Why should a city with a team like the Bengals be worried about flying pigs?" and the *Wall Street Journal* headlining an article, "Perhaps New York Would Accept The Pigs in Trade for 'Tilted Arc.'"[29] Smelling PR opportunities, Chabot mustered his political resources and, acting as chair of the Urban Development Committee, called for a public hearing on the pigs in city council chambers on 12 January 1988.

The predicted pig roast, however, turned into a resounding porcine pep rally, with the largest attendance for a public hearing since the 1976 police strike. Over two hundred people turned out, ranging from Taft Museum Director Ruth Meyer and bank CEO Bill Rowe to local artists and teachers. Most were pro-pig, and many wore pig snouts, carried piglets, and sang (à la John Lennon), "All we are sa-a-a-a-ying is give pigs a chance." Students from the University of Cincinnati carried cardboard pigs on wooden sticks with the messages "Pro-Art" and "Let the Pigs Fly" written on them, and one pro-pig protester explained, "It is not the issue of pigs being anti-Cincinnati. It's the idea of art censorship." Posters plastered around council chambers read "Don't get taken. Back the bacon," and "Swine are divine. This hearing is hogwash." Three of the five city council representatives on the Urban Development Committee wore pig hats and pig noses, and Arn Bortz put a canned ham and a piggy bank on the table. Presenting the case for the pigs, Dennis Barrie said Leicester's sculpture had "wit, harmony, and elegance," and the crowd cheered. Arguing against the pigs, Milton Bortz said, "The issue is whether the pig statues will subject our city, our businesses and our people to public scorn," and the crowd jeered. Councilman Bortz responded to his cousin by commenting, "If we're the major-league town we think we are, we need to be able to be a little more self-assured about ourselves and our place in history, and be able to laugh at ourselves."[30] Finally Chabot, who was remarkably quiet throughout the hearing (and did not wear a pig hat), polled the audience, and the pro-pig forces yelled and clapped for twenty seconds. Pig detractors couldn't produce the same response, and the hearing came to an end with *Cincinnati Gateway*'s proposed flying pigs acquitted.

"The flying pigs had captured the imagination—or at least the attention—of the masses in a way that few sculptures ever could," reporter Mary McCarty commented a few months after the hearing. "Some people hated Andrew Leicester's sculpture, which inspired another tier of people to embrace it as their emblem of civic freedom." Leicester offered the following explanation for the controversy: "There is a very up-and-coming conservative faction in Cincinnati that wants to look very groovy and modern, up-to-date and high-tech. To have these pigs must have really irked them." In some ways Cincinnati's debate over flying pigs resembled that over Dorfeuille's Western Museum in the 1830s. Leicester, however, was not forced to abandon the public art project, and the people of Cincinnati did not acquiesce to dour pockets of concern over their "image." Instead a process of public discussion was generated, highlighted by humor but accompanied by a certain degree of serious attention to issues such as freedom of expression, censorship, artistic and civic control in the development of public culture, and notions of civic identity. And eventually, as Leicester remarked, "people started saying, 'This is ridiculous, this has gotten way out of hand. There is nothing wrong with the pig.' Then there was a natural, sensible reaction and people began taking the pig in the humorous way in which it was intended."[31]

Indeed, within a few months broad public perception of *Cincinnati Gateway* shifted from civic albatross to local pride. The flying pigs were quickly appropriated for civic and commercial use—all with the full approval of the GCBC, of course, which eagerly embraced the graphic lift Leicester had provided their entire Bicentennial Commons project as the boon that it was. As GCBC member Bill Liggett remarked of the controversy, "That episode was the most fortunate thing that ever could have happened. It focused the attention of the media and the community on what we were trying to accomplish."[32]

Soon flying pigs were featured in ads for the Cincinnati Symphony Orchestra ("You'll squeal with delight") and Economy Markets ("All pork items made from 'genuine flying swine'"), and as floats in parades. Con-

■ 77. Flying pig T-shirts. Photo: Andrew Leicester.

testing the logo domination of the Cincinnati Reds, they appeared on T-shirts, coffee mugs, dish towels, beer steins, refrigerator magnets, key rings, pencils, tie clasps, and other souvenir items (Fig. 77). McAlpin's and a few other local department stores quickly sold out their "Commemorative Bicentennial Pewter Creations" of flying pig paraphernalia, which ranged from limited-edition plates to crystal bells; "this little piggy flew to market" was the ad copy for the best-selling $24.95 pewter figurine of a flying pig on a tall stack. Elmo's Bar and Grill began offering "pig wing" appetizers—pork ribs halved and marinated like chicken wings. Sales of pet pigs and plastic pig snouts boomed. Record stores couldn't keep Gene Krupa's recording of "The Cincinnati Dancing Pig" in stock. Children's story hour at the downtown public library consisted of repeated readings of *Charlotte's Web*. At their spring graduation ceremony, children at Seven Hills School sang "The Ballad of the Flying Pigs":

Porkopolis she once was called,

her slaughterhouses jammed,

with spirits of so many pigs

who gave their lives to ham.

Porkopolis, Porkopolis,

your name is ever fair,

lift up your head and now behold

winged pigs up in the air!

In perhaps the ultimate signal of public acceptance, the Myth of Pigasus was immortalized in a children's book called *A Pig Tale of Porkopolis*, featuring the adventures of a sculptor named Andrew and his pal, a flying pig.[33] More than 350,000 people turned out for the official opening of Bicentennial Commons on 4 June 1988, many drawn to the park by the controversy over the flying pigs, most entering Sawyer Point through the massive canal locks—and under the flying pigs—of *Cincinnati Gateway*.

Put simply, the pigs of *Cincinnati Gateway* appealed to Cincinnatians on a variety of levels and for a variety of reasons. But they also rendered a sense of civic identity, albeit humorous and initially (for some) unwanted. The symbol of the flying pig galvanized public response to

Cincinnati Gateway and added to the civic meaning of this work of public art. Leicester remarked, "It is the community that has decided the importance of the work. They have adopted it. It is very difficult for an artist from out-of-town to do this. The challenge, of course, is to find an image that will resonate within that community and effect people quite profoundly—and be hotly debated."[34] In Cincinnati that image was the flying pig; elsewhere it would be another symbol, another animal, another history. As Leicester points out, the real challenge in public art is to discover the symbols—the visual hooks—that will take effect in specific communities and can create some degree of heightened emotionalism. Rather than impose an aesthetic onto Cincinnati—either his own or that suggested by those who wanted to soft-pedal the city's Porkopolis past—Leicester drew on the hints and clues and emotional reactions that he received throughout the process of making this public art project. He facilitated Cincinnati's civic consciousness—its historical memories, legends, and traditions—and helped orchestrate the development of civic identity through public art. By so doing he helped to *create* community.

Clearly *Cincinnati Gateway* is a challenge to the generic, inert model of much contemporary public art. It is specifically oriented to its physical setting and its particular audience; it is acutely aware of the needs and concerns of the Cincinnati community—the needs for public space, civic dialogue, and historical reclamation, the concerns over image and propriety. The vociferous public debate that surrounded *Cincinnati Gateway* raised those needs and concerns, and the public sculpture itself, finally embraced as a resounding civic emblem, met them. *Cincinnati Gateway* ultimately emerged, then, as a critically attuned and intensely pragmatic work of public art.

As a result some see *Cincinnati Gateway* as being more about economic boosterism than about civic dialogue and citizen agency. True, the entire public art project was commissioned and financed by a cadre of Cincinnati's corporate elite, and the GCBC's primary objective was to turn Sawyer Point into a viable sports and recreation complex—with *Cincinnati Gateway* as the visual come-on. And Dennis Barrie's decision to follow the NEA's "tried-and-true" public art selection process led Milton Bortz and Steve Chabot—somewhat justifiably—to get on their pseudopopulist bandwagons and denounce the elitism of an art world practice of speaking to rather than talking with the people about public culture. Elsewhere the next chapter in this public art story would have been fairly predictable: The entire *Cincinnati Gateway* sculpture project would have come to a screeching halt (as in Blum's *Three Pavilions* proposal for Boulder), it would have been resituated (as in *Free Stamp*), it would have been built and then treated with civic resignation (as in *Spirit Poles* and *Effigy Tumuli*), or it would have been built and then neglected (as in *Paradise*). But because of Leicester's commitment to process, from soliciting citizen participation in the design and development of public art to encouraging citizens to shape the meaning of that art through debate and discussion, *Cincinnati Gateway* avoided the fate of some of the other projects discussed in this book. It remains well attended, well liked, and still a source of debate, as visitors to Bicentennial Commons (now attracting 5,000 people daily) continue to ask questions about the historical imagery and the cultural significance of the sculptural gateway that they pass through and walk upon.

Some chastise *Cincinnati Gateway* for being a kind of Disneyesque kitsch, an artified amusement park. They suggest that public preference for Leicester's referential, hands-on sculpture, a kind of approval which they castigate as "giving the people what they want," makes it more difficult for the works of abstract sculptors (such as Richard Serra) to survive in the public sphere. But audience response to the *Vietnam Veterans Memorial* suggests the fallibility of that argument. Likewise, specious assumptions that narrative forms of public art are not as critically informed as those of nonobjective art are undercut by less biased attention to the exact nature of that narrative in *Cincinnati Gateway*, where the historical recovery of the city's Native American past and its pigs = profits antebellum mind-set was part of Leicester's larger scheme to spur public dialogue about Cincinnati's contemporary sense of self. If *Cincinnati Gateway* resonates more with its audience than *Tilted Arc* did with its, it is not simply because Leicester created a narrative, anecdotal, and interactive work of art. Rather *Cincinnati Gateway* is meaningful and accessible because, in the words of artist Houston Conwill, it functions as a forum for "self-critique and self-renewal."[35] *Cincinnati Gateway* does not just "give the people what they want" but encourages people to imagine the social and cultural possibilities of becoming a *community*— a difficult enough feat in a town with a longtime reputation for being conservative and contentious.

In 1987 Polish artist Krzysztof Wodiczko wrote that the aim of

critical public art is neither a happy self-exhibition nor a passive collaboration with the grand gallery of the city, its ideological theater and architectural social-system. Rather, it is an engagement in strategic challenges to the city structures and mediums that mediate our everyday perception of the world: an engagement through aesthetic-critical interruptions, infiltrations and appropriations that question the symbolic, psychopolitical and economic operations of the city.[36]

Asked how he challenges the entrenched physical and ideological structures of cities in his own public artworks, which include light projections and vehicle designs for the urban homeless, Wodiczko responded that he relies on the processes of intervention and negotiation, coordinating both as he works with and challenges cultural norms.

With *Cincinnati Gateway,* Leicester followed a similar sort of approach. Treating the public art project as a forum for community dialogue and negotiation, Leicester searched for processes and images capable of evoking public engagement. Collaborative activity and symbols such as the flying pig infiltrated and interrupted public consciousness, galvanizing civic debate and activism. The essence of *Cincinnati Gateway,* with its plethora of challenging, oppositional historical referents, was to create a physical and psychological environment out of which community could be, and was, formed.

Indeed, the agenda of civic dialogue and agency initiated by Leicester in this public art project may well have provided a model for citizen activism in Cincinnati: The same community that came out to embrace *Cincinnati Gateway* in winter 1988, for example, would take to the streets in spring 1990 to protest the vice squad raid on the Robert Mapplethorpe exhibition at the Contemporary Art Center and Dennis Barrie's subsequent grand jury indictment for turning the CAC into a house of smut.[37] About two hundred people showed up in front of the Cincinnati courthouse, where Barrie went on trial that September. Even the placards they held up were similar to those that had been carried when *Cincinnati Gateway* had gone on trial a few years earlier: "Welcome to Censornati," and "Another Monkey Trial." Like the flying pigs, Barrie was acquitted. If this rejection of the moralizing agenda of the religious right is one indication of a renewed faith in the possibilities of cultural democracy in contemporary America, so too is the story of *Cincinnati Gateway.*

Public Art in Little Tokyo
Part Two

O n 22 June 1989 the Little Tokyo Community Development Advisory Committee (LTCDAC) voted unanimously to reject Barbara Kruger's proposal to paint a gigantic mural on the south wall of the Temporary Contemporary (TC), an adjunct of the Museum of Contemporary Art (MOCA) situated on the fringe of Los Angeles's largest Japanese American neighborhood. In another such scenario public art might have ended here, with the artist and anyone else involved either ignoring civic agency disapproval or taking it as a sign that Little Tokyo's public sphere was simply too contested, too problematic, to try to "do" public art. Instead Kruger and MOCA were stimulated to debate further the merits of the project with the advisory committee, to negotiate its design with the Little Tokyo community, and eventually to realize the potential of an engaging and critically attuned public art project. To open and close this book with the story of how Kruger's outdoor mural came to be made in Little Tokyo seems especially appropriate, because it is ultimately the story of public art and democratic culture.

Kruger's original proposal (see Fig. 1) consisted of an 8.8 meters (29 feet) tall by 66.4 meters (218 feet) long mural in the shape of a U.S. flag, a behemoth billboard in red, white, and blue featuring the Pledge of Allegiance and nine particularly provocative questions: "Who is bought and sold? Who is beyond the law? Who is free to choose? Who follows orders? Who salutes longest? Who prays loudest? Who dies first? Who laughs last? Who does time?" Called *Untitled (Questions)*, the mural was planned as a sign for the TC and was aimed at raising consciousness about how words and pictures—such as the pledge and the flag—affect American identity.

It was especially intended as a rejoinder to the culture wars that raged in the 1980s, as neoconservative politicians and right-wing fundamentalists seized democratic slogans and symbols such as the Pledge of Allegiance and the U.S. flag to affirm their own power and authority, and corporate America did much the same in ads linking consumerism with patriotism—such as Chrysler's "The Pride Is Back, Born in America Again" campaign and Philip Morris's equally transparent appropriation of the Bill of Rights. Yet, while "the mythology of democracy" was amplified for political and corporate purposes in the 1980s, widespread public participation in that democracy steadily declined. Among current democracies the United States has the lowest rate of voter participation. "Seen in this light," says critic Richard Bolton, "the 'spontaneous' rebirth of patriotism in the United States seems like nothing more than the *management* of citizenship."[1] In *Untitled (Questions)* Kruger challenged this neoconservative and corporate management of democracy in large-scale letters asking "who" really has control in the public sphere.

But Kruger was trying to give a civics lesson about the significance of the U.S. Constitution in what is the most multicultural of American cities. Los Angeles is perhaps the most poly-ethnic place in America— some eighty-six languages were recently counted among its schoolchildren.[2] It is a city where day-to-day survival takes precedence over abstract discussions about democracy—although the two are obviously related. And it is a city where there are no commonly held values and views about the meaning of democracy, of citizenship, of individual rights, of the concept of the state. Kruger assumed that her Los Angeles audience shared her concerns about the contemporary appropriation of democratic symbols and slogans, and that they shared as well the critical tools necessary to enter into some sort of debate about those symbols and slogans. Speaking for the public rather than with them in the insistent language of her brand of political art, Kruger privileged art world polemics over the complexities of a multicultural public sphere.

The crux of Kruger's problem—maybe the most important problem in contemporary public art—was how to make democracy meaningful in multicultural America, how to tie day-to-day struggles and differing values to the broader concept of democracy. For some the immediacy of her words-on-the-wall approach was too one-dimensional to address the complex meaning of democracy in contemporary, multicultural America. The words themselves were presumptuous and perhaps insulting: asking "Who is free to choose?" for example, implies freedom of choice, an issue that right-to-lifers and abortion-rights activists have been arguing about for decades. The anticapitalist overtones of a question such as "Who is bought and sold?" may not have gone over particularly well in a Japanese American community like Little Tokyo, currently prospering under capitalism. And asking these questions alongside the Pledge of Allegiance changed Kruger's general critique of the manipulation of democratic signs and symbols into a more specific critique (or so some thought) about the American-ness of the Little Tokyo community. While Kruger was certainly trying to remind her potential audience that freedom—whether freedom of choice or free trade—is tenuous in democracies, she assumed that they would share her concern with these moral, legal, and economic issues. As she discovered, these concerns, and even the larger sense of what America is all about, are hardly agreed upon or even definable. There is and always has been a dynamic to democracy.

It is not surprising, then, that Kruger's efforts to raise consciousness about democracy were immediately embroiled in controversy. Nationally, uncompromising racial and ethnic hostilities have overshadowed naive melting pot ideals of egalitarianism and more appealing notions of multicultural tolerance. Nor has much recent attention been given those ideals and notions—save by politicians and admen eager to appropriate a more or less "democratic" image and political artists who often have had equally self-serving agendas. And if democracy per se was an especially multifaceted (and perhaps conflicted) concept for most Los Angelenos, this was especially true in Little Tokyo—where the Constitution had been completely trounced upon some fifty years earlier.

In light of the memories that the redress movement roused of how the U.S. government had violated the civil and human rights of some 120,000 Japanese Americans during World War II, it is not surprising that the LTCDAC rejected Kruger's initial design. They read it as an insult, as malicious defamation. Posed right on the edge of Little Tokyo and framed as a gigantic U.S. flag, it seemed specifically to question the authenticity of *Japanese American* patriotism and loyalty—both in the wartime past and in the context of contemporary Japan bashing. Using the Pledge of Allegiance in a neighborhood where rights had been denied, said the LTCDAC, was inappropriate. One speaker at their June meeting observed that MOCA's mural proposal was tantamount to putting a swastika on a Jew's front lawn.

Like several of the other artists discussed in this book, Kruger interpreted the volatile reaction to the proposed mural as a vital part of the public art process. "I don't think the process started negatively," she explains. "My whole artistic life has been a series of negotiations to try to be effective. To be effective you need a reality test. The process is most important. It's a real social relationship, bringing different histories together and challenging stereotypes."[3] Since public reaction revealed that her mural proposal was not effective—at least not as she intended, as a critique of how certain words and images were being manipulated to shape the meaning of democracy in the late 1980s—Kruger was anxious to stay with the project and work it through. The museum was anxious as well, since comments at the June LTCDAC meeting revealed that many in Little Tokyo felt that MOCA was extraordinarily elitist—out of touch and seemingly unconcerned with specific community concerns and local history. On 12 July 1989 a special public meeting was held at the Japanese American Cultural and Community Center, where Kruger (who had flown out from New York), and representatives from the LTCDAC and MOCA, met with members of the Little Tokyo neighborhood, and larger Los Angeles, to discuss the proposed public art project.

At this meeting Kruger explained that her artistic practice focuses on process, the process of exchanging views and opinions. *Untitled (Questions)*, she said, was specifically intended to demonstrate the process of democracy:

> This project draws attention to the meanings of democracy and its fragile amalgam of freedom and responsibility, of pride and tolerance. I believe we must maintain a good-humored vigilance in protecting the generosities of democracy, its complexities, its intelligence, its respect for *all* the races, sexes, and economic groupings that make up our diverse cultural life. I want this project to contribute to the debate that sees democracy as an ongoing process, a *real* part of people's lives; not an empty slogan, a deep dark secret that must be kept from the people.[4]

Democracy—as a concept—is actually more freewheeling than fragile, but Kruger's point was clear: Public art, like democracy, should be the product of debate and dialogue, not an "empty slogan" and "deep dark secret" being kept from "the people." While Kruger probably didn't count herself among those keeping that secret from "the people," she and MOCA had proposed the mural without first engaging the public in any sort of debate about it and then were quite surprised at the outcry it created. Now, however, both Kruger and the museum insisted that dialogue was instrumental to the public art project.

Audience response to Kruger's comments and the proposed public art project centered on the mural's size, duration, and meaning. Some Little Tokyo residents felt that the gigantic scale of the mural might be too overwhelming. Others questioned how long it would appear: MOCA had promised that *Untitled (Questions)* was to be a temporary, two-year project since construction for First Street North, a mixed-use development that will eventually surround the Temporary MOCA building, was scheduled to begin in 1991. Several LTCDAC members worried that some future arts group might want the mural to stay up longer—thereby delaying development. They also criticized MOCA's steamroller approach to public art—the fact that no one at the museum had done the groundwork to ascertain whether an outdoor mural on the fringe of Little Tokyo was appropriate, or even desired.

But the biggest concern expressed at the public meeting was over the mural's content, specifically the inclusion of the Pledge of Allegiance. The pledge had been used as a mode of humiliation for Japanese Americans in the internment camps, one person reminded everyone. To paint it so large in Little Tokyo would be insensitive, like rubbing salt into an open wound, said another. Combined with the nine questions, the pledge seemed to suggest that democracy and patriotism were questionable in Little Tokyo. Kruger responded by saying she was open to making design changes that would enhance the mural's critical and visual effectiveness. When the LTCDAC asked if she would return in August with several alternative design proposals, she readily agreed.

In the weeks before the next meeting, MOCA staff took the opportunity to work on community relations—touching base with members of the Japanese American Citizens' League, the Little Tokyo Chamber Association, the Japanese Chamber of Commerce, the Little Tokyo Businessmen's Association, the Japanese American Cultural and Community Center, and various other neighborhood organizations, asking for their input about the project and assuring them that the mural would be temporary. The museum's efforts at engaging the community at this point in the project might be cynically interpreted as the orchestration of local opinion, and Kruger might be accused of the same by appealing to democratic process after the mural project was well under way. But both the museum and the artist now realized that Little Tokyo's concerns were of the utmost importance in this public art process. By the time Kruger returned to Los Angeles for the 24 August 1989 meeting, she had redesigned the proposed mural accordingly.

She presented two plans, both in the shape of the U.S. flag and both retaining the nine original questions. In one, a smaller version of the Pledge of Allegiance bordered the now greatly enlarged questions, and in the other the huge questions stood alone, big white words against a bright red wall, with a smaller blue rectangle reading "MOCA at the Temporary Contemporary" painted in the upper-left-hand corner (Fig. 78). The second design was stronger and more convincing, with the words to the nine questions clearly standing out as the white stripes of the U.S. flag and, hence, standing in as critical flash points raising concerns about the meaning of popular democratic symbols. And it dropped the slogan that had roused such local wrath. Kats Kunitsugu—the LTC-DAC member who had made the motion rejecting Kruger's original public art design in June—was so impressed with this new design, with MOCA's new spirit of community interaction, and with Kruger's participation in democratic process that she led the vote of support for the second proposal. Other LTCDAC votes followed, and the TC mural was given the Little Tokyo advisory committee's official backing.

There were more steps involved before the mural could be painted, however, such as resubmitting the design to the Cultural Affairs Commission (CAC), Los Angeles's central arts board. Having perfunctorily approved the original proposal—with the pledge—some months earlier, the CAC was now particularly sensitive about their role (and reputation) in this public art process. At their September 1989 meeting, CAC members decided they could not approve the new project until they had spoken directly with the artist at a special public hearing. A meeting was scheduled for 14 December 1989, and Kruger flew back to L.A.

It was a highly emotional meeting, a condensed version of the intense debate that the proposed mural had stirred for over eight months. Commissioners and audience members alike recounted Japanese American internment camp experiences and those of the Jewish holocaust, condemned current right-wing attacks on the National Endowment for the Arts, and celebrated the apparent new freedoms in Eastern Europe. Debate over the mural, in other words, generated a discussion about democracy. The open exchange of ideas and information helped constitute

■ 78. **Barbara Kruger,** *Untitled (Questions),* Version 3, August 1989; proposed 8.8 meters (29 feet) by 66.4 meters (218 feet) mural design for south wall of the Temporary Contemporary, Los Angeles. Photo courtesy The Museum of Contemporary Art, Los Angeles.

the public audience essential to the existence of an authentic public sphere.

Kruger began by thanking MOCA and the "Little Tokyo communities" for her participation in "a really gratifying democratic process." A CAC commissioner asked her to discuss the mural's content, and she explained that the questions

> address power and its misuses, but they also strike a note for the ringing allowances and dispensations of a democratic process. A process that makes sure that these questions are asked so that power is not abused . . . and also the ability of this country, and its incredible flexibility to be able to celebrate questions rather than repress them. Whether it's through a conversation, whether it's through a democratic, electoral process, or whether it's through the allowing of art to be seen in a free society.

Redirected from a specific critique of democratic symbols to a more generalized appeal to democratic expression, debate over Kruger's design became an issue of free speech. Noting the five years he spent in internment camps, James Niho, design director for the Japanese American National Museum, tearfully remarked, "These are questions the common person in the street should be asking. I don't see why people don't understand. Look, go with this thing."[5] After listening to other testimonials, CAC members voted 5 to 1 in favor of the mural.

One reporter described the December meeting as "an extraordinary microcosm of Los Angeles: here were six or seven ethnic groups, seeking a compromise on a significant and problematic piece of public art." After the vote Rodri Rodriguez, a Cuban immigrant and naturalized U.S. citizen, made the following impassioned comments:

> I just want you all to understand how significant it is that in the United States of America we are allowed to put up a mural like this. Perhaps it means that America can learn from its mistakes. We came without money, clothes, religion, parents—and this country welcomed us, and treated us with dignity. Those of you who have lived here all your lives may not understand what America means; those of us who have been taken in by the United States cannot speak highly enough of this country.[6]

Now open-ended enough to inspire the variety of interpretations that democracy embodies—from Niho's call for vigilance to Rodriguez's celebration of freedom—*Untitled (Questions)* was more fitting for multicultural Los Angeles. Shorn of the pledge, it omitted the subject that had aroused such negative Little Tokyo reaction, although it also omitted a critique of that democratic slogan's political and corporate appropriation. Kruger comments that this was part of the process of public art negotiation. "I don't feel that I compromised with the design," she explains. "What I proposed—the questions large—is what I had originally proposed. I wanted to get those questions on the wall. I was glad to see that design finally succeed."

Only one person at the December CAC meeting—a Little Tokyo property owner who said the proposed mural was some thirteen times larger than permissible signage in downtown Los Angeles—raised any significant objections to the new design. Cranky because he had been forced to remove an oversize billboard on his own property, Robert Volk remarked, "This thing is so totally out of scale." Kruger responded that contemporary artists utilize both the scale and the style of billboards: "The artist's problem is how to intervene in the public space. How can I be effective if I don't make it big?"[7] Still, Volk's insistence on taking his turn at the democratic process led to months of further debate about the proposed mural. Not until 1 May 1990, after the design was approved (as art, not signage) by two more L.A. agencies—the Cultural Redevelopment Agency and the Building and Safety Commission—did MOCA receive final approval to make the mural. *Untitled (Questions)* was painted between 18 and 27 June 1990 and was unveiled just in time for the Fourth of July (Fig. 79).

■ 79. **Barbara Kruger,** *Untitled (Questions),* June 1990–July 1992; final version (version 3) of 8.8 meters (29 ft) by 66.4 meters (218 ft) mural painted on south exterior wall of the Temporary Contemporary, Los Angeles. Photo courtesy The Museum of Contemporary Art, Los Angeles.

During its two-year tenure, the mural was glimpsed in more than a few MTV videos. It even got a bit part in *The Trials of Rosie O'Neill,* a CBS prime-time drama that starred Sharon Gless as a feisty public defender. In one fall 1990 episode, O'Neill is assigned the defense of a particularly noxious sexual offender. Walking to work, presumably to the Los Angeles City Hall and courthouses up the hill from the TC, she stops to look at MOCA's mural. As the camera pans the nine questions, her boss drives by, rolls down his window, and remarks, "One could spend an entire lifetime doing nothing but investigating those questions."[8] O'Neill nods and continues up the hill to the halls of justice.

If network TV used *Untitled (Questions)* as a thought-provoking backdrop to plot development, the mural also had an impact on subsequent public art projects proposed in the Little Tokyo area. One piece in particular, a controversial war memorial featuring the names of the Nisei soldiers of the 442nd Regimental Combat Team, has recently undergone rigorous public scrutiny. Inspired by the process of public debate that surrounded Kruger's project, Kats Kunitsugu says more members of the Japanese American community have become convinced that their opinions count. "Some feel only the war dead should be honored in the memorial, not all the veterans," she remarks. "Others feel that Nisei vets in other service units (like the Air Force) or other wars (like Vietnam) should be represented. We've heard from lots of different people about the memorial at our LTCDAC meetings."[9] It will be interesting to see how the $2.5 million project—slated for dedication on Veterans Day 1995, in a central plaza across from the TC—actually turns out, and who is honored by it.

Finally, the process of painting a public mural on the outside of the TC has had an important impact on the museum itself. Curator Ann Goldstein remarks that it "was an incredible learning experience for all of us. There were problems of communication with the neighborhood and the audience that this project revealed." In 1992, Goldstein says, in-house talk about making *Untitled (Questions)* a permanent piece was quickly rebuffed: "MOCA felt that it would have been irresponsible and disrespectful to the public art process that had been established to have even proposed keeping it up. We needed to finish the project off as honestly and as clearly as we could." True to their word, in July 1992 MOCA had the mural painted over. In a press release MOCA Director Richard Koshalek expressed no regret at seeing it go and emphasized, instead, the importance of community relations: "This project has been particularly important to MOCA and to Barbara Kruger both in terms of gaining greater insight into the complex dynamics of realizing a work in the public sector and also as a critical lesson in the importance of the community in that process."[10]

For MOCA and Kruger, participation in that process embodied the critical issue facing contemporary public art: "the indignity of speaking for others" rather than engaging in the free and open debate that is the hallmark of democratic conversation.[11] Given that Kruger's mural was commissioned for MOCA's 1989 exhibition "A Forest of Signs: Art in the Crisis of Representation," the manner in which it became embroiled in the politics of representation was entirely appropriate, although it is interesting to speculate why neither the artist nor the museum considered that when the mural was first proposed. Via the process of public art, Kruger addressed the crisis of representation as she negotiated the painting of certain democratic signs and symbols, and tried to sustain their critique, in Little Tokyo. "I want this project to contribute to the debate that sees democracy as an ongoing process," Kruger had said after her proposal had elicited so much response. While ultimately shaped (but not, it seems, inspired) by that process, the story of *Untitled (Questions)* is certainly informative about the workings of contemporary cultural democracy.

Like the other stories recounted in this book, that of public art in Little Tokyo tells how culture is contested and created in the public sphere. Today cultural debate obviously continues—a sampling of a few recent public art controversies includes the vandalism of Sheila Oettinger's 1990 sculpture *The Normal Family* in Normal, Illinois (where drunk college students kneecapped clay figures of parental authority) and the removal of three bronze statues by John Ahearn from the front of the 44th Precinct police station in the South Bronx (where objections were raised over Ahearn's "reaffirmation of stereotypes" by depicting local kids with boom boxes, basketballs, and pit bulls). In Miami Beach citizens are arguing over whether to accept the "gift" of a thirty-three-story statue of Columbus (taller than the Statue of Liberty) by Russian émigré artist Novy Svyet. And in Seattle recent debates over public art range from the somber to the simply strange. While some unamused citizens called Mowry Baden's *Wall of Death,* a carnivalesque sculpture of junky cars and cone-shaped columns, a public menace, others were absolutely delighted when, in September 1993, local street personality Subculture Joe shackled a 319-kilogram (700-pound) ball and chain to the ankles of yet another controversial public sculpture, Jonathan Borofsky's 14.6 meters (48 feet) tall *Hammering Man,* in front of the Seattle Art Museum. The local press, the museum, and the Seattle Arts Council were all besieged with complaints when the irons were cut two days later, and souvenir ball-and-chain pins have since become all the rage.[12]

These stories show that the public sphere is hardly the passive or inclusive place that postwar liberals imagined. It is nuanced and complicated, frequently conflicted and constantly in flux. The case of public art in Little Tokyo indicates how essential it is to recognize the complex ingredients that make up identity formation and race relations in specific public places. Ethnic publics are no more monolithic than the country as a whole. There is no unified and seamless America (there never has been), and democracy is too complex to be represented (or accommodated) in any single way.

At the same time one of the greatest dangers facing American democracy, critic Eleanor Heartney writes, is "the decay of the public sphere and the disintegration of the public interest into an atomized collection of narrow, localized, and often ethnically defined special interests." Many of the objections to Kruger's mural were based on its perceived anti–Japanese American overtones. Similar tensions surrounded the removal of Ahearn's sculptures in the South Bronx, where some African American residents and a group of black urban professionals who had moved out of the neighborhood protested the artist's decision to put what they felt were "outrageously racist" sculptures of street kids up on a pedestal—rather than their preferred monuments to "college kids" or civil rights figures.[13]

Yet both Kruger's mural and Ahearn's sculptures were commissioned for public spaces that cannot be reduced to the context of racial tensions alone; both MOCA's museum in Little Tokyo and the 44th Precinct police station are parts of a larger and more complicated public culture. Limiting the debate over that public culture to issues of race (or sex, or gender, or ethnicity) prohibits more expansive conversations about democracy, and power, and participation in the public sphere. Making democracy meaningful in multicultural America obviously necessitates more inclusive conversations, which recognize and critique the deep inconsistencies and contradictions of American history. But it also necessitates a willingness to converse, to engage in debates about democracy and democratic expression.

Contemporary public art has the capacity to stimulate those conversations. If the abiding cynicism and heartless social Darwinism of the greed decade encouraged hardly any debate at all, there seems to be a new hunger for democratic dialogue and renewed interest in the possibilities of a more democratic culture today. As Herbert Muschamp wrote shortly before Bill Clinton took office in January 1993, "The yearning for a public realm figures strongly in the mythology of the baby boomers."[14] Prominently featured in that realm, public art—and the debates that surround and shape it—manifests itself as an outstanding example of how cultural democracy is being rediscovered and reconsidered. In this respect public art is far less a luxury than an important element in the revitalization of the experiment that is and remains democracy.

It is hard work: The dynamics of contemporary multiculturalism make easy assumptions about the public out of the question and demand instead more critical and nuanced analyses—and artworks. Some in the art world scoff at the idea of public art, mistakenly equating it with consensus and wary of speaking for anyone except themselves. However, as this book has shown, an authentic public art is based not on absolute agreement or the monolithic construction of identity but on the willingness to share and tolerate differing opinions and competing agendas. Barbara Kruger, for one, disowns titles such as "public artist" and "public art." "I don't do public art," she says. "I don't exactly know what that term means." Rightfully objecting to the "deadening" effect of categorization, her reluctance to define and claim her role in the public realm nonetheless betrays a profound ambivalence about that realm—an ambivalence played out in the early chapters of the Little Tokyo mural project.

Truly public art hinges on public advocacy: understanding who the public is and what culture means to them; critiquing the relationships at work between public artists, their patrons, and their audiences; and ascertaining how culture can be created in a multicultural democracy. Public art has the unique potential to encourage the public to realize their voice—their power—in the public sphere. And public artists are equally empowered to invent that sphere as a place where ideas about cultural democracy can be debated and refreshed, tested and tried anew.

■■■

Notes

Prologue

1. Richard Koshalek, "Foreword," in *A Forest of Signs: Art in the Crisis of Representation* (Los Angeles: Museum of Contemporary Art, 1989), 11.

2. Barbara Kruger, interview by author, telephone, 27 January 1994. Unless otherwise noted all subsequent quotations from Kruger come from this conversation. See also Jeanne Siegel, "Barbara Kruger: Pictures and Words," *Arts* 61, no. 10 (June/Summer 1987): 19.

3. Nicolaus Mills, "The Culture of Triumph and the Spirit of the Times," in *Culture in an Age of Money: The Legacy of the 1980s in America,* ed. Nicolaus Mills (Chicago: Ivan R. Dee, 1990), 25. See also *Culture Wars: Documents from the Recent Controversies in the Arts,* ed. Richard Bolton (New York: New Press, 1992), 344–45.

4. Albert Boime, "Waving the Red Flag and Reconstructing Old Glory," *American Art* 4, no. 2 (Spring 1990): 23. See Steven C. Dubin, "Rally 'Round the Flag," in *Arresting Images: Impolitic Art and Uncivil Actions* (New York: Routledge, 1992), 102–24, for an excellent overview of American debate about the flag and an account of the Scott Tyler episode.

5. For information on Little Tokyo see John Modell, *The Economics and Politics of Racial Accommodation: The Japanese of Los Angeles, 1900–1942* (Urbana: University of Illinois Press, 1977), 18, 67–69. See also the entry in *Japanese American History: An A–Z Reference from 1868 to the Present,* ed. Brian Niiya (New York: Facts on File, 1993), 216–17, and Ichiro Mike Murase, *Little Tokyo: One Hundred Years in Pictures* (Los Angeles: Visual Communications/ Asian American Studies Central, 1983).

6. Michi Weglyn, *Years of Infamy: The Untold Story of America's Concentration Camps* (New York: William Morrow, 1976). Ickes is quoted from a 1946 newspaper interview, p. 316, n. 21.

Weglyn notes (p. 21) that some 120,000 Japanese Americans were eventually incarcerated in the camps during World War II, including 5,981 who were born in the camps. Relocation centers for East Coast Japanese Americans were in Arkansas; people of Japanese ancestry were also held in Texas, Oklahoma, North Dakota, Tennessee, Maryland, North Carolina, Louisiana, and Alaska.

7. On the "Nipponization" of the Southern California economy in the 1980s see Mike Davis, *City of Quartz: Excavating the Future in Los Angeles* (New York: Verso, 1990), 74, 135–38. For information on Little Tokyo's recent development see the "Biennial Report, 1988–1990" of the Little Tokyo Community Development Agency of the City of Los Angeles (Los Angeles: Community Development Agency, 1990).

8. Mission statement of the Japanese American National Museum, quoted in *Museum News: A Quarterly Calendar of Activities,* 4th quarter 1992, n.p.

9. Allan Parachini, "MOCA's Writing on the Wall," *Los Angeles Times,* 21 July 1989, sec. 4, p. 15.

10. Roger Daniels, *Prisoners Without Trial: Japanese-Americans in World War II* (New York: Hill and Wang, 1993), 68–69; Sandra C. Taylor, *Jewel of the Desert: Japanese American Internment at Topaz* (Berkeley: University of California Press, 1993), 148–50; Weglyn, *Years of Infamy,* 136.

11. Kats Kunitsugu, interview by author, telephone, 1 February 1994, and quoted in Parachini, "MOCA's Writing," 15.

12. On Japan bashing see the following review articles: Robert B. Reich, "Is Japan Really Out to Get Us?" and Robert Nathan, "Rising Sun," *New York Times Book Review,* 9 February 1992, 1, 22, 24–25; Karl Tao Greenfeld, "Return of the Yellow Peril," *Nation,* 11 May 1992, 636–38; Ian Buruma, "It Can't Happen Here," *New York Review of Books,* 23 April 1992, 3–4. On redress see Taylor, *Jewel of the Desert,* xi, 282–83; Daniels, *Prisoners Without Trial,* 88–106; and Philip S. Foner and Daniel Rosenberg, *Racism, Dissent, and Asian Americans from 1850 to the Present* (Westport: Greenwood Press, 1993), 290–98.

13. Koshalek quoted in Parachini, "MOCA's Writing," 15.

Chapter 1: Contemporary Public Art Controversy

1. On Greenough see Russell Lynes, *The Art-Makers: An Informal History of Painting, Sculpture and Architecture in Nineteenth Century America* (New York: Dover, 1970), 119–21; on the Washington Monument see Kirk Savage, "The Self-made Monument: George Washington and the Fight to Erect a National Memorial," *Winterthur Portfolio* 22, no. 4 (Winter 1987): 235.

2. On the *Maine Memorial* see Michele Bogart, *Public Sculpture and the Civic Ideal in New York City, 1890–1930* (Chicago: University of Chicago Press, 1989), 202; on 1930s murals see Karal Ann Marling, *Wall-to-Wall America: A*

Cultural History of Post-Office Murals in the Great Depression (Minneapolis: University of Minnesota Press, 1982); M. Sue Kendall, *Rethinking Regionalism: John Steuart Curry and the Kansas Mural Controversy* (Washington, D.C.: Smithsonian Institution Press, 1986); Erika Doss, *Benton, Pollock, and the Politics of Modernism: From Regionalism to Abstract Expressionism* (Chicago: University of Chicago Press, 1991); on the Iwo Jima monument see Karal Ann Marling and John Wetenhall, *Iwo Jima: Monuments, Memories, and the American Hero* (Cambridge, Mass.: Harvard University Press, 1991), 195.

3. Habermas's thesis first appeared in *Strukturwandel der Oeffentlichkeit* (Frankfurt: Hermann Luchterhand Verlag, 1962), in English, *The Cultural Transformation of the Public Sphere: An Inquiry into a Category of Bourgeois Society*, trans. Thomas Burger and Frederick Lawrence (Cambridge, Mass.: MIT Press, 1989); Nancy Fraser, "Rethinking the Public Sphere: A Contribution to the Critique of Actually Existing Democracy," in *The Phantom Public Sphere*, ed. Bruce Robbins (Minneapolis: University of Minnesota Press, 1993), 1–32.

4. Michael North, *The Final Sculpture: Public Monuments and Modern Poets* (Ithaca: Cornell University Press, 1985), 25.

5. Avis Berman, "Public Sculpture's New Look," *ARTnews* 90 (September 1991): 104.

6. *Response of the National Endowment for the Arts to the March 22, 1979, Report of the Surveys and Investigations Staff House Appropriations Committee* (Washington, D.C.: NEA, 1979), 6–8.

7. Calvin Tomkins, "The Art World: *Tilted Arc*," *New Yorker*, 20 May 1985, 95.

8. Dixie L. Griffin, "Plop Art: A New Trend in Art Coming to a Neighborhood Near You," *Icon* [Denver] *The Arts Alternative* 2, no. 7 (November 1989): 1.

9. Cindy Eberting, "S.J. May Cast Aside Statue, Capt. Fallon Monument Rankles Some Hispanics," *San Jose Mercury News*, 25 August 1990, sec. B, p. 1; Lucy R. Lippard, "Facing Up," *Z Magazine*, June 1991, 72–75; Pancho Epstein, "Defending Chicano Culture, Awareness," *Albuquerque Pasatiempo*, 28 June–4 July 1991, 45.

10. Karen Stanger, "Glenna Goodacre Sculpts Vietnam Women's Memorial," *American Artist* 57, no. 613 (August 1993): 66; "Santa Fe Sculptor Glenna Goodacre Battles Nonsense," *Art-Talk* [Albuquerque], March 1991, 17.

11. Gary Schwan, "Public Art's Changing Landscape," *Palm Beach Post*, 15 September 1991, sec. L, pp. 1–2.

12. Ed Quillen, "Paradise with a Prison View," *MUSE: The Arts Newspaper for Colorado* 44 (October–November 1986): 1, 8–9, 18; and Lucy Lippard, "Sniper's Nest, Captive Audience," *Z Magazine*, June 1989, 90–93. See also Mark Starr, "Build a Jail, Buy Some Art," *Newsweek*, 20 March 1989, 35.

13. Bill Gertz, "Cryptic Sculpture Spooks CIA Employees," *Washington Times*, 8 April 1991, sec. E, p. 1.

14. Ronald Lee Fleming and Renata von Tscharner, *PlaceMakers: Creating Public Art That Tells You Where You Are* (New York: Harcourt Brace Jovanovich, 1987), 1; Michael Hough, *Out of Place: Restoring Identity to the*

Regional Landscape (New Haven: Yale University Press, 1990), 87.

15. Patricia Phillips, "Out of Order: The Public Art Machine," *Artforum* 27 (December 1988): 93; on placemaking see Fleming and von Tscharner, *Place-Makers,* and Mike Lipske, *Places as Art* (New York: Publishing Center for Cultural Resources, 1985), a book commissioned by the Design Arts Program, National Endowment for the Arts.

16. Kate Linker noted Wines's coinage of this term in "Public Sculpture: The Pursuit of the Pleasurable and Profitable Paradise," *Artforum* 19 (March 1981): 65, 73; Marling quoted in Karal Ann Marling and Robert Silberman, "The Statue Near the Wall: The Vietnam Veterans Memorial and the Art of Remembering," *Smithsonian Studies in American Art* 1 (Spring 1987): 19.

17. Peter Steinfels, *The Neoconservatives* (New York: Simon and Schuster, 1979), 55; Reagan is quoted from an August 1980 speech, noted in Rowland Evans and Robert Novak, *The Reagan Revolution* (New York: E. P. Dutton, 1981), 204.

18. Donald Wildmon quoted in Bruce Selcraig, "Reverand Wildmon's War on the Arts," *Sunday New York Times Magazine,* 2 September 1990, sec. 6, p. 24.

19. Jayne Merkel, "Report from Cincinnati: Art on Trial," *Art in America* 78, no. 1 (December 1990): 41–51.

20. Laura Bergheim, "Pluggies," in *Culture in an Age of Money: The Legacy of the 1980s in America,* ed. Nicolaus Mills (Chicago: Ivan R. Dee, 1990), 94.

21. Richard Serra, "*Tilted Arc* Destroyed," *Art in America* 77, no. 5 (May 1989): 36.

22. Perot quoted in John Bodnar, *Remaking America: Public Memory, Commemoration, and Patriotism in the Twentieth Century* (Princeton: Princeton University Press, 1992), 5; *Vietnam Veterans Memorial Official Park Guide* (Washington, D.C.: National Park Service, U.S. Department of the Interior, 1986), n.p.

23. Michael Clark, "Remembering Vietnam," *Cultural Critique,* no. 3 (Spring 1986): 68; Scruggs quoted in Kurt Andersen, "A Homecoming at Last," *Time,* 22 November 1982, 45.

24. Stanger, "Glenna Goodacre," 68.

25. Serra quoted in Douglas Crimp, "Richard Serra's Urban Sculpture: An Interview," *Arts Magazine* 55, no. 3 (November 1980): 118; Michael Brenson, "The Messy Saga of *Tilted Arc* Is Far from Over," *New York Times,* 2 April 1989, sec. 2, p. 33.

26. Deborah Solomon, "Richard Serra, Our Most Notorious Sculptor," *New York Times,* 8 October 1989, sec. 6, p. 39; Harriet Senie, "The Right Stuff," *ARTnews* 83 (March 1984): 58. See Robert Storr, "*Tilted Arc:* Enemy of the People?" in *Art in the Public Interest,* ed. Arlene Raven (Ann Arbor: UMI Research Press, 1989), p. 283, n. 8, for an account of contaminated water at the Federal Complex.

27. Senie, "The Right Stuff," 55. Historian Casey Nelson Blake offers a similar assessment of Serra's antipublic attitudes in "An Atmosphere of Effrontery: Richard Serra, *Tilted Arc,* and the Crisis of Public Art," in *The Power of Culture: Critical Essays in American History,* eds. Richard Wightman Fox and T. J. Jackson Lears (Chicago: University of Chicago Press, 1993), 247–89.

28. Serra, "*Tilted Arc* Destroyed," 35–36; Diamond quoted in "Trying to Move a Wall of Art," *New York Times,* 13 March 1988, sec. 1, p. 48.

29. Diamond quoted in *New York Post,* 17 March 1989, as noted in Serra, "*Tilted Arc* Destroyed," p. 45, n. 1.

30. Rosalyn Deutsche, "*Tilted Arc* and the Uses of Public Space," review of *The Destruction of Tilted Arc: Documents,* ed. Clara Weyergraf-Serra and Martha Buskirk, in *Design Book Review* 23 (Winter 1992): 26.

31. Harriet Senie, "Richard Serra's *Tilted Arc:* Art and Non-Art Issues," *Art Journal* 48, no. 4 (Winter 1989): 301.

32. T. J. Jackson Lears, "The Concept of Cultural Hegemony: Problems and Possibilities," *American Historical Review* 90, no. 3 (June 1985): 588.

Chapter 2: Public Spirit and *Spirit Poles*

1. Avalos quoted in *Democracy: A Project by Group Material,* ed. Brian Wallis (Seattle: Bay Press, 1990), 177.

2. John Blosser, "*Enquirer* Contest Winners Pick . . . America's Ugliest Sculptures—And Your Taxes Pay for 'Em," *National Enquirer,* 6 March 1990, 5. On the *Concord Heritage Gateway* see Hawley Holmes, "Media Advisory on *The Concord Heritage Gateway*" (Concord: Concord Arts Committee/Art in Public Places Program, 1989), n.p. Unless otherwise noted all information on the project, including artists' comments, is derived from this or other Concord Arts Committee documents (survey responses, press releases, etc.) as mentioned in the text.

3. Blosser, "*Enquirer* Contest Winners," 5. Information also from Blosser's files and notes.

4. Gilkinson quoted in Alan Ehrenhalt, *The United States of Ambition: Politicians, Power, and the Pursuit of Office* (New York: Random House, 1991), 56.

5. Chapter 3 of Ehrenhalt's *United States of Ambition* deals exclusively with Concord's city council in the 1980s, 42–64. The Human Relations Commission is discussed on p. 2 of the February 1987 *City of Concord Newsette.*

6. Ehrenhalt, *United States of Ambition,* 20, 34.

7. Harry C. Boyte, *CommonWealth: A Return to Citizen Politics* (New York: Free Press, 1989), 10.

8. Paul Mattick, Jr., "Arts and the State," *Nation* 251, no. 10 (1 October 1990): 348; Carolyn Newbergh, "Freeway Exit Could Showcase City's Image," *Oakland Tribune,* 10 July 1986, sec. C, p. 1.

9. Jürgen Habermas, "The Public Sphere: An Encyclopedia Article," *New German Critique* 1, no. 3 (Fall 1974): 53.

10. W. J. T. Mitchell, "The Violence of Public Art: *Do the Right Thing,*" *Critical Inquiry* 16, no. 4 (Summer 1990): 886.

11. Clement Greenberg, "Avant-Garde and Kitsch," *Partisan Review* 6, no. 5 (Fall 1939): 34–39, reprinted in John O'Brian, ed., *Perceptions and Judgement, 1939–1944,* vol. 1 of *Clement Greenberg: The Collected Essays and Criticism* (Chicago: University of Chicago Press, 1986), 5–22.

12. Clement Greenberg, "The Present Prospects of American Painting and

Sculpture," *Horizon* (October 1947), reprinted in John O'Brian, ed., *Arrogant Purpose, 1945–1949*, vol. 2 of *Clement Greenberg: The Collected Essays and Criticism* (Chicago: University of Chicago Press, 1986), 160–70.

13. See, for instance, Serge Guilbaut, *How New York Stole the Idea of Modern Art: Abstract Expressionism, Freedom, and the Cold War* (Chicago: University of Chicago Press, 1983), especially chap. 4 and conclusion; and Erika Doss, *Benton, Pollock, and the Politics of Modernism: From Regionalism to Abstract Expressionism* (Chicago: University of Chicago Press, 1991), chaps. 5 and 6.

14. Sampson quoted in Donald W. Thalacker, *The Place of Art in the World of Architecture* (New York: Chelsea House, 1980), xii. On the origins of the GSA see John Wetenhall, "Camelot's Legacy to Public Art: Aesthetic Ideology in the New Frontier," *Art Journal* 48, no. 4 (Winter 1989): 304–5.

15. Kathy Halbreich, "Stretching the Terrain: Sketching Twenty Years of Public Art," in Jeffrey L. Cruikshank and Pam Korza, eds., *Going Public: A Field Guide to Developments in Art in Public Places* (Amherst, Mass.: Arts Extension Service, 1988), 9. See also John Beardsley, "For Example: Grand Rapids and Seattle," *Art in Public Places* (Washington, D.C.: Partners for Livable Places, 1981), 14–24. Ford's comments are quoted in Wolf Von Eckardt, "The Malignant Objectors," *Public Interest* 66 (Winter 1982): 24. On "official culture" see John Bodnar, *Remaking America: Public Memory, Commemoration, and Patriotism in the Twentieth Century* (Princeton: Princeton University Press, 1992), 13–14.

16. Joel Garreau, "Edge Cities," *Landscape Architecture* 78, no. 8 (December 1988): 48–55; see also his book *Edge Cities* (New York: Doubleday, 1991).

17. Roger Stevens, testimony before a subcommittee of the Committee on Appropriations, House of Representatives, U.S. Congress, House, Department of Interior and Related Agencies, *Hearings,* 90th Cong., 2d sess., March 1980, quoted in C. Richard Swaim, "The National Endowment for the Arts: 1965–1980," in *Public Policy and the Arts,* eds. Kevin V. Mulcahy and C. Richard Swaim (Boulder: Westview Pres, 1982), 181.

18. Mike Davis, *City of Quartz: Excavating the Future in Los Angeles* (New York: Verso, 1990), 227.

19. Sam Hunter, "Preface," in Thalacker, *Place of Art,* ix; Douglas Stalker and Clark Glymour, "The Malignant Object: Thoughts on Public Sculpture," *Public Interest* 66 (Winter 1982): 17.

20. Cruikshank and Korza, *Going Public,* 5, 27.

21. Kevin V. Mulcahy, "Government and the Arts in the United States," in *The Patron State: Government and the Arts in Europe, North America, and Japan,* eds. Milton C. Cummings, Jr., and Richard S. Katz (New York: Oxford University Press, 1987), 314; Nixon quoted in *National Endowment for the Arts, 1965–1985: A Brief Chronology of Federal Involvement in the Arts* (Washington, D.C.: Office of Public Information, National Endowment for the Arts, 1985), 27; Edward C. Banfield, *The Democratic Muse: Visual Arts and the Public Interest* (New York: Basic Books, 1984), 62.

22. Michael Hall, "Weights and Measures: Public Art," in *Stereoscopic Perspective: Reflections on American Fine and Folk Art* (Ann Arbor: UMI Research

Press, 1988), 53; Janet Kardon, "Introduction," in *Urban Encounters: A Map of Public Art in Philadelphia, 1959–1979* (Philadelphia: Falcon Press, 1980), n.p.

23. Arthur Danto, "Public Art and the General Will," *Nation* 241 (28 September 1985): 288.

24. Robert H. Knight, "The National Endowment for the Arts: Misusing Taxpayers' Money," *Heritage Foundation Reports* (Washington, D.C.: Heritage Foundation, 1991), 1; James Melchart, "Visual Arts," *National Endowment for the Arts Annual Report 1980* (Washington, D.C.: National Endowment for the Arts, 1980), 277; AIPP awards are listed on pp. 281–82. It should be noted that Melchart also said that the NEA had "seen some regrettable results when the artwork is an afterthought, commissioned and installed after all else is completed" and suggested that in the 1980s the Endowment would be committed to site-specific works of public art. Further, in the late 1980s the NEA added the following to their own guidelines: "[The NEA] must not, under any circumstances, impose a single aesthetic standard or attempt to direct artistic content," and the 1990s have seen increased NEA funding for representational art, such as public murals.

For discussion of the NEA preference for abstract modern art see Mary Eleanor McCombie, "Art and Policy: The National Endowment for the Arts's Art in Public Places Program, 1967–1980" (Ph.D. diss., University of Texas, Austin, 1992).

25. Barbara Hoffman, "Law for Art's Sake in the Public Realm," *Critical Inquiry* 17, no. 3 (Spring 1991): 542. See Ronald Lee Fleming and Renata von Tscharner, *PlaceMakers: Creating Public Art That Tells You Where You Are* (New York: Harcourt Brace Jovanovich, 1987), 176, for reference to the NEA's ban on commemorative art; see Hoffman, n. 3, for reference to Philadelphia.

26. Hoffman, "Law for Art's Sake," 542.

27. Edward Arian, *The Unfulfilled Promise: Public Subsidy of the Arts in America* (Philadelphia: Temple University Press, 1989), 8–9. On the Oakland mural see Fleming and von Tscharner, *PlaceMakers*, 154–55; on the Villa Nueva tapestry see Arthur Levitt, Jr., "Introduction," in *Public Money and the Muse: Essays on Government Funding for the Arts*, ed. Stephen Benedict (New York: W. W. Norton, 1991), 28.

28. Kevin Mulcahy, "The Rationale for Public Culture," in Mulcahy and Swaim, *Public Policy and the Arts*, 41. On p. 40 Mulcahy explains, "The basis for these conclusions is an independent evaluation commissioned by the Research Division of the National Endowment for the Arts in 1978. This report examined 270 audience studies of the performing arts and museums to determine the general characteristics of the 'culture-consuming public.' The arts public was found to differ from the general public on several measures of socio-economic status."

29. Hall, "Weights and Measures," 47.

30. Clifford Geertz, *The Interpretation of Culture* (New York: Basic Books, 1973), as noted in Myron J. Aronoff, "Conceptualizing the Role of Culture in Political Change," in Myron J. Aronoff, ed., *Culture and Political Change*, vol.

2 of *Political Anthropology* (New Brunswick, N.J.: Transaction Books, 1983), 14.

31. Cary Tennis, "Poles Apart: Public Art vs. the Public in Concord," *San Francisco Weekly* 8, no. 47 (13 December 1989): 7.

32. See Letters to the Editor, *Contra Costa Times,* 31 October 1989, and *Concord Transcript,* 18 and 25 October 1989.

33. Tennis, "Poles Apart," 7.

34. "Sutherland, Hyde Win Re-election to Council," *Tacoma News Tribune,* 6 November 1985, sec. A, p. 1. See also Nancy D. Kates's case study for the John F. Kennedy School of Government, "Tacoma Neon Wars: Procuring Public Art" (Cambridge, Mass.: Harvard University, 1987).

35. Donna Joy Newman, "New York Sculptor Picked for City Art Project," [Boulder] *Daily Camera,* 10 December 1982, sec. B, p. 3.

36. Donna Joy Newman, "Artist's Dream Is About to Become Reality," [Boulder] *Daily Camera,* 12 December 1982, sec. C, pp. 1–2; Diane O'Donnell, "A Public Nuisance or a Work [of] Art," [Boulder] *Colorado Daily,* 15 April 1983, pp. 32, 34; Donna Joy Newman, "Blum Backers Take Issue with Critics," [Boulder] *Daily Camera,* 24 April 1983, sec. B, pp. 1, 5; Donna Joy Newman, "NO! Sculpture Poll's Overwhelming Verdict Proves Art Has Become Boulder's Latest Conversation Piece," [Boulder] *Daily Camera,* 1 May 1983, sec. C, pp. 14–15; Daryl Gibson, "Blum Sculpture Critics Blast Arts Commission," [Boulder] *Daily Camera,* 19 May 1983, sec. B, p. 1; Daryl Gibson, "Panel Rejects Controversial Sculpture Plan," [Boulder] *Daily Camera,* 21 June 1983, sec. A, pp. 1, 11. See also Carol Kliger, *A Public Art Primer for Artists of the Boulder-Denver Area* (Boulder: Carol Kliger, 1993), 11–16.

37. "Is America's Ugliest Tax-Funded Sculpture the Laughingstock of YOUR Hometown?" *National Enquirer,* 5 December 1989, 29.

38. Blosser, "*Enquirer* Contest Winners," 5. Information also from Blosser's files and notes.

39. Mary Mazzocco, "'Spirit Poles' Stay in Concord," *Contra Costa Times,* 8 November 1990, sec. A, p. 1. On the Blum episode see Dana Wilkie, "Assembly Backs Foes of 'Split Pavilion,'" *San Diego Union-Tribune,* 20 August 1993, sec. B, pp. 1, 4; and Dayna Lynn Fried, "Carlsbad Elated with a 'Split' Decision," *San Diego Union-Tribune,* 11 December 1993, sec. B, pp. 1, 14.

40. David Forst, "No Longer *Poles* Apart," *ARTnews* 91 (April 1992): 29.

41. Letter to the Editor, *Contra Costa Times,* 6 June 1990, sec. A, p. 16.

42. Forst, "No Longer *Poles* Apart," 30.

Chapter 3: Public Art in the Corporate Sphere

1. Oldenburg and Whitehouse quoted in Helen Cullinan, "Sohio Puts Its Stamp on City Art," [Cleveland] *Plain Dealer,* 1 August 1985, sec. A, p. 10; Whitehouse also quoted in James Braham, "The Wrong Impression? Does a 48-Ft. Rubber Stamp Say 'Standard Oil'?" *Industry Week,* 28 April 1986, 28.

2. William Hall, "BP Grasps Its U.S. Nettle; Standard Oil," *Financial Times,* 9 July 1986, sec. 1, p. 20.

3. Mark Russell, "Free Stamp Sculpture Gets Spot by City Hall," [Cleveland] *Plain Dealer,* 23 April 1991, sec. A, p. 6.

4. Miriam Horn, "Today's Medicis Wear Suits and Ties," *U.S. News and World Report,* 19 October 1987, 72; Richard Bolton, "Enlightened Self-interest: The Avant-Garde in the 1980s," *Afterimage* 16, no. 7 (February 1989): 14; John Taylor, "Prisoners of Success: The Art World of the Eighties," in *Circus of Ambition: The Culture of Wealth and Power in the Eighties* (New York: Warner Books, 1989), 53–99.

5. "Make a Sound Investment," brochure published by the Business Committee for the Arts, 1988, as noted in Bolton, "Enlightened Self-interest," 13; Mobil Oil spokesperson Sandra J. Ruch noted in Carol Squiers, "Wheel of Fortune," *American Photographer* 19, no. 4 (October 1987): 16.

6. Bolton, "Enlightened Self-interest," 13.

7. On the relationship between public art and private development in New York see, especially, Rosalyn Deutsche, "Uneven Development: Public Art in New York City," *October* 47 (Winter 1988): 3–52.

8. Reagan quoted in *Speaking My Mind: Selected Speeches* (New York: Simon and Schuster, 1989), 60–61; Haynes Johnson, *Sleepwalking Through History* (New York: W. W. Norton, 1991), 186.

9. Reagan quoted in *A Time for Choosing: The Speeches of Ronald Reagan, 1961–1982* (Chicago: Regnery Gateway, 1983), 255; Bakshian quoted in *New York Times,* 9 August 1981, sec. B, p. 16, as noted in Kevin V. Mulcahy, "The Attack on Public Culture: Policy Revisionism in a Conservative Era," in *Public Policy and the Arts,* eds. Kevin V. Mulcahy and C. Richard Swaim (Boulder: Westview Press, 1982), 316.

10. Mulcahy, "Attack on Public Culture," 311–14.

11. Carol Vance, "Reagan's Revenge: Restructuring the NEA," *Art in America* 78, no. 11 (November 1990): 49; Biddle quoted in John Friedman, "A Populist Shift in Federal Cultural Support," *New York Times,* 13 May 1979, sec. 2, p. 35. See also Biddle, "Chairman's Statement," *National Endowment for the Arts Annual Report 1979* (Washington, D.C.: NEA, 1980), 2–3.

12. Hilton Kramer, "A Note on *The New Criterion*," *New Criterion* 1, no. 1 (September 1982): 1–5; "Notes and Comments: September 1991," *New Criterion* 10, no. 1 (September 1991): 3.

13. Kramer, "Note on *The New Criterion*," 4; Hilton Kramer, "Postmodern: Art and Culture in the 1980s," *New Criterion* 1, no. 1 (September 1982): 42.

14. See Pat Buchanan's "How Can We Clean Up Our Art Act?" *Washington Post,* June 19, 1989, as quoted in Carol Vance, "The War on Culture," *Art in America* 77, no. 9 (September 1989): p. 41, n. 14. See also Allan Sekula's remarks on *The New Criterion* in "Some American Notes," *Art in America* 78, no. 2 (February 1990): 39–45.

15. Samuel Lipman quoted in Derek Guthrie, "Lipman Speaks: The Conservative Voice of the National Endowment," *New Art Examiner* 12, no. 1 (October 1984): 32; Kramer, "Note on *The New Criterion*," 4.

16. Vance, "War on Culture," 41.

17. George Lipsitz, "Precious and Communicable: History in an Age of Popu-

lar Culture," in *Time Passages: Collective Memory and American Popular Culture* (Minneapolis: University of Minnesota Press, 1989), 27.

18. Samuel Lipman, "Funding the Arts: Who Decides?" *New Criterion* 2, no. 2 (October 1983): 7, and "Cultural Policy: Whither America, Whither Government?" *New Criterion* 3, no. 3 (November 1984): 14.

On Kramer's participation in the NEA's Visual Arts Criticism Seminar in September 1983 see his "Criticism Endowed: Reflections on a Debacle," *New Criterion* 2, no. 3 (November 1983): 1–5. See also subsequent letters from other seminar participants (including Kenneth S. Friedman and Doug Davis), and Kramer's reply, in *New Criterion* 2, no. 7 (March 1984): 84–88. For other accounts see Niki Coleman, "National Council Roasts Critics Fellowships," *New Art Examiner* 11, no. 3 (December 1983): 31; Martha Gever, "New Criteria for NEA's Visual Arts Program," *Afterimage* 11, no. 5 (December 1983): 3, 21; Grace Glueck, "Endowment Suspends Grants for Art Critics," *New York Times,* 5 April 1984, sec. C, p. 16; Max Kozloff, Kay Larson, and Donald Kuspit, "Forum," *Artforum* 22, no. 9 (May 1984): 77–79; and Martha Gever, "Blowing in the Wind: The Fate of NEA Critics Fellowships," *Afterimage* 12, nos. 1 and 2 (Summer 1984): 3, 37.

19. The Heritage Foundation report is discussed in Richard Bolton, "The Cultural Contradictions of Conservatism," *New Art Examiner* 17, no. 10 (June 1990): 28; and Vance, "Reagan's Revenge," 49.

20. Samuel Lipman, "Redefining Culture and Democracy," *New Criterion* 8, no. 4 (December 1989): 14, 18.

21. Lipman, "Cultural Policy," 14.

22. Jürgen Habermas, "Neoconservative Cultural Criticism in the United States and West Germany," in *The New Conservatism: Cultural Criticism and the Historians' Debate,* ed. and trans. by Shierry Weber Nicholsen (Cambridge, Mass.: MIT Press, 1989), 25–26.

23. Lipman, "Funding the Arts," 7–8; Lipman, "Cultural Policy," 15.

24. "*Irises* to Getty," *Art in America* 78, no. 5 (May 1990): 43; Ben Heller, "The *Irises* Affair," *Art in America* 78, no. 7 (July 1990): 45–53.

25. Bolton, "Enlightened Self-interest," 13; Cathleen McGuigan et al., "A Word from Our Sponsor," *Newsweek,* 25 November 1985, 96–98; Ian Pears and Lorraine Glennon, "The Museum and the Corporation: New Realities," *Museum News* (January–February 1988): 39; "In Sum: Corporate Support for Art," *Art in America* 76, no. 7 (July 1988): 55–59.

26. Hans Haacke, "In the Vice," *Art Journal* 50, no. 3 (Fall 1991): 49–55.

27. Pears and Glennon, "The Museum and the Corporation," 37–39.

28. Nicolaus Mills, "The Culture of Triumph and the Spirit of the Times," in *Culture in an Age of Money: The Legacy of the 1980s in America,* ed. Nicolaus Mills (Chicago: Ivan R. Dee, 1990), 11; Johnson, *Sleepwalking Through History,* 215.

29. Paul Mattick, Jr., "Arts and the State," *Nation* 251, no. 10 (1 October 1990): 348.

30. For a description of Haacke's 1975 work *On Social Grease* see Brian Wallis, ed., *Hans Haacke: Unfinished Business* (New York: New Museum of

Contemporary Art, 1986), 152–55; the executive quoted is Robert Kingsley (d. 1980). AT&T advertisement, *ARTnews* 86, no. 1 (January 1987): 25.

31. Richard Bolton, "The Contradictions of Corporate Culture," *New Art Examiner* 17, no. 8 (April 1990): 18–21; Roger Kimball, "Art and Architecture at the Equitable Center," *New Criterion* 5, no. 3 (November 1986): 24–32; Donald J. Barr, "Letter from the Publisher," *Sports Illustrated,* 27 October 1986, 4; Donna Graves, "Representing the Race: Detroit's *Monument to Joe Louis,*" in *Critical Issues in Public Art: Content, Context, and Controversy,* eds. Harriet F. Senie and Sally Webster (New York: Icon Editions, HarperCollins, 1992), 215–27.

32. Tom Wolfe, "The Worship of Art: Notes on the New God," *Harper's* 269, no. 1613 (October 1984): 66; Haacke quoted in an interview with Connie Samaras, "Sponsorship or Censorship," *New Art Examiner* 13, no. 3 (November 1985): 22.

33. Advertisement, *Art in America* 72, no. 9 (October 1984): 138–39. Italics added. For a different look at this ad, considering "the contradiction faced by a corporation in representing a liberal view of primitivism," see Brian Wallis, "Institutions Trust Institutions," in *Hans Haacke: Unfinished Business,* 59.

As cigarette sales declined among upper- and middle-class Anglo Americans, Philip Morris targeted African American consumers. This was done through direct product advertising and through sponsorship of art exhibitions anticipated to reach African American audiences, such as the 1984 "Primitivism" exhibition and the 1991 "Romare Bearden" show at the Studio Museum in Harlem.

34. Mattick, "Arts and the State," 348; Haacke, "In the Vice," 49–55; Steven C. Dubin, *Arresting Images: Impolitic Art and Uncivil Actions* (New York: Routledge, 1992), 260–61.

35. Herbert Schiller, *Culture, Inc.: The Corporate Takeover of Public Expression* (New York: Oxford University Press, 1989), 67 and passim.

36. John Koch, "Helping Malls Offer More Than Commerce," *Boston Globe,* 13 December 1990, sec. L, p. 79; Kim Masters, "NEA Funds Arts in Shopping Malls," *Washington Post,* 9 November 1990, sec. C, p. 1; Barbara Hoffman, "Law for Art's Sake in the Public Realm," *Critical Inquiry* 17, no. 3 (Spring 1991): p. 572, n. 83.

37. Cornelius F. Foote, Jr., "Artful Office Landscapes," *Washington Post,* 19 December 1987, sec. E, p. 1.

38. Blair Gately, "How to Tone Up a Building: Commission Some Art," *Washington Business Journal,* 5 May 1986, sec. B, p. 1.

39. Tom Precious, "National Notebook: Alexandria, Va.; Offices with a River View," *New York Times,* 7 June 1987, sec. 8, p. 1.

40. Peter Collier and David Horowitz, *The Rockefellers: An American Dynasty* (New York: Signet, 1976), 65–70.

41. Carol Poh Miller and Robert Wheeler, *Cleveland: A Concise History, 1796–1990* (Bloomington: Indiana University Press, 1990), 166–79.

42. Miller and Wheeler, *Cleveland,* 182, 186. For an excellent account of Cleveland city planning during the 1970s, when "neighborhood advocacy" was pursued, see Norman Krumholz and John Forester, *Making Equity Planning*

Work: Leadership in the Public Sector (Philadelphia: Temple University Press, 1990). Krumholz was planning director in Cleveland from 1969 through the 1970s.

43. George F. Will, "Oh, Cleveland!" in *The Pursuit of Virtue and Other Tory Notions* (New York: Simon and Schuster, 1982), 344; David D. Van Tassel and John J. Grabowski, eds., *The Encyclopedia of Cleveland History* (Bloomington: Indiana University Press, 1987), 809–10. See also John Bodnar's account of controversy in Public Square in *Remaking America: Public Memory, Commemoration, and Patriotism in the Twentieth Century* (Princeton: Princeton University Press, 1992), 93–95.

44. Obata quoted in "Innesca il centro urbano la cattedrale della Sohio: Sede direzionale della Standard Oilo a Cleveland, Ohio," *L'Architettura* 33, no. 12 (December 1987): 866–78 (my translation). Architect Jerry Sincoff and engineer William O'Neal discussed the building in "The Sohio Building: A Distinctive, Revitalizing Force," *Modern Steel Construction* 25, no. 2 (2d quarter 1985): 19.

45. Obata commented on this in *L'Architettura*, 873.

46. James G. Archuleta, spokesman for the Oil, Chemical and Atomic Workers Union, quoted in Kenneth R. Sheets, "Oil Profits Running Wild?" *U.S. News and World Report,* 5 November 1979, 24; Wolfe, "Worship of Art," 64.

47. Schmertz quoted in Pears and Glennon, "The Museum and the Corporation," 40; on Haacke's Mobil installations see *Hans Haacke: Unfinished Business,* 156–65, 206–9, 238–41, 272–77. See also Haacke's essay "Museums, Managers of Consciousness," 60–72, and Schmertz's book *Good-bye to the Low Profile: The Art of Creative Communication* (Boston: Little, Brown, 1986), especially the chapter titled "Affinity-of-Purpose Marketing: The Case of *Masterpiece Theater.*"

48. Kerry Cooper and R. Malcolm Richards, "Investing the Alaskan Project Cash Flows: The Sohio Experience," *Financial Management* 17, no. 2 (Summer 1988): 58–70; Sheets, "Oil Profits Running Wild?" 24. See also Paul D. Phillips et al., "Financing the Alaskan Project: The Experience at Sohio," *Financial Management* 8, no. 3 (Autumn 1979): 7–16.

49. Whitehouse quoted in S. K. List, "Rubbing Out the Rubber Stamp," *RubberStampMadness* [Newfield, N.Y.], 6, no. 29 (September–October 1986): 3.

50. Claire Ansberry, "If Cleveland Is Sick of Bad Jokes, Why Is It Making This So Easy?" *Wall Street Journal,* 26 August 1985, sec. 2, p. 19. Oldenburg and van Bruggen quoted from "Notes on the *Free Stamp,*" a prospectus written for Sohio in 1985; van Bruggen quoted in *HQ* (September 1985), 2, a Standard Oil Company Cleveland-area employee newsletter. Unless otherwise noted, all their comments are taken from these in-house documents.

51. Will, "Oh, Cleveland!" 344.

52. Oldenburg quoted in Cullinan, "Sohio Puts Its Stamp on City Art," 10.

53. Cartoon by Osrin, [Cleveland] *Plain Dealer,* 4 August 1985, sec. D, p. 4. Editorial, "Public Square's Rubber Stamp," [Cleveland] *Plain Dealer,* 3 August 1985, sec. A, p. 14. Ernest Holsendolph, "Stamp Sohio's Sculpture 'Approved,' at Least So Far," [Cleveland] *Plain Dealer,* 4 August 1985, sec. B, p. 3; Sally

Norman, "Art Choice Leaves Stamp on the City," [Cleveland] *Plain Dealer*, 11 August 1985, sec. P, pp. 1, 4.

54. Letter to the Editor, [Cleveland] *Plain Dealer*, 26 August 1985, sec. B, p. 4.

55. Letters to the Editor, [Cleveland] *Plain Dealer*, in the order cited: 9 August 1985, sec. B, p. 10; 15 August 1985, sec. B, p. 4; 6 August 1985, sec. B, p. 4; 12 August 1985, sec. B, p. 6; 11 August 1985, sec. B, p. 5.

56. Whitehouse quoted in *HQ*, 2; Joseph Ceruti of the Cleveland Fine Arts Committee quoted in Ansberry, "If Cleveland Is Sick," 19. On *Free Stamp*'s fabrication see Ron Grossman, "In Defense of Stomped Stamp Art," *Chicago Tribune*, 29 July 1986, sec. Tempo, pp. 1, 3.

57. On Sohio and the 1980s oil bust, see Cooper and Richards, "Investing the Alaskan Project Cash Flows," 58–70.

58. Gary Putka, Ralph Winter, and Gregory Stricharchuk, "Taking Charge: How and Why BP Put Its Own Commanders at Standard Oil Helm," *Wall Street Journal*, 7 March 1986, 1, 14; Horton quoted in Hall, "BP Grasps Its US Nettle," 20. On BP America's cancellation of *Free Stamp* see Helen Cullinan, "Standard Oil Seeks New Pad for Desk Stamp Sculpture," [Cleveland] *Plain Dealer*, 25 April 1986, sec. A, p. 16.

59. Editorial, "The Shake-up at Standard Oil," [Cleveland] *Plain Dealer*, 1 March 1986, sec. A, p. 16; Letters to the Editor, [Cleveland] *Plain Dealer*, 1 May 1986, sec. A, p. 24.

60. Helen Cullinan, "*Stamp* Fans Stump for Art," [Cleveland] *Plain Dealer*, 3 May 1986, sec. E, pp. 1, 7; Cullinan, "Standard Oil Seeks New Pad," pp. 1, 16; Cullinan, "STAMPED OUT!" [Cleveland] *Plain Dealer*, 4 May 1986, sec. P, pp. 1, 4; Grossman, "In Defense of Stomped Stamp Art," pp. 1, 3; Braham, "Wrong Impression?" 29. Starr quoted in Cullinan, "*Free Stamp* Offered Home at Oberlin," [Cleveland] *Plain Dealer*, 26 April 1986, sec. A, p. 1; James Demetrion and Martin Friedman quoted in Cullinan, "STAMPED OUT!" 4.

61. Oldenburg quoted in Cullinan, "Standard Oil Seeks New Pad," 1, and Cullinan, "STAMPED OUT!" 4.

62. Letter from Council President Jay Westbrook to Oldenburg and van Bruggen, 25 May 1990. Courtesy City of Cleveland City Hall Legislative Department. Unless otherwise noted all quotations from Westbrook come from this letter or other City Council documents.

63. On George Forbes see Krumholz and Forester, *Making Equity Planning Work*, 8, 10–14.

64. "Free Stamp Still Unwanted," UPI Wire Service, 18 December 1990, n.p.

65. Mike Polensek, interview by author, telephone, 17 July 1992. Unless otherwise noted all quotations from him come from this interview. Oldenburg and van Bruggen quoted in Amy Sparks, "The *Free* Free Stamp," *Cleveland Edition*, 11 April 1991, 25.

66. Bill Patmon, interview by author, telephone, 25 August 1992. Unless otherwise noted all quotations from Patmon come from this interview.

67. Kathleen Coakley, interview by author, telephone, 14 July 1992. Statistics on Cleveland in Krumholz and Forester, *Making Equity Planning Work*, 17–18.

68. Sparks, "*Free* Free Stamp," 25.

69. Mark Russell, "Free Stamp Sculpture Gets Spot by City Hall," [Cleveland] *Plain Dealer,* 23 April 1991, sec. A, pp. 1, 6; Clifford Anthony, "Familiar Stamping Grounds Change," [Euclid, Ohio] *Sunscoop Journal,* 21 November 1991, sec. A, pp. 1–2.

70. Bodnar, *Remaking America,* 17.

71. Richard Bolton, "What Is to Be Un-done, Rethinking Political Art," *New Art Examiner* 18, no. 10 (June/Summer 1991): 25.

72. Noted in Miller and Wheeler, *Cleveland,* 190.

73. Richard A. Melcher, "Bob Horton May Have 'Americanized' BP Too Well," *Business Week,* 13 July 1992, 44.

74. Samir al-Khalil, *The Monument: Art, Vulgarity and Responsibility in Iraq* (Berkeley: University of California Press, 1991), 132.

Chapter 4: Sculptures from Strip Mines

1. Klaus Kertess, "Earth Angles," *Artforum* 24, no. 6 (February 1986): 76–79.

2. Heizer quoted in Douglas C. McGill, *Michael Heizer: Effigy Tumuli* (New York: Harry N. Abrams, 1990), 11, 22, 43; Harriet F. Senie, *Contemporary Public Sculpture: Tradition, Transformation, and Controversy* (New York: Oxford University Press, 1992), 170.

3. Heizer quoted in McGill, *Effigy Tumuli,* 41.

4. Douglas C. McGill, "Illinois Project to Transform Ruined Forest into Sculpture," *New York Times,* 3 June 1985, sec. A, 1, 19.

5. Thornton and Heizer quoted in McGill, "Illinois Project," 1, 19; Alice Thorson, "A Paragon of Art in the '80s," *ARTnews* 85 (January 1986): 11–12; Kertess, "Earth Angles," 79; Heizer quoted in McGill, *Effigy Tumuli,* 23.

6. Amway ad, *Life,* May 1993, 7; Ford ad, *People Weekly,* 18 January 1993, inside back cover; Working Assets Long Distance ad, *Utne Reader,* May–June 1993, 40.

7. Dominique G. W. Mazeaud and Robert B. Gaylor, *Revered Earth* (Santa Fe: Center for Contemporary Arts of Santa Fe, 1990); Barbara C. Matilsky, *Fragile Ecologies: Contemporary Artists' Interpretations and Solutions* (New York: Rizzoli, 1992); Robin Cembalest, "The Ecological Art Explosion," *ARTnews* 90 (Summer 1991): 99.

8. Robert Smithson, "Untitled, 1971," "Untitled, 1972," and "Proposal, 1972," in *The Writings of Robert Smithson,* ed. Nancy Holt (New York: New York University Press, 1979), 220–21.

9. Mierle Laderman Ukeles, "A Journey: Earth/City/Flow," *Art Journal* 51, no. 2 (Summer 1992): 13; Jude Schwendenwien, "Breaking Ground: Art in the Environment," *Sculpture* 10, no. 5 (September–October 1991): 41.

10. Robert Morris, "Notes on Art as/and Land Reclamation," *October* 12 (Spring 1980): 98, 100, 102; Robert Morris, "Robert Morris Keynote Address," in *Earthworks: Land Reclamation as Sculpture* (Seattle: Seattle Art Museum, 1979), 16.

11. Suzi Gablik, "The Ecological Imperative," *Art Journal* 51, no. 2 (Summer 1982): 49. See also Deborah Bright, "The Machine in the Garden Revisited: American Environmentalism and Photographic Aesthetics," ibid., 70.

12. Gablik, "Ecological Imperative," 49; Daniel J. Kevles, "Some Like It Hot," *New York Review of Books,* 26 March 1992, 36.

13. Schwendenwien, "Breaking Ground," 42; Matilsky, *Fragile Ecologies,* 104–7.

14. Matilsky, *Fragile Ecologies,* 5; Marianna Torgovnick, *Gone Primitive: Savage Intellects, Modern Lives* (Chicago: University of Chicago Press, 1990), 245.

15. Ward Churchill, "Spiritual Hucksterism: The Rise of the Plastic Medicine Men," in *Fantasies of the Master Race: Literature, Cinema, and the Colonization of American Indians* (Monroe, Maine: Common Courage Press, 1992), 218. Sun Bear's workshops drew outrage from many American Indians, as did his claims that Native American spiritual knowledge helped him win at the craps tables in Las Vegas.

16. John W. Simpson, "The Emotional Landscape and Public Law 95-87," *Landscape Architecture* 75, no. 3 (May–June 1985): 60; James Krohe, "Reclamation Initiatives," *Landscape Architecture* 79, no. 5 (June 1989): 40–41.

17. Harriet Shapiro, "It May Be Dirty Work, but Sculptor Michael Heizer Breaks New Ground Indoors and Out," *People,* 19 August 1985, 108; John Gruen, "Michael Heizer: 'You Might Say I'm in the Construction Business,'" *ARTnews* 76 (December 1977): 99.

18. Michael Heizer, interview by author, telephone, 9 March 1986; David Bourdon, "Working with Earth: Michael Heizer Makes Art as Big as All Outdoors," *Smithsonian,* April 1986, 74.

19. Gruen, "Michael Heizer," 99.

20. Michael Heizer, "The Art of Michael Heizer," *Artforum* 8 (December 1969): 37. See also John Beardsley, *Earthworks and Beyond: Contemporary Art in the Landscape,* 2d ed. (New York: Abbeville Press, 1989).

21. Michael Heizer, interview by Julia Brown, in *Michael Heizer: Sculpture in Reverse,* ed. Julia Brown (Los Angeles: Museum of Contemporary Art, 1984), 11.

22. Bourdon, "Working with Earth," 74.

23. Dwan quoted in Calvin Tomkins, "Maybe a Quantum Leap," in *The Scene: Reports on Post-Modern Art* (New York: Viking Press, 1976), 135.

24. Patricia Nelson Limerick, *The Legacy of Conquest: The Unbroken Past of the American West* (New York: W. W. Norton, 1987), 324.

25. Warren Susman, "Did Success Spoil the United States? Dual Representations in Postwar America," in *Recasting America: Culture and Politics in the Age of Cold War,* ed. Lary May (Chicago: University of Chicago Press, 1989), 19–37; Heizer quoted in Brown, *Michael Heizer,* 11, and Gruen, "Michael Heizer," 99.

26. Dwan quoted in Tomkins, "Maybe a Quantum Leap," 135; Heizer quoted in Brown, *Michael Heizer,* 15–16; and see Paula Deitz's essay "Downtown in the Desert" in this catalog for a description of the making of *Double Negative,* 81.

27. Joseph Mascheck, "The Panama Canal and Some Other Works of Work," *Artforum* 9 (May 1971): 41; Michael Auping, "Michael Heizer: The Ecology and Economics of 'Earth Art,'" *Artweek* 8, no. 23 (18 June 1977): 1. See also Mark C. Taylor, "Rend(er)ing," in *Michael Heizer: Double Negative* (New York: Rizzoli, 1991), 12–22. For other critiques of earthworks see Allen Carlson, "Is Environmental Art an Aesthetic Affront to Nature?" *Canadian Journal of Philosophy* 16, no. 4 (December 1986): 635–50; Donald Crawford, "Nature and Art: Some Dialectical Relationships," *Journal of Aesthetics and Art Criticism* 42, no. 1 (Fall 1983): 49–58; and Peter Humphrey, "The Ethics of Earthworks," *Environmental Ethics* 7, no. 1 (Spring 1985): 5–21.

28. Edmund Thornton, interview by author, telephone, 14 December 1992. Unless otherwise noted all subsequent quotations from Thornton come from this conversation.

29. Heizer quoted in Brown, *Michael Heizer,* 42–43. Paula Deitz estimated this *Double Negative* attendance figure in "Downtown in the Desert," 75. On Wolfe's view of the art world see Tom Wolfe, *The Painted Word* (New York: Bantam, 1975), 26.

30. Limerick, *Legacy of Conquest,* 324.

31. Umberto Eco, "Travels in Hyperreality," in *Travels in Hyperreality: Essays* (New York: Harcourt Brace Jovanovich, 1991), 4–5.

32. Beardsley, *Earthworks,* 9; Panza quoted in Deitz, "Downtown in the Desert," 76. See also Bright, "Machine in the Garden Revisited."

33. Heizer quoted in Howard Junker, "The New Sculpture: Getting Down to the Nitty Gritty," *Saturday Evening Post,* 2 November 1968, 42.

34. Heizer quoted in Brown, *Michael Heizer,* 33, 38; and Gruen, "Michael Heizer," 98.

35. Limerick, *Legacy of Conquest,* 55.

36. Heizer quoted in Roy Bongartz, "Earth Art," *Nation,* 24 December 1973, 700; Scull quoted in David L. Shirey, "Impossible Art—What It Is," *Art in America* 57, no. 3 (May–June 1969): 34. In "Maybe a Quantum Leap," Tomkins discussed gallery interest in *Double Negative;* apparently in 1971 Swiss dealer Bruno Bischofberger had hoped to buy and then sell the sculpture for some $65,000. See p. 130.

37. Douglas Davis, "The Earth Mover," *Newsweek,* 18 November 1974, 113.

38. Robert Heilbroner quoted in Peter N. Carroll, *It Seemed Like Nothing Happened: The Tragedy and Promise of America in the 1970s* (New York: Holt, Rinehart and Winston, 1982), 135.

39. Heizer quoted in Brown, *Michael Heizer,* 33–34.

40. Or even among Atlantic Richfield board members. Apparently, when the project was proposed, they voted 7 to 1 against it, but the (then) vice president's vote—and project initiative—carried.

41. Bert Johns, interview by author, 22 August 1985, at the Anaconda Minerals Company moly plant, Tonopah, Nevada.

42. McGill, *Effigy Tumuli,* 16.

43. Jeff L. Nelson and Jeffrey D. Robertson, "Abandoned Mines," *Landscape Architecture* 75, no. 3 (May–June 1985): 51.

44. McGill, *Effigy Tumuli*, 22.

45. McGill, *Effigy Tumuli*, 37; Kertess, "Earth Angles," 77; Bourdon, "Working with Earth," 76.

46. McGill, *Effigy Tumuli*, 23, 24.

47. Heizer quoted in McGill, *Effigy Tumuli*, 34.

48. Ryan quoted in Susan Blake, "The Art of Reclamation: Michael Heizer Digs in Illinois," *New Art Examiner* 13, no. 5 (January 1986): 33; Thornton quoted in Thorson, "Paragon of Art," 11; Cole quoted in JoAnn Hustis, "Earthen Sculptures Dedicated," *Ottawa* [Illinois] *Daily Times,* 30 October 1985, 2.

49. Wes Smith, "Land Mine: Downstate Feud over Dirt-Bike Paradise Lost to Art May Be About to Explode Again," *Chicago Tribune,* 30 July 1992, sec. 5, pp. 1–2.

50. Evelyn Muffler, interview by author, 17 April 1993, Ottawa, Ill. Unless otherwise noted subsequent quotations from Muffler, Kelly Dempsey, and Jim Farrell come from this conversation.

51. The company also abandoned similar factories in Athens, Georgia, and Queens, New York.

Joseph Kelly started the Radium Chemical Company in New York in 1913; Radium Dial and Luminous Process were divisions of the original company, today owned and operated by Joseph Kelly III in New York City. Radium Chemical used "dozens of office and factory locations" throughout Queens and midtown Manhattan, and across the country, from the 1910s through the 1980s. See "Queens Firm Mishandling Radium," UPI, Dateline NY, 4 October 1987, and "Radiation Detected in Midtown Building," UPI, Dateline NY, 5 May 1988.

52. Daphne Mitchell, interview by author, telephone, 28 June 1993.

53. Charlie Morey, "Easy Riding," *Dirt Rider,* September 1992, 7.

54. Charlie Morey, "Project Stealth: It's Up to Us," *Dirt Rider,* May 1993, 11.

55. Charlie Morey, "S.21: Many Dollars, No Sense," *Dirt Rider,* June 1993, 4, and "Stop the Madness," *Dirt Rider,* July 1993, 6. See the Honda advertisement in *Dirt Rider,* September 1992, 7, for the entire Tread Lightly pledge.

56. Morey, "S.21: Many Dollars, No Sense," 4; and "Stop the Madness," 6.

57. Edward Abbey, *The Monkey Wrench Gang* (New York: Avon, 1975). *Ecotage* refers to the actions—tearing down billboards, spiking trees, pouring sand into bulldozer crankcases—of radical environmentalists.

58. Paul Smith quoted in Wes Smith, "What in the Name of Art Are They Doing to That Dirt?" *Chicago Tribune,* 10 June 1985, sec. C, p. 1.

59. Smith, "Land Mine," 2.

60. Paul Smith quoted in Smith, "Land Mine," 2.

61. Judy Schoenenberger, interview by author, 17 April 1993, at the *Effigy Tumuli* sculpture park, Ottawa, Ill. Unless otherwise noted subsequent quotations from Schoenenberger come from this conversation.

62. When I was visiting *Effigy Tumuli* in spring 1991, the muck dissolved my shoes.

63. JoAnn Hustis, interview by author, telephone, 18 December 1992.

64. Heizer quoted in McGill, *Effigy Tumuli,* 43.

65. Thornton quoted in McGill, "Illinois Project," 1.

66. Wes Smith, "Roadside Distraction: Billboard of Junk Turns Heads on Downstate Highway," *Chicago Tribune,* 18 October 1992, sec. C, pp. 1, 7.

67. Leicester quoted in Erika Doss, "Andrew Leicester's Mining Memorials," *ARTS Magazine* 61, no. 5 (January 1987): 34.

68. Andrew Leicester, interview by Carol Kliger, in Carol Kliger, *A Public Art Primer for Artists of the Boulder-Denver Area* (Boulder: Carol Kliger, 1993), 57.

Chapter 5: Raising Community Consciousness with Public Art

1. QUAD Consultants, *Data-Base: City of Guadalupe General Plan Update* (City of Guadalupe, 1990).

2. Baca quoted in Russ Spencer, "Guadalupe History in Four-Part Harmony," *Santa Barbara News Press Scene Magazine,* 9 June 1989, 22.

3. Judy Baca, interview by author, 2 February 1990, Boulder, Colo. Unless otherwise noted subsequent quotations from Baca come from this conversation or from comments made on 28 September 1993, in Los Angeles. Likewise, quotations from Guadalupe citizens come from author interviews conducted in Guadalupe from 23 to 27 September 1993.

4. Suzanne Lacy, "Interlinked Narratives (If There Was No Mural This Would Still Be Art)," in *World Wall: A Vision of the Future Without Fear* (Venice, Calif.: SPARC [Social and Public Arts Resource Center], 1991), 13.

5. Steve Dalzell, "A Renaissance Begins for Guad's LeRoy Park," *Santa Maria* [California] *Times,* 8 March 1988, sec. B, p. 7.

6. Pico Iyer, "Is It Really That Wacky? A Flaky Image Hides a Deeper Truth; Bright Sunshine Casts Dark Shadows," *Time,* 18 November 1991, 109–10; "A Hobo Jungle with Class: Santa Barbara, Reagan's Neighbor, Wrestles with 2,000 Homeless," *Time,* 31 March 1986, 29.

7. Victor Garcia, "Surviving Farm Work: Economic Strategies of Mexican and Mexican American Households in a Rural California Community" (Ph.D. diss., University of California, Santa Barbara, 1990), 152. He notes that in 1988, according to federal guidelines, a household of five was impoverished at an income level of $14,435.

8. Baca quoted in Lisa McKinnon, "Words of Advice for Local Mural Projects," *Valley* [Lompoc, Calif.] *Living,* 10 February 1989, T5.

9. Ethel-May Dorsey, "Colorful History of Guadalupe," *Santa Maria Times,* 15 October 1966, sec. B, p. 8. For further information on Guadalupe see V. F. Carlson, *This Is Our Valley* (Santa Maria, Calif.: Santa Maria Valley Historical Society, 1959); Thomas F. Collison and H. R. Reynolds, *Guadalupe, California* (Guadalupe: Valley Vidette Print, 1930); and *Reproduction of Thompson and West's History of Santa Barbara and Ventura Counties, California, With Illustrations and Biographical Sketches of its Prominent Men and Pioneers* (1883; reprint, Berkeley: Howell-North, 1961).

10. Quotation from the "Fiesta Guadalupana" Souvenir Program of Our Lady of Guadalupe, 12 and 13 December 1936, n.p.

11. Stephanie Finucane, "Guadalupe Journal: Under the Dunes, a City by De-Mille," *New York Times,* 26 November 1990, sec. A, p. 14; Brian Fagan, "Digging DeMille," *Archaeology* 44, no. 2 (March–April 1991): 16–20. See also *The Ten Commandments: A Movie, a Mystery, a Slice of Santa Maria History* (Santa Maria, Calif.: Santa Maria Valley Historical Society, 1985).

12. Garcia, "Surviving Farm Work," 50, 144.

13. California State Advisory Committee to the U.S. Commission on Civil Rights, *The Schools of Guadalupe . . . A Legacy of Educational Oppression* (Washington, D.C.: U.S. Commission on Civil Rights, 1973).

14. Tom Mooneyham, "Guadalupe Raid," *Santa Maria Times,* 1 December 1983, sec. A, p. 1; Kim Miller, "Drug Bust in Guadalupe: Police Snare 46 in Morning Raid," *Santa Maria Times,* 5 June 1986, sec. A, p. l.

15. Collison and Reynolds, *Guadalupe,* 1.

16. Anne Estrada, "Judy Baca's Art for Peace," *Hispanic,* May 1991, 17; Diane Neumaier, "Judy Baca: Our People Are the Internal Exiles," in *Cultures in Contention,* eds. Douglas Kahn and Diane Neumaier (Seattle: Real Comet Press, 1985), 63–64.

17. From SPARC's newsletter, *SPARC Plug* 1, no. 1 (January 1991): 1, and 2, no. 3 (May 1992): insert. For more on SPARC see Nancy Angelo, "A Brief History of SPARC," in Kahn and Neumaier, *Cultures in Contention,* 71–72.

18. Carrie Rickey, "The Writing on the Wall," *Art in America* 69 (May 1981): 57. For other descriptions see Alan W. Barnett, *Community Murals: The People's Art* (Philadelphia: Art Alliance Press, 1984), 280; Emily Hicks, "The Artist as Citizen," *High Performance* 9, no. 35 (1986): 36; Evagene H. Bond, "A Successful Art Product with a Social Impact: The Great Wall of Los Angeles," in *La Comunidad: Design, Development, and Self-Determination in Hispanic Communities,* ed. Evagene H. Bond (Washington, D.C.: Partners for Livable Places, 1982), 13–24; and *Walking Tour and Guide to the Great Wall of Los Angeles* (Venice, Calif.: SPARC, 1983), 1–18.

19. Baca quoted in *Walking Tour and Guide,* 1.

20. Baca quoted from a lecture at the "Mixing It Up" symposium, University of Colorado, Boulder, 7 April 1989. See also Erika Doss, "Raising Community Consciousness with Public Art: Contrasting Projects by Judy Baca and Andrew Leicester," *American Art* 6, no. 1 (Winter 1992): 62–80.

21. Angelo, "Brief History of SPARC," 72. On funding for the *Great Wall* see Bond, "Successful Art Product," 18, and Rebecca Yule, "From Revolution to Assimilation: Judy Baca, Leo Tanguma, Chicano Culture, and Contemporary Art in the Late Twentieth Century" (M.A. thesis, University of Colorado, Boulder 1991), 11, 50, 61.

22. Baca quoted in Neumaier, "Our People Are the Internal Exiles," 72; Ableser quoted in *Walking Tour and Guide,* 17. On Rollins and K.O.S. see Phyllis Rosser, "Education Through Collaboration Saves Lives," in *Art in the Public Interest,* ed. Arlene Raven (Ann Arbor: UMI Research Press, 1989), 127–38.

23. Avila quoted in *Walking Tour and Guide,* 17.

24. Baca quoted in Bond, "Successful Art Product," 16.

25. Bond, "Successful Art Product," 24.

26. Baca quoted in Neumaier, "Our People Are the Internal Exiles," 67, and in Frances Pohl, "Judith F. Baca: Site and Insights, 1974–1992," catalog essay for exhibition *Judith F. Baca: Site and Insights, 1974–1992* (Claremont, Calif.: Montgomery Gallery, Pomona College, 7 March–4 April 1993), n.p.

27. Ramón A. Gutiérrez, "Community, Patriarchy and Individualism: The Politics of Chicano History and the Dream of Equality," *American Quarterly* 45, no. 1 (March 1993): 45–46. See also Rodolfo Acuña, *Occupied America: A History of Chicanos* (New York: Harper and Row, 1988).

28. Amalia Mesa-Bains, "El Mundo Femenino: Chicana Artists of the Movement—A Commentary on Development and Production," in *Chicano Art: Resistance and Affirmation, 1965–1985,* ed. Richard Griswold del Castillo (Los Angeles: Wight Art Gallery, University of California, Los Angeles, 1991), 131. See also Judith F. Baca, "Murals/Public Art," in *Chicano Expressions: A New View in American Art* (New York: INTAR Latin American Gallery, 1987).

29. Amalia Mesa-Bains, "Quest for Identity: Profile of Two Chicana Muralists Based on Interviews with Judith F. Baca and Patricia Rodríguez," in Eva Sperling Cockcroft and Holly Barnet-Sánchez, eds., *Signs from the Heart: California Chicano Murals* (Venice, Calif.: SPARC, 1990), 81.

30. Baca quoted in Neumaier, "Our People Are the Internal Exiles," 68.

31. Bond, "Successful Art Product," 19.

32. Hicks, "Artist as Citizen," 36.

33. Judy Baca, "Public Art in a Multicultural Society," *SPARCplug* 2, no. 3 (May 1992): 12; Baca quoted in Mesa-Bains, "Quest for Identity," 79.

34. Neumaier, "Our People Are the Internal Exiles," 67; Spencer, "Guadalupe History," 23.

35. Baca, "Public Art in a Multicultural Society," 12, and quoted in Neumaier, "Our People Are the Internal Exiles," 69. On cultural democracy see Don Adams and Arlene Goldbard, *Crossroads: Reflections on the Politics of Culture* (Talmage, Calif.: DNA Press, 1990); and Lucy Lippard's review, "Cultural Policy," in *Art in America* 80, no. 5 (May 1992): 43, 45.

36. Baca quoted from Yvette Martinez's 1989 video, *Guadalupe.*

37. Spencer, "Guadalupe History," 23.

38. Nelson George, *Buppies, B-Boys, Baps and Bohos: Notes on Post-Soul Black Culture* (New York: HarperCollins, 1992), 115.

39. bell hooks, *talking back: thinking feminist, thinking black* (Boston: South End Press, 1989), 29.

40. Baca quoted in Pohl, "Judith F. Baca," n.p.

41. David Trend, *Cultural Pedagogy: Art/Education/Politics* (New York: Bergin and Garvey, 1992), 84.

42. Mikhail Bakhtin, *The Dialogic Imagination: Four Essays by M. M. Bakhtin,* ed. by Michael Holquist, trans. Michael Holquist and Caryl Emerson (Austin: University of Texas Press, 1981). See also George Lipsitz, "Against the Wind: Dialogic Aspects of Rock and Roll," in *Time Passages: Collective Mem-*

ory and American Popular Culture (Minneapolis: University of Minnesota Press, 1990), 99–132.

43. Michael Kimmelman, "Of Candy Bars, Parades and Public Art," *New York Times,* 26 September 1993, sec. H, p. 43.

44. Trend, *Cultural Pedagogy,* 85.

45. Harry C. Boyte, ed., *The New Populism: The Politics of Empowerment* (Philadelphia: Temple University Press, 1986), 12.

Chapter 6: Public Art and Flying Pigs

1. John P. Frankenstein, *American Art: Its Awful Attitude* (Cincinnati, 1864), quoted in Daniel Aaron, *Cincinnati: Queen City of the West, 1819–1838* (Columbus: Ohio State University Press, 1992), 256.

2. Stern quoted in Dennis Love, "How Sawyer Point Started from Scratch," *Cincinnati Post,* 4 June 1988, sec. A, p. 7; GCBC mandate included among the GCBC Papers, Box 15, Blegen Library Archives, University of Cincinnati. Unless otherwise noted subsequent references to the GCBC and the Bicentennial Commons public art project can be found among these papers and in boxes 36, 37, and 38.

3. Christine Wolff, "A Sculptor's-eye View of 'Porkopolis,'" *Cincinnati Enquirer,* 1 November 1987, sec. A, pp. 1, 12.

4. Leicester pronounced "Lester." For headlines see Jim Calhoun, "Pig in a Poke or a Work of Art?" *Cincinnati Enquirer,* 29 December 1987, sec. A, p. 6; Marty Bonvechio, "In the Sty of the Beholder," *Naples* [Florida] *Daily News,* 3 January 1988, sec. A, p. 1; Sarah Sturman, "They Wax Po(rk)etic in Praise of Flying Pigs," *Cincinnati Post,* 11 January 1988, sec. A, p. 1. On Cincinnati's moralizing tendencies see Cynthia Carr, "With Mapplethorpe in Cincinnati," in *On Edge: Performance Art at the End of the Twentieth Century* (Hanover, N.H.: Wesleyan University Press, 1993), 264–80.

5. Ruth Meyer, "Introduction," in *Proposals for Sawyer Point Park* (Cincinnati: Contemporary Arts Center exhibition catalog, 8 October–27 November 1977), n.p.

6. Dennis Barrie, interview by author, Contemporary Arts Center, Cincinnati, 26 March 1991. Unless otherwise noted subsequent quotations from Barrie come from this conversation.

7. Barrie quoted in Mary McCarty, "Cincinnati Does So Have a Sense of Humor," *Cincinnati,* March 1988, 78; and Owen Findsen, "Political Guns Keep Sights Trained on Controversial Flying Pigs," *Cincinnati Enquirer,* 10 January 1988, sec. H, p. 1.

8. Barrie quoted in Findsen, "Political Guns," 1.

9. Barrie quoted in McCarty, "Cincinnati Does So," 78.

10. Derek Woodham, interview by author, telephone, 9 March 1991; Gotoff quoted in Mark A. Davis, "Students Help Mold Riverfront's Future," *Horizons* [University of Cincinnati School of Art, College of Design, Architecture, Art and Planning Newsletter], May 1988, n.p.

11. Andrew Leicester, interview by author, Boulder, 14 March 1989. Unless otherwise noted subsequent quotations from Leicester come from this conversation.

12. Benjamin Drake and Edward Deering Mansfield, *Cincinnati in 1826* (Cincinnati: Morgan, Lodge, and Fisher, 1827).

13. Aaron, *Cincinnati*, 232–33, 276–79. See also Robert Vitz, *The Queen and the Arts: Cultural Life in Nineteenth-century Cincinnati* (Kent, Ohio: Kent State University Press, 1989).

14. *Cincinnati: A Guide to the Queen City and Its Neighbors* (Cincinnati: Wiesen-Hart Press, 1943), 57–61; Steven J. Ross, *Workers on the Edge: Work, Leisure, and Politics in Industrializing Cincinnati, 1788–1890* (New York: Columbia University Press, 1985), 11, 14–15; Aaron, *Cincinnati*, 15.

15. Frances Trollope, *The Domestic Manners of the Americans* (1832; reprint, New York: Vintage Books, 1960), 105, 88–89.

16. J. S. Buckingham, *The Eastern and Western States of America*, 2 vols. (London: 1842), 2:394, as quoted in Ross, *Workers on the Edge*, 120.

17. Quoted in Ross, *Workers on the Edge*, 122.

18. Andrew Leicester, "Contextual Art," *VINYL Arts* [Minneapolis] *Magazine* 4, no. 7 (October 1987): 10.

19. Leicester quoted in Owen Findsen, "Sculptor Defends His 'Little Piggies,'" *Cincinnati Enquirer,* 15 January 1988, sec. A, back page; Leicester, "Contextual Art," 10.

20. Leicester, "Contextual Art," 10.

21. See also David Lyman's account in "Huffing and Puffing over Four Little Pigs," *New Art Examiner* 16, no. 2 (October 1988): 43–44.

22. Wolff, "A Sculptor's-eye View," 1, 12.

23. Carr, "With Mapplethorpe," 266; see also Steven C. Dubin, *Arresting Images: Impolitic Art and Uncivil Actions* (New York: Routledge, 1992), 181–90.

24. Leicester quoted in Christine Wolff, "Bicentennial Pigs to Stay," *Cincinnati Enquirer,* 12 November 1987, sec. D, p. 1; Letters in *Cincinnati Enquirer,* 8 November 1987, sec. A, p. 4; and *Cincinnati Post,* 1 December 1987, sec. A, p. 9; 15 December 1987, sec. D, p. 1; and 8 January 1988, sec. A, p. 15.

25. Letters to *Cincinnati Enquirer,* 25 November 1987, sec. A, p. 7; and *Cincinnati Post,* 1 December 1987, sec. A, p. 9; 15 December 1987, sec. D, pp. 1, 7.

26. Letters to *Cincinnati Enquirer,* 22 November 1987, sec. H, p. 4; and *Cincinnati Post,* 15 December 1987, sec. D, pp. 1, 7.

27. Mayor Charles Luken to Richard Greiwe, executive director of the GCBC, 16 November 1987, Box 36, GCBC Papers; Jim Calhoun, "Flying Pigs Raise Bicentennial Fuss at Mayor's Office," *Cincinnati Enquirer,* 17 November 1987, sec. A, p. 6.

28. Chabot quoted in Calhoun, "Pig in a Poke," 6; Clare Ansberry, "Perhaps New York Would Accept the Pigs in Trade for 'Tilted Arc,'" *Wall Street Journal,* 19 January 1988, 33; Joe Kay, "'Pigasus' Statue Stirs Up a Stink in Cincinnati," [Cleveland] *Plain Dealer,* 10 January 1988, sec. A, p. 12; Sturman, "They Wax Po(rk)etic," 1. Leicester quoted in Bonvechio, "In the Sty of the Beholder," 2.

29. Andrew Leicester quoted in Bob Musselman, "Going Hog Wild?" *Cincinnati Post,* 24 November 1987, sec. A, p. 5. For polls see "Pig Poll Ends with Photo Finish," *Cincinnati Post,* 15 December 1987, sec. A, p. 1, and sec. D, pp. 1, 7; McCarty, "Cincinnati Does So," 75, 77; Camilla Warrick, "Flying Pigs Shoot Down City's Humor," *Cincinnati Enquirer,* 3 January 1988, sec. B, p. 1. For national attention see Ansberry, "Perhaps New York," 33. Gumbel made his comments on *Today*'s 8 January 1988 show.

30. Al Salvato, "Pigs Aplenty Send Council Squealing," *Cincinnati Post,* 13 January 1988, sec. A, p. 1; Lew Moores, "Cincinnati Voices Its Pig Beefs," *Cincinnati Post,* 13 January 1988, sec. B, p. 1; Karl J. Karlson, "'Pig People' Poke Fun at Artist's 'Porkopolis,'" *St. Paul Dispatch,* 13 January 1988, sec. B, p. 2.

31. McCarty, "Cincinnati Does So," 75; Andrew Leicester quoted in an interview with Mason Riddle, *Artpaper* 7, no. 9 (May 1988): 7.

32. Love, "How Sawyer Point Started," 7.

33. See Lew Moores, "Hot Pink, Cincinnati Wallows in Glow of Pig-mania," *Cincinnati Post,* 18 July 1988, sec. A, p. 1; and Christine Wolff, "C'mon Lass— Buy a Pig," *Cincinnati Enquirer,* 20 May 1988, sec. D, p. l. The ballad was written by Cindy Ramirez-Martyi. *A Pig Tale of Porkopolis: The Untold Story of How the Flying Pigs Became Famous* (Cincinnati: Word Watchers, 1988) was written by bandleader Bill Walters and illustrated by Peggy Heimlich.

34. Leicester quoted in Riddle's interview in *Artpaper,* 7.

35. Houston Conwill, "Act of Faith," *Art Journal* 48, no. 4 (Winter 1989): 337.

36. Krzysztof Wodiczko, "Strategies of Public Address: Which Media, Which Publics?" in *Discussions in Contemporary Culture,* no. 1, ed. Hal Foster (Seattle: Bay Press, 1987), 42.

37. For contrasting views on the solidarity of the Cincinnati community regarding the Mapplethorpe trial see Carr, "With Mapplethorpe," 264–80; Dubin, *Arresting Images,* 184–90; Jayne Merkel, "Report from Cincinnati: Art on Trial," *Art in America* 78, no. 1 (December 1990): 41–51; Elizabeth Hess, "Art on Trial," *Village Voice,* 23 October 1990, 109–12; and David Lyman, "Post-Mapplethorpe Blues in Cincinnati," *New Art Examiner* 18, no. 5 (January 1991): 56.

Epilogue

1. Richard Bolton, "Advertising Democracy," *Ten.8* 1, no. 35 (Winter 1989–90): 30, 35.

2. Mike Davis, *City of Quartz: Excavating the Future in Los Angeles* (New York: Verso, 1990), 81.

3. Barbara Kruger, interview by author, telephone, 27 January 1994. Unless otherwise noted all subsequent quotations from Kruger come from this conversation.

4. Statement from Barbara Kruger, from *Untitled (Questions)* File, Museum of Contemporary Art, Los Angeles.

5. Kruger quoted from transcript of the 14 December 1989 CAC meeting, *Untitled (Questions)* File, MOCA; Niho quoted in Marc Porter Zasada, "Emotions Run High in Mural Debate," *Downtown* [Los Angeles] *News,* 18 December 1989, 9.

6. Rodriguez quoted in Zasada, "Emotions Run High," 40.

7. Volk and Kruger quoted in Zasada, "Emotions Run High," 9.

8. David Deitcher, "Barbara Kruger: Resisting Arrest," *Artforum* 29, no. 6 (February 1991): 86.

9. Kats Kunitsugu, interview by author, telephone, 1 February 1994. See also Gary Libman, "Dispute Simmers as Design Is Picked for War Memorial in Little Tokyo," *Los Angeles Times,* 15 January 1991, sec. B, p. 8; and David McCombs, "World War II Memorial Splits Japanese American Community," *Downtown* [Los Angeles] *News,* 28 January 1991, 1, 12. Thanks also to Mike Several for sharing information on this project with me.

10. Ann Goldstein, interview by author, telephone, 12 January 1994; Koshalek quoted in MOCA press release, 10 June 1992, *Untitled (Questions)* File, MOCA.

11. Craig Owens, "The Discourse of Others: Feminists and Postmodernism," in *The Anti-Aesthetic: Essays on Postmodern Culture,* ed. Hal Foster (Port Townsend: Bay Press, 1983), 69. Owens refers (p. 80, n. 37) to a conversation between Gilles Deleuze and Michel Foucault in which Deleuze remarked, "You were the first . . . to teach us something absolutely fundamental: the indignity of speaking for others." See also Owens, "'The Indignity of Speaking for Others': An Imaginary Interview," *Art & Social Change, U.S.A.* [Oberlin, Ohio: Allen Memorial Art Museum Bulletin] 40, no. 2 (1982–83): 85.

12. On Ahearn's case see Jane Kramer, "Whose Art Is It?" *New Yorker,* 21 December 1992, 80–109; and Rayne Roper, "Public Art Conflict and the Politics of Race and Representation in John Ahearn's *South Bronx Sculpture Park*" (M.A. thesis, University of Colorado, Boulder, 1993). On the Miami Beach sculpture see David Adams, "The Columbus Monster Monument," *South Florida Magazine,* January 1993, 34–36. On Baden's *Wall of Death* see Sally MacDonald, "Beholders See No Beauty in This Art," *Seattle Times,* 13 November 1993, sec. A, pp. 1, 11; on Subculture Joe see Eric Scigliano, "Unchain My Foot," *Seattle Weekly,* 22 September 1993, 15–16.

13. Eleanor Heartney, "The New Word Order," *New Art Examiner* 18, no. 8 (April 1991): 25; Kramer, "Whose Art Is It?" 81, 95–96, 98–99.

14. Herbert Muschamp, "Thinking About Tomorrow and How to Build It," *New York Times,* 10 January 1993, sec. 2, p. 1.

■■■

Index